THE FREUDIAN ETHIC

Other books by RICHARD LaPIERE

Technical

SOCIAL PSYCHOLOGY (*with Paul R. Farnsworth*)

COLLECTIVE BEHAVIOR

SOCIOLOGY

A THEORY OF SOCIAL CONTROL

Novels

SON OF HAN

WHEN THE LIVING STRIVE

THE FREUDIAN ETHIC

By

Richard LaPiere

duell, sloan and pearce

new york

To HELEN

who also advocates
individual enterprise

Preface

THIS BOOK IS not another addition to the massive literature on Sigmund Freud and psychoanalysis. The theories evolved by Freud have already been paraphrased, interpreted, and dissected, and both lauded and condemned, by a profusion of authors, a number of whom have been far better qualified than I to deal with the intricacies of the Freudian doctrine and all of whom have been far more tolerant of the devious thought ways of metapsychological speculation.

Nor is this book concerned with the value of psychoanalysis as a therapeutic procedure. The question of value is not without import, if for no other reason than that millions of dollars are spent annually in the hope that psychoanalysis can relieve mental distress. But so far, at least, the evidence on the effectiveness of this procedure, or of any of the various competitive psychotherapeutic techniques, is fragmentary, contradictory, and unreliable; and there is no firmer basis than faith upon which to evaluate its worth.

Freudianism has become, however, more than a theory of the causes of mental disorders and a therapy claimed to resolve them. It has become, as Freud so obviously hoped that it would, a doctrine of the nature of man that its adherents believe applicable to all mankind. And it has of late years become remarkably popular with both laymen and scientists, particularly here in the United States.

The widespread acceptance of Freudianism has not, of course, gone unnoted. The proponents of the doctrine hold that its popularity is deserved and say in effect and in many words that truth will out. Those less beguiled by Freudianism have been inclined to find the explanation for its popularity in its exotic content; and a few observers have related its popularity, vaguely but perhaps with

viii PREFACE

some validity, to the current American ethos with its liberality toward self-indulgence and irresponsibility. But no systematic effort has been made to relate the growing popularity of Freudianism to other changes that are occurring in our society or to explore what this particular change reflects and suggests. It is with these matters, with the social implications of Freudianism, rather than with Freudianism per se, that this book is concerned.

The growing popularity of Freudianism as an explanation of and justification for human conduct is only one of many social changes, but it is a change of paramount significance; for Freudianism provides a unique idea of the nature of man, of his potentialities, and of his relations to society. Those who adopt this new idea and act upon it *ipso facto* regard themselves and the world about them in a way that differs radically from the traditional view. They are perforce constrained to renounce many established values and sentiments and to accept, as logical correlates of the Freudian idea of man, a new set—values and sentiments that are, for convenience and with an eye to precedent, here designated as the "Freudian ethic."

Science presumes that there is some sort of order in the universe, can we but perceive it; and thus it follows that there is some sort of pattern in social change, however chaotic it may seem. The emergence of the Freudian ethic is not an isolated, independent development. On the contrary, there is a concordance between the emergence of this new ethic and a number of educational and organizational changes, changes which *in toto* seem likely to stultify individual enterprise and which might very well bring American society into an era of stagnation.

But concordance and cause are not synonymous; and nowhere in the pages that follow is there any intent to imply that Freud, Freudianism, or the Freudian ethic is the cause of concordant changes in our family life, in education, in judicial practices, or in our class, economic, or political organization. To do so would, in the first place, employ the prescientific idea of simple cause and effect, and so violate the scientific principle of multiple and interdependent variables. And it would, in the second place, attribute to Freud, his disciples, and his doctrine greater credit for good or ill than is due any man, any body of men, or any system of ideas.

Contents

ix

PART I

THE ETHIC

The Protestant Ethic

THE INTELLECTUALS of the nineteenth century were for the most part men of courage, confidence, and strong convictions. They had rejected the Christian myth of special creation and along with it the doctrine of the fall of man, and many of them had gone so far as to deny the existence of any god, Christian or otherwise. Karl Marx, one of the more radical of the lot, contended that the very idea of God is a degrading social fiction that reconciles the mass of men to being exploited and deters them from taking the violent action that would bring them the ease and plenty of a communal society.

Whatever the extent of their faith in God, the intellectuals of the nineteenth century did not, however, lack any faith in man himself. Almost all the great social thinkers of that century were confident not only that man could determine his social destiny but that, moreover, he was, perhaps for the first time in human history, exercising this power to the end that he was bringing into being the perfect social order. Long before Darwin, the idea of social evolution was embodied in Western social thought; and although there was little agreement concerning the course of social evolution and still less regarding the exact mechanism by which evolution occurs, few doubted that man was the active agent and that social perfection was the ultimate consequence.

The roster of late eighteenth- and nineteenth-century social thinkers (whether they were philosophers or scientists depends upon one's point of view) is long and illustrious: France contributed such great men as Saint-Simon, Condorcet, Comte, Durkheim, and Tarde; Britain such men as Adam Smith and his many notable followers and Herbert Spencer, Darwin, and Kidd; Germany Marx, but also Wundt,

Weber, and Tönnies; and although the United States was and tradi-tionally has continued to be stronger on action than on reflection, it contributed the remarkable William Graham Sumner and the im-posing Lester F. Ward.

All these men, as well as many others, had faith in man and be-lieved that, in one way or another, man was evolving his society toward perfection. In this belief they gave intellectual reflection to the then prevailing, though by no means universal, ideal of the human character. In that ideal the human individual is physically, mentally, and morally sturdy. Being sturdy, he is self-reliant; and being self-reliant, he is also responsible. And let it be observed at once, in anticipation of what will be analyzed in detail later, that this nine-teenth-century idea of man is in all salient respects the exact antith-esis to a view of man that has emerged during the present century and that seems to be well on the way toward becoming the pre-vailing ideal of the twentieth century.

Social Change

The philosopher-scientists of the nineteenth century viewed all things social—past, present, and future—through the mental frame-work of evolutionism. And because they believed in evolution and, further, because each had tremendous confidence in his own reason-ing powers, they ingeniously, and each in his own way, fitted into the evolutionary framework such social facts as came their way. Be it a war, a revolution, a famine, or even a plague, one or another of them was certain to find in the event further proof that human society was moving steadily from good to better on its way toward perfection.*

The past half century has brought many changes in the societies of the West, and one of the more significant of these has been the

---

* A detailed history of the idea of progress is provided by J. B. Bury in *The Idea of Progress* (New York: Dover Publications, Inc., 1956). Bury believes that the idea of progress provided much of the motivation for the social changes that followed the Reformation; in current sociological terms, that the idea of progress was "a self-fulfilling prophecy." It was certainly an aspect of, or at least an assumption underlying, the Protestant ethic as that ethic will be described in the present work. Bury's interpretation is, however, overly partic-ularistic and thus far too simple to encompass the historical facts.

abandonment of the doctrine of social evolution. With the development of the social sciences, the easy and optimistic generalizations of the social evolutionists crumbled under the weight of adverse evidence, and today no social scientist can be confident that our society is changing for the better. As the findings of social scientists have accumulated, it has become evident that any unitary theory—evolutionary or otherwise—of society and of the changes that occur in society is untenable and that any attempt to forecast the future or to predict the consequences of any particular change is, thus, an act of faith or fear.

There is, of course, no dearth of social diagnosticians and social prognosticators, and in keeping with the illusions of the day many of them operate under the rubric of science. They can prove to their own satisfaction that the reputed rise in juvenile delinquency is caused by authoritarianism in the home, or by premature weaning, or by exposure to too many—or too few—television programs; that the recent (since 1940) rise in the American birth rate was brought about by the growing insecurity of social life, or by the growing *anomie* of life in our modern urban communities, or perhaps by the increasing availability of consumer credit; and so on. They can also predict, with apparent confidence, that forcible desegregation in the schools in the South will hasten the amalgamation of Negroes and whites in the South; that if the United States keeps ahead in the armaments race, the advent of another world war will be indefinitely postponed; and that if American mothers will shower their offspring with love and affection and demand nothing at all in return, the American population will be composed within a few generations of people who are happy, content, co-operative, and, presumably, also prosperous. But from the scientific point of view, all such views, assertions, and predictions stem from ignorance, sophistry, or wishful thinking.

It is currently impossible to say, on demonstrable scientific grounds, that "this" is the cause of "that," or that this social change will bring forth these social consequences. What can be said is that any society, even a so-called simple primitive one, is so complex and its elements are all so interdependent that a change—deliberate or inadvertent—in one element will bring about changes in many other elements and that every change that is positively attempted—that is, planned and deliberately undertaken—is an effort to resolve a disequilibrium that has become manifest and, hence, defined as a problem needing solution. A dynamically balanced social system is like a healthy organism in that it is composed of a great many interdependent "parts"—institutions, customs, value systems, etc. (not persons)—comparable to the cells, organs, etc., in an organism; and, like a healthy organism, it tends to correct for any disturbance to its balance by compensatory changes. In the body, the process of re-establishing balance—homeostasis—takes such familiar forms as the rise in respiratory rate that normally accompanies an increase in physical activity and the rise in body temperature that is a normal sign of defense against bacterial invasion. Sociologists have not yet coined a term to apply to comparable adaptive changes in society; they can only be described, when identified, as adaptive or functionally effective.

The social evolutionists proceeded on the reassuring assumption that all social changes are in the direction of greater functional effectiveness. But even as in a healthy organism there is always some possibility that the body's reaction to an unbalance will aggravate the disturbance rather than correct for it (*e.g.*, a muscle spasm that is more disabling than the sprain that set it off, an allergic response that is an overcorrection to an irritant), so a society may adopt changes that aggravate the problems that they were intended to cure (*e.g.*, a political revolution that leads to increased political repression, a legal prohibition that results in greater consumption of what was prohibited). Social change is not, therefore, synonymous with progress. One change may improve the working of the social system; another may only destroy the effectiveness of one or many of its parts.

No doubt a great many of the changes that are occurring in contemporary American society are adaptive in character and are thus contributing to the health, the wealth, or the happiness of its members. But there is reason to believe that some of the changes that have occurred over recent years are reducing, as does hardening of the arteries in the human body, the adaptive powers of the American social system. Whether this means that American society is in grave danger of losing its dynamic character is a matter that can be postponed until these changes have been examined in detail.

The Individual and Innovation

The starting point for this analysis is the postulate that every positive change—planned and deliberately undertaken—within a society has its origin in a specific innovation either achieved by some individual within the society or borrowed by some individual from another society. The corollary to this proposition is that the amount of adaptive change that occurs depends upon the extent to which the social system fosters the production of individuals who can and will innovate or borrow. In terms of this postulate, the social stagnation of contemporary Spain stems from those characteristics of Spanish society that preclude the emergence of innovative minds or that effectively discourage innovation and borrowing by those who might otherwise do so. Conversely, the highly dynamic character of American society is attributable to social characteristics that have so far provided a favorable climate for the genesis of an extraordinary number of innovative minds and that have given sanction to their endeavors.

From the fact, easily demonstrated, that all the societies of the past have changed very slowly and that many of them have maintained almost complete stability over centuries of time, it is an easy inference that innovative endeavor is socially atypical. Most of the members of any society are and have always been traditionalists in all salient regards. Thus for well over a thousand years the intellectuals of China contributed nothing to the social thought of Chinese society; all that they did was embellish Confucian philosophy and hand it down intact from generation to generation. Through the same period the peasants continued to cultivate their land by the same techniques, to own it in the same fashion, to build their huts in the same way, and otherwise to repeat through the generations what their ancestors had done.

The idea that innovative endeavor is socially atypical has led to the assumption, widely accepted by scientists until a generation or two ago, that the innovator is a biological sport—a genius, a person born with exceptional mental abilities. In this view, the failure of Chinese and other societies to produce innovators of note was simply a social reflection of the biological mediocrity of the members of those societies. But it has proved impossible to explain in biological terms actual occurrences of innovativeness—to explain, for example, such facts as that the many changes of the Renaissance were worked by people who had for centuries produced no geniuses and who shortly slipped back into the traditionalism from which the Renaissance had lifted them; as that the next great spurt of innovativeness appeared among the peoples of Northern Europe, who had previously displayed little ability in this direction; and as that many innovators have been considered commonplace dullards by their contemporaries, while many judged to be intellectually superior have created nothing at all.

The biological theory of innovation has, therefore, been discarded for a social interpretation.* Every normal human being is, presumably, biologically capable of innovation, of arranging into a unique pattern or combination a number of pre-existing cultural elements— words, actions, mechanical parts, chemical elements, or whatever— to the end that a new and useful idea, action, device, or substance is produced. In actuality, however, very few members of any society are inclined to attempt anything new because the social training of most induces them to accept as normal, natural, and complete the practices and devices of their society and in the process culturally blinds them to the possibility of any other practices and devices. The innovative individual is, it now appears, one who has for reasons peculiar to his time and place been imperfectly trained into acceptance of the traditional and at the same time inadvertently motivated to attempt to discover something previously unknown, to invent a new idea, form of action, or device, or to put to practical use something that has been discovered or invented by others.

Every society produces at least some members who are personally ambitious, men who are more highly motivated than their fellows. A personally ambitious person is seldom, however, one who makes a creative contribution to the development of society. Ordinarily he

---

* Such an interpretation is provided by Homer Barnett in *Innovation: The Basis of Cultural Change* (New York: McGraw-Hill Book Co., 1953).

accepts things as they are and simply endeavors in socially conventional ways to improve his position within the existing social context. He may do this by working harder than most, by being more ruthless, or by trickery and deceit. The more successful of such men have from time to time won great wealth and power; and many are remembered as historically important princes, kings, generals, popes, conquerors, dictators. It is men of this sort who in the modern world are acclaimed in the headlines and are reputed to be the shapers of human destiny. They do stand out above their· fellows; but they seldom contribute to the making of enduring and significant social changes.

The person who makes some change, however slight, in his society does so through endeavor of an original, rather than conventional, sort. He is not simply more industrious, more determined, more ruthless, or more skilled in some traditional art or craft than the majority of men; he is enterprising. The man of enterprise is distinctive in that he has both high motivation and initiative; and this latter attribute would seem to be the result of socially produced detachment from, or discontent with, some aspect of society plus a socially atypical faith in his own acumen. For unless a man believes that he is in his own right superior to the authority of custom, convention, tradition, and the people who embody that authority— father, king, or priest—he will be unlikely to apply himself to improve upon what they represent.

Just what social circumstances will induce in an individual confidence in himself and distrust of social authority sufficient to induce him to undertake to work a change in his society is not clear. It is evident, however, that the man of enterprise does in this manner set himself apart from ordinary men and that if his endeavor is to bear fruit in successful discovery, invention, or practical application of discovery or invention, he must have this faith in himself to an inordinate degree. For enterprise is seldom socially encouraged until it has proved itself; and the proof is usually slow to come and sometimes may never be achieved. That the man of enterprise must have both great and enduring faith in his own judgment and skills and a certain contempt for the opinion of his fellows is illustrated by the life histories of even the more successful of recent discoverers, inventors, and developers; they have all struggled long and suffered many failures, and they have often been ignored and even persecuted before they have achieved their self-set goals. Nonetheless, it has been just such rare and atypical men—Columbus, Luther, Watt, Whitney, Carnegie, and countless other men of enterprise, mostly unknown by name—who have worked the changes that make modern society so much more fruitful than was the society of the Middle Ages.

Weber and the Ethic of the West

The rates of social changes in Western Europe were, in so far as they can be ascertained, exceedingly low from about A.D. 500, by which time the feudal system had become widely established, to about 1100, when the Crusades began to reflect, and in turn to intensify, the restiveness of Western peoples. By the fourteenth century, when all Europe was ravaged by a succession of highly destructive plagues, many changes were occurring both in the technology and in the social organization of Western peoples. Political consolidation had begun, world exploration had been undertaken, the seeds of scientific investigation had been planted, and some beginnings had been made in the development of regional specialization of production and in interregional commerce.

The next few centuries brought what appears, upon looking backward, to have been fairly steady development in all these aspects of Western social life. Princes rose and fell, wars were won and lost, social movements of one sort and another came and went; but through all the clutter of historical events the salient aspects of modern society were slowly and quite gradually emerging. And then, toward the close of the eighteenth century, the rates of change rose abruptly. Watt invented the steam engine; Whitney invented the cotton gin; Scheele and Priestley discovered the element oxygen; Cavendish synthesized water; Franklin advocated republican government to the Americans; and there was in almost every sphere of life an unprecedented upsurge of enterprise. During the nearly two centuries since the initial acceleration in the rates of change, the rates have in most instances continued upward.

It is a comparatively simple matter to document the idea that the rates of change in many aspects of our culture have been accelerating over the past century or two; it can be done in terms of the growth of Western populations, of the rising per capita consumption of coal, oil, and iron, of the progressively increasing power of steam engines, of the rise in the divorce rate, of the growth of cities, etc. It is far more difficult to explain why there should have begun, in one place and period, a great outburst of enterprise which has mushroomed into the atomic age. The explanation accepted by the nineteenth-century evolutionists is no longer tenable; and the frequently advanced theory that it has been changes in the technology of production that have forced into being all the other changes ignores the need to explain why those changes in technology occurred. This technological theory no doubt stems from the fact that the most striking of the initial changes did occur in productive methods, which earned for the period the designation "industrial revolution." But antecedent to, accompanying, and following these initial technological changes were a host of less striking but no doubt equally significant changes in social organization and ideology.

The most impressive, if not altogether convincing, explanation for the industrial revolution that has so far been advanced is that of the German sociologist Max Weber.* From a comparative study of the social history and the social institutions and ideologies of the West with those of India and China, in which no comparable changes had occurred, he came to the conclusion that the significant variable—that is, what most distinguishes the West from these Eastern societies—is the ethic of the West. As here used, the term "ethic" designates a people's character or ideals of character, rather than a code of morality.

In Eastern societies at the time that Weber made his study the ideal man was a passive conformist to tradition; the more closely he adhered to traditional forms of conduct, the more closely he approached the ideal man. His energies and intellect were applied

---

* Weber's thesis is developed through the three volumes of his *Gesammelte Aufsätze zur Religionssoziologie,* published in 1920-21, which has been translated as *The Protestant Ethic and the Spirit of Capitalism* by Talcott Parsons (London: Allen and Unwin, 1930).

to the meticulous fulfillment of his assigned or, as in the case of the Chinese scholar, his achieved station in society. The individual, be he peasant or prince, who deviated from the role requirements of his particular station in life thereby violated the social ideal; and the entire social system operated toward establishing in the individual member of society those attitudes, values, and motivations appropriate to his social roles.

During the Middle Ages the ethic of Western society had differed, Weber thought, only in detail from that of the Eastern societies. It, too, had called for a passive conformity to the traditional. The perfect embodiment of the ideal man of the Middle Ages was the monastic monk, a man who took so literally the theological doctrine of man's fall from grace and who accepted so complacently the theological thesis that this life is an ordeal to be endured in order to gain the kingdom of heaven that he joined with others to sit out that ordeal in poverty, hardship, and prayer. It is perhaps significant that, while the majority of medieval people did meet life with some zest and courage, they also honored and respected the man who took refuge from it in a monastery.

The industrial revolution and the commercial "revolution" that preceded it were wrought, Weber realized, by men of enterprise. What, then, brought about the emergence of sufficient men of enterprise to work these great changes? A decline, he decided, of the medieval ethic and the rise of a new ideal of man. In the official medieval view, man is a weak and incompetent creature, prone to sin, incapable of distinguishing God's will from the temptations of the Devil. He is, in fact, born of sin; and his will—theoretically "free"—is so infirm that he must be constantly guided in the path of righteousness by a higher authority, the Church. The world into which he is born was originally created for his welfare; but because he failed his creator, it is for him a world of suffering which he should endure without protest. He has but one defense against this world, and that is prayer; he should not, indeed in theory he cannot, shape the world to his own interests. If plague strikes him down, as it did repeatedly during the Middle Ages, such is the will of God and such is to be borne with patience and humility. If the land grows sterile, if rodents destroy the harvest, if there be floods or droughts or other disasters of nature, these, too, are to be endured with passive acceptance; for they have been visited upon man as punishment for his sins, original or subsequent.

Some few members of medieval society deviated widely from the medieval ethic, for some few were men of enterprise. Copernicus explored the heavens with his own eyes, rather than through the dogma of the Church; Columbus violated every canon of good sense and sailed west to get east; Machiavelli dared to advise the ambitious prince on the arts of political survival; and numerous merchants and craftsmen struggled against the Church and the general social lethargy in the effort to exploit new markets and even perhaps to improve upon their products. Nonetheless, according to Weber, the medieval ethic was generally adhered to until the Protestant Reformation, when there began to emerge a new ethic, which gradually became accepted by those peoples of northern and western Europe who abandoned the authority of the Church in favor of the doctrines of Luther and Calvin. Since this new ethic was, in Weber's view, historically associated with Protestantism, he gave to it the name the *Protestant ethic;* and as such it has been known by scholars ever since. The term is rather unfortunate, for it suggests that the values and sentiments that constitute the ethic are irrevocably identified with Protestantism, held only by those of the Protestant faith, and adhered to universally by all professed Protestants.

Weber did not, however, advance a simple, particularistic explanation for the emergence of the Protestant ethic. He recognized that the values and sentiments incorporated in this ethic had existed in latent and uncodified form prior to the rise of Protestantism; and he also recognized that Protestantism was itself a product of many antecedent changes, all of which had been brought about by men of enterprise. Indeed, Luther and Calvin were themselves men of great enterprise, and they gave representation to the ethic that, in Weber's view, their religious endeavors fostered. What the Protestant religion did was provide a favorable intellectual climate for the acceptance of the ethic, a theological rationale, and, through the Protestant clergy, a body of more or less persistent advocates.

Luther rebelled against the economic and political corruption and the empty ceremonialism of the medieval Church. He wished, like many another rebel before and since, to purify a venal institution —in this instance to revitalize the essence of Christian piety; and to this end he challenged the authority of the Church. In place of the authority of an organization grown old and decrepit and indifferent to all but its own survival, he would substitute the variable but vital conscience of the individual Christian. In this Luther was, no doubt, one of the first individualistic philosophers of post-feudal Europe; and he was certainly the first churchman to make the individual theologically superior to the Church.

If it be true that the conscience of the individual Christian is the only valid guide to the Christian life, then it follows that the medieval concept of the individual as a weak and incompetent creature is false; and since this concept is the rational premise upon which the whole of the medieval ethic rests, Luther's doctrine of individual competence and responsibility is at once an attack upon the medieval ethic and a premise upon which to erect a new ethic.

Neither Luther nor Calvin had actually enunciated the Protestant ethic. Weber found, however, that by the seventeenth century many Protestant preachers were holding forth on the virtues of individual self-reliance and responsibility in matters secular as well as religious, and that in the course of time they came to identify the godly life with the life of enterprise. And although Weber did not remark upon this fact, it is to a practice established by Luther that we may trace the religious sanctioning of the Protestant ethic. Luther had intended to purify the Church from within; but he soon discovered that a venal organization is easier to replace than to reform, and his suspicion of theologians was so great that in the new churches he established he insisted that laymen play a dominant role and that each church have considerable local autonomy. Thus began the practice, continued in the Protestant sects to this day, of having a board or council of local laymen direct the affairs of the church. Since in many instances such councils were composed of the more responsible—in financial and other respects—members of the local congregation, it is understandable that Protestant clergymen often gave sanction to the characteristics of responsible men and deprecated those of men who were, for reasons of ignorance, sloth, or personal misadventure, incapable of achieving and maintaining membership in the company of respected men.

The Incentives to Enterprise

The Protestant ethic, as seen by Weber, consists of a complex of interrelated values, sentiments, and beliefs that are in marked contrast to those sanctioned by the medieval Church and, in fact, by any other form of institutionalized religion. None of the elements of this complex is uniquely Protestant; what is new is their synthesis into an ethic and the making of adherence to this ethic a religious imperative.

The idea of man upon which the new ethic rests is an admixture of Spartan and humanitarian elements. In the Spartan view, man is by nature a sturdy, durable creature; or, to put the same idea in modern terms, man is the dominant animal because he is organically the most complex and competent animal. Such being the case, society can demand much of the individual member and insist that he fulfill those demands. In Sparta, as in Rome during its ascendancy and in other militant societies, the individual was thought to be by nature courageous and indifferent to physical danger; and the man who fell short of this expectation was treated with contempt. This idea of man, or of what was worthy in man, was central to the ideology and practices of such recent totalitarian political regimes as that of the Fascists in Italy and the Nazis in Germany; and it seems to be, contrary to the philosophy of Marx, enforced upon the peoples of Russia by their Communist masters.

In the Protestant ethic, however, this Spartan view of man is modulated by the humanitarian idea of the inherent dignity and integrity of the individual. The result is an idea of man that makes him by nature independent and individually self-reliant; man has, in this view, great capacity for moral courage as distinct from the simple, brutish ability to endure socially imposed physical hardships and to submit, when the occasion demands, to violent death. It is such a man, the man of moral courage and stamina, who has the capacity to be lord and master of all that he surveys. The contrast between this idea of the nature of man and that which obtained under the Church during the Middle Ages is self-evident; and almost as marked is the contrast between this idea of man and that which seems to have replaced it in Western societies over the past half century.

Since man has, in the Protestant view, the capacity to be independent and self-reliant, the worth of any individual, to his fellows and in the sight of God, is measured by his accomplishments in this life—by how fully he utilizes this capacity. And in the Protestant system of values, accomplishment means the overcoming of obstacles, physical or otherwise, to the satisfactions of man's mundane needs. The man who passively submits to hardships is an unworthy creature; if his larder is empty and his family hungry, he should go forth and seek food, not just pray and wait in the medieval manner for God's benevolence or sit and wait in the modern mode for the next unemployment check. The ideal man in the Protestant ethic is, thus, a man of action rather than of passive acceptance; he is a man who is strongly motivated and has both the courage and the confidence to seek the satisfaction of his needs.

Thus the Protestant ethic is a codification of those personal qualities—strong motivation, freedom from social preconceptions, self-confidence, foresightfulness, etc.—that together constitute individual initiative and lead to enterprising conduct of some sort or other. In accordance with the ethic, that man is best who applies himself most energetically and with the greatest ingenuity to the accomplishment of some worthwhile task; that man is of least worth who does little and does that little in a routine, inefficient way. A correlate to this stress upon individual enterprise is the conviction that every man is himself responsible for his own welfare. God has not decreed that this life should be harsh and unrewarding, that he should live here in misery and secure his reward for passive patience in the afterlife. God has, rather, given man the ability to make of this life what he will. If he fails to exercise the enterprise that will make his life pleasant and rewarding, it is no one's fault but his own; he has only himself to blame.

To the extent, highly varied even in the heyday of the ethic, that the members of society honor the Protestant ethic, they encourage enterprise by rewarding through approval and otherwise the individual who displays it and by punishing the individual who does not make the fullest use of his opportunities. Thus the man who undertakes a venture can anticipate that if he is successful he will gain wealth or position and, as a sort of bonus, the satisfaction of being recognized as one who has succeeded by his own efforts. And the one who is tempted to lie abed of a morning can look forward to the dual punishments of failure to earn his daily bread and the contempt of his fellows.

But the incentives to enterprise transcend the mundane. For the Protestant ethic identifies the good life with the godly; and the idea that one gets what he deserves in this life is projected into the eternal life of the spirit. For in this as in other religious beliefs men make God in their own image. The Protestant god is, on the whole, demanding. He is, in effect, a god of achievement over adversity. He has given men this earth on which to dwell, an earth that is distinctly neutral toward man. And he has given them the ability—reason and freedom of will—to make of this earth what they will. If a man does little with it, he has, in the sight of God, demonstrated his unworthiness, and he will not be welcomed into the company of heaven. If he exploits his opportunities to the utmost, he will be rewarded in heaven as he was on earth.*

Medieval Christianity made life in heaven a compensation for the ungratifying and inescapable trials and tribulations of this life, thus to some extent encouraging passive submission to whatever circumstances the individual was subject. The Protestant ethic, on the contrary, makes the afterlife a spiritual supplement to the rewards, presumably earned, of this life. In this sense, at least, Protestantism does not operate as "the opiate of the people," to use Marx's phrase. To the extent that it is effective, it serves rather

---

* The Calvinistic doctrine of predestination was incorporated, in some form or other, into the theology of all the Protestant sects. Its logical implication is that nothing that man does in this life will affect his spiritual status after death; and in some times and places the doctrine of predestination may have served as the basis for religious self-abasement, such as that which is reflected in many of the old Baptist hymns. But on the whole, Protestants have given no more than lip service to the doctrine and have proceeded operationally on the assumption that achievement in the eyes of man is rewardable achievement in the eyes of God.

to encourage the individual to seek by his own efforts the maximum possible achievement, since those who do not do so suffer both before and after death, and those who do do so will be doubly rewarded—first here and then in heaven. In this system of beliefs and values, it is obviously of no consequence that "you can't take it with you."

And so we come to another basic aspect of the Protestant ethic: the fact that it makes achievement a means to an end rather than an end in itself. In the Protestant ethic there is no such nonsense as "art for art's sake." Men exert themselves as a means to the end that they may gain something to which they aspire; and in this view both aestheticism and asceticism are but feeble rationalizations of unwillingness or inability to tackle life with zest and self-confidence. Depending upon time, place, and circumstance, the means may be the taming of the wilderness to the end that future generations may prosper, the making of a monetary profit to the end that wealth may be accumulated, the achieving of high position to the end that—among other things—one's name will be remembered by posterity, or the extension of scientific knowledge to the end that the welfare of man may be improved.*

Such stress on endeavor toward some end has a number of interrelated consequences. In the first place, it makes today subordinate to tomorrow; it leads to foresightful conduct, to the sacrifice of current satisfactions for future satisfactions—e.g., to the repairing of the roof today in order that it will be sound when rain does come, and to the invention during the winter of a new kind of plow in the hope that it will aid in the spring plowing. In the second place, it leads to the continual accumulation of satisfactions rather than to the consumption of them as they are acquired. This latter result is most easily demonstrated when the satisfactions are measured in terms of material wealth. In the Protestant ethic the production of wealth is not so much for the satisfactions to be obtained directly from the

---

* Robert K. Merton has summarized the historical evidence that indicates an association between Protestantism and the rise of science in eighteenth-century England and discusses the general problem in his *Social Theory and Social Structure* (Glencoe, Illinois: The Free Press, 1957), Chapter XVIII, "Puritanism, Pietism, and Science."

consumption of wealth as it is a means to the accumulation of wealth. One might ask what is the value of accumulated wealth, if it is not to be consumed; the answer is that success, in the material realm, is measured by the amount of wealth that one has amassed rather than by the display of expended wealth—"conspicuous consumption," as Veblen called it. Thus, under this system of values, a penny saved *is* the equivalent of a penny earned.*

Capitalism and the Social Climate

The critics of Weber, most especially the English economic historian Tawney, attacked his thesis on the grounds that capitalistic forms of economic activity—*i.e.*, of production for market, marketplace determination of values, etc.—had appeared here and there in Europe prior to the Protestant Reformation. This being so, they argued, the Protestant ethic was not essential to the rise of capitalism. But the fact is that Weber did not undertake to explain the rise of capitalistic society as such, or, for that matter, to explain the rise of any other specific forms of social organization. He endeavored, rather, to ascertain why Western societies around the eighteenth century entered upon a period of exceptionally rapid change, or, in his own phrase, a period in which there appeared the *Geist*, or spirit, of capitalism. It was that spirit, or as we would now term it "social climate," which concerned him. The social climate was, as it has at least until recently continued to be, one favorable to individual enterprise in most fields of human endeavor—arts and sciences, social thought and organization, technology and commerce.

Weber undoubtedly overestimated the role of Protestantism in bringing about and maintaining the Protestant ethic. His proof that

---

* Critics of capitalism have often contended that this particular aspect of the Protestant ethic may have contributed to the accumulation of venture capital, necessary in the early phase of the industrial revolution, but that it has since operated to retard consumption and thus delay the full flowering of the industrial age. Such critics take a myopic view of the Protestant ethic. The idea that effort is a means to an end is just as essential to success in technological innovation or scientific discovery as it is in commerce or industry; for without it the many failures that normally precede success in such endeavors would be discouraging of further effort.

there was a historical concordance between Protestantism and the ethic is, however, indisputable. The major changes that occurred during the eighteenth and nineteenth centuries in the technologies, organizations, sciences, and philosophies of Western peoples for the most part originated among Protestants; and many of those developments are still restricted in use to Protestant lands. This does not mean that Jews, Catholics, and men of no particular religious faith have not been enterprising; indeed, it is easy to demonstrate that in some realms non-Protestants have been disproportionately represented—as is certainly the case of Jews in science and philosophy. But it was people who were preponderantly Protestant who gave rise to and acceptance to most of the changes that came about in the West; and it was for the most part among such people that non-Protestant men of enterprise made their appearance and achieved their success. It is to be observed, by way of negative example, that nowhere in the New World did the Spanish, who had not then and have not yet discarded the beliefs, values, and sentiments of the Middle Ages, develop the lands that they discovered. They conquered the native peoples and imposed upon them both religious and military systems of exploitation. But they never conquered the land and set about exploiting its resources; and even now, long after the break with Spain itself, Latin America is still in many respects a very old New World.

Weber's error, or oversight, was in ignoring the organizational, as distinct from ideological, circumstances that were favorable to the rise of men of enterprise in Western Europe. The early, pioneering men of enterprise slowly produced organizational circumstances conducive to the rise of more men of enterprise; and in this and other ways they contributed to the codification of the values, sentiments, and beliefs that became the Protestant ethic. The Protestant Reformation was itself an expression of social changes that were already in process; and Luther was as an individual a man of enterprise; unlike the vast majority of his fellow priests, he had acquired those personal characteristics that together constitute individual initiative. And had there not already been, in his time and place, numbers of others so constituted, his enterprise in the reformation of Christianity would probably have come to nothing.

That there was a body, however small, of enterprising men in sixteenth-century Germany and Switzerland prior to the rise of Protestantism is indicated by the fact that in establishing his churches Luther turned for support and guidance to the more "progressive" secular leaders, both political and commercial, of the regions into which Protestantism spread. The acceptance of Protestantism was itself an indication that in these regions changes, organizational in nature, were already occurring; and the importance to the evolution of the Protestant ethic of the organizational innovation of subordinating the new church to lay authority has already been indicated. Equally important to the rise of Protestantism and in turn to the ethic was the pre-existing development of secular written languages and of a secular, and largely anti-Church, literature. For it was through this that the intellectual authority of the Church was being broken and an occasional individual was being exposed to nontraditional ideas and facts.

It would seem essential to the development of any significant number of enterprising men that the channels of communication between men be free and unhampered. Wherever those channels have been monopolized by a single organization, such as the Church during the Middle Ages and the classical scholars in old China, the monopoly has invariably been used to maintain the intellectual and social *status quo*. This end is accomplished by rigorous indoctrination of those who are to have access to the existing body of knowledge and ideas and by the preservation of that body of knowledge and ideas from contamination. It was to the latter end that all through the Middle Ages the Church persecuted those who dared to advance ideas or even sense evidences that were at variance with Church dogma regarding matters religious or mundane. Only as the monopoly of the Church over the minds of medieval men was gradually broken was it possible for many individuals to begin in significant ways to think for themselves—that is, to become intellectually enterprising. And the emergence of Protestantism was more a culmination than a "cause" of this development. Critical items in this development were the invention of the printing press, itself a reflection of unusual enterprise, and the growth among the rising merchant class of methods of writing in the local spoken language; for until then written documents were few and held mainly by churchmen, and the writing was in Latin.

Closely allied to the ease and freedom of communication between the members of society is the extent to which the class system is open, offering opportunities for individual movement up and down the class ranks. Where, as was the case in medieval Europe, the class categories are rigidly defined, the differences between the classes are great, and class membership is determined by parentage, there is little occasion or opportunity for individual enterprise. Under such circumstances, the individual, whatever his class position at birth, is effectively indoctrinated into the values, sentiments, beliefs, and so on of that class and is isolated from those of the other classes. He is, therefore, unlikely to acquire those socially atypical attributes that make for individual initiative; and should he happen to do so, his endeavors are certain to take more, rather than less, conventional directions. For, whether his class position be high or low, his knowledge and understandings will inevitably be class-bound and thus narrow and distorted; and any efforts that he might make to break from the constrictions of his class position will be discouraged by the members of his class and by those of the class superior to him.

By the time of Luther the class structure of Western Europe had become confused and sufficiently open to enable some individuals to rise through their own efforts to a class position higher than that to which they had been born. The old medieval class system had been profoundly disturbed by plagues that swept through Europe during the fourteenth century, which reduced the population by one half or more and resulted in an acute scarcity of labor, thus giving to the laboring classes, both rural and urban, a new and improved status. Further disturbance to the old order was occasioned by the subsequent rise of new classes composed of artisans, mercantilists, and such professionals as scribes and legal scholars who provided services needed by the mercantilists.

The Reformation was as much a consequence as a cause of these changes in the class system: Protestantism reflected the liberalism of the new men of enterprise; it broke the Church's hold on usury and enabled Christians to engage in finance; and, finally, it gave religious sanction, as has been shown, to their enterprise. In so doing Protestantism did, of course, accelerate the changes, class and otherwise, that were already occurring. But there were still many circumstances that discouraged the appearance of men of initiative and that limited the scope of individual enterprise. Wars, many of them having religious implication, were frequent and devastating; and monarchical political control persistently favored the old hereditary aristocracy and the peasantry against the interests and ambitions of the new urban artisan and mercantile classes. Moreover, the latter soon developed the protective support of guild organization, and this in turn resulted in monopolization of production and commerce, discouraging enterprise and slowing down the rates of social change. For two centuries and more the Protestant ethic was, therefore, more an ideal than an actuality; and until the latter part of the eighteenth century, European men of enterprise were constrained to direct their efforts into colonial developments rather than the modification of European technology, trade, and organization.

Enterprise in America

It is perhaps significant that when Weber sought an example of adherence to the Protestant ethic he found it in Colonial America rather than in preindustrial Europe. To Weber, Benjamin Franklin, author, editor, scientist, inventor, politician, and social philosopher, was the ultimate man of enterprise. He was active in a wide variety of endeavors; to each he brought a remarkably open mind; and to many he contributed in an innovative manner. Moreover, he was perhaps the first and certainly the most vocal publicist to advocate the Protestant ethic.

It may be debated whether the Protestant ethic flourished more fully in America than in England and Continental countries; the main impetus for the industrial revolution came in England, and it was there that most of the crucial early inventions in industrial technology occurred. But for whatever reasons, the earliest and most persistent propaganda on behalf of the Protestant ethic was American. Benjamin Franklin established the precedent for this propaganda in his *Pennsylvania Gazette* (the predecessor of the still existent *The Saturday Evening Post*) and in his *Poor Richard's*

Almanac, which he larded with homilies glorifying the virtues of adherence to the ethic and the rewards to be so secured. By way of Franklin's publications came many of those now old-fashioned maxims that were handed down from father to son (or, more often perhaps, from mother to son) for generations: A penny saved is a penny earned; Early to bed and early to rise makes a man healthy, wealthy, and wise; A fool and his money are soon parted; Do not postpone to tomorrow what should be done today; etc.*

To what extent Franklin's advocacy of the Protestant ethic simply reflected the prevailing sentiments and values of his time it is impossible to say. Perhaps, like all good journalists, he printed for his readers what they wanted to read, although it is just possible that his efforts on behalf of the Protestant ethic contributed to its acceptance in America. At any event, he did set a journalistic fashion that was to persist for nearly a century and a half. One of the most successful and widely known of the later advocates of the Protestant ethic was the textbook writer McGuffey, who supplied many generations of school children with "Readers" heavily weighted with little tales demonstrating the virtue of enterprise and with maxims in the Franklin tradition. Long before the vogue for McGuffey Readers ran out, Horatio Alger began to provide the schoolboys and young men of America with a series of enterprising heroes to emulate.†

---

* There seems to be a tendency to associate the Protestant ethic with Puritanical grimness; but in point of fact the former need not lead to a harsh and inflexible outlook. Franklin, who throughout his life advocated—and himself adhered to—the Protestant ethic, was tolerant and not without humor.

† Horatio Alger was himself a rather enterprising man; but his enterprise took the direction of advocacy rather than innovation. In 1807, he wrote and published a story, *Ragged Dick,* in which the youthful hero demonstrates his honesty, his thrift, his industry, his reliability, and his self-reliance in such obvious ways that his virtue is ultimately recognized and rewarded. (Not, however, by society; for that would be too complex for youthful comprehension. Alger represents society in the person of a benevolent and wealthy gentleman.) For more than forty years Alger republished this story, slightly modified and with new titles, until he had a bibliography of well over a hundred books, which had sold to more than ten million readers.

A perceptive and amusing article on the role of Alger in the maintenance of the Protestant ethic, with some asides on its current decline, is Clifton Fadiman's "The Road to Success" (*Holiday,* February, 1957).

Journalistic support of the Protestant ethic continued well into the present century in America. The revived *The Saturday Evening Post,* under the durable and vigorous editorship of George Horace Lorimer, was dedicated to the principles of its original founder. Almost every issue had at least one article, biographical, autobiographical, or general, that either demonstrated or else lauded the virtues of honesty, personal integrity, industry, originality, and other items of individual enterprise; and many of the stories seem now to have been published more for their moral implications than for their entertainment value. Throughout the same period there were a number of periodicals designed for young people that held up for emulation heroes and heroines embodying all the attributes of individual initiative and engaging in a highly enterprising way in study, work, or even play.

In other ways, too, the American people have in the past indicated their acceptance of, if not actual adherence to, the Protestant ethic. The political tradition that a presidential candidate ought to have been born in a log cabin, to have acquired an education the hard way, and to have risen to high station by his own individual efforts is peculiarly American; and that tradition persisted into the present century. Many, but certainly not all, of the semi-mythological heroes of America have likewise been men of enterprise; there are, for example, Daniel Boone, Johnny Appleseed, David Crockett, and the entirely mythological Paul Bunyan.

To what extent a people's popular literature, political images, and mythological heroes reflect the ideals toward which they actually strive is not clear. But that the American people, including the millions who came as immigrants from Europe and Asia, displayed a high level of enterprise is self-evident. In less than two centuries they settled and subdued a territory four times the size of all Western Europe, built a vast and reasonably efficient physical plant —towns, cities, factories, roads, etc.—and, at the same time, achieved and adopted a wide variety of technological and organizational innovations. England was the center of the industrial revolution, and for a time Germany made the major contributions to the sciences of physics, chemistry, and biology. But what others began, the people of the United States rapidly and most vigorously developed. And following World War II, the United States embarked upon the greatest enterprise of all history—the attempt to serve as the cultural center, to use an anthropological term, for more than half the peoples of the world and to protect, to support, and to guide them into the American Way without at the same time subordinating them to American political, military, or economic interests.

An End to Enterprise?

Many conditions, including the possession of vast physical resources and a comparative freedom from the constraints of old institutions and the dead hand of history, have contributed to the rise of modern American society. But these conditions have provided only opportunity; and, in the terms of an old American maxim, opportunity may knock, but there must be someone to open the door to it. It has been the enterprise not of a few great men but of a historically atypical proportion of the population that has kept American society dynamic and so wrought the multitudinous changes that all together make the difference between Colonial America and the America of today. And for individual enterprise no substitute has yet been found, despite the attempts of the political masters of contemporary Russia and China to achieve by force what has so far in human experience been obtained only through the free expression of individual initiative. Unless and until such a substitute is discovered, the future of American society, and indirectly of at least half the people of the world, depends in large part upon the maintenance of the values and sentiments of the Protestant ethic and of the organizational and other circumstances favorable to the rise and social acceptance of men of enterprise. For without a large number of such men to keep it changing constantly toward greater functional equilibrium, American society will most certainly enter upon a cycle of adversity, thus following the route already taken by France and Britain.

It can no longer be said of American society, as has been truly said of many societies in the past, that in the midst of plenty there is hunger. It is practically impossible for any modern American, however incompetent or willfully determined to starve himself to death, to suffer hunger for long. Once discovered, the hungry man will be fed, forcibly if necessary, at public expense. But it can be said of American society that in the midst of constant and impressive changes, worked by men of enterprise, circumstances are arising that seem to jeopardize the future, since they threaten to bring to an end the production and acceptance of men of enterprise.

There is no scientific basis upon which to forecast the social future; the most that can be done with due regard for scientific integrity is to hypothesize the future consequences of selected current trends—in this case, trends in social change. But whether any or all of the current trends in social change will continue into the future or be canceled out by other and new developments it is, of course, impossible to know in advance. So all that follows here is contingent upon the assumption that what are singled out for analysis are long-term trends, although in fact one may hope or fear—depending upon personal values—that they may shortly come to naught.

2

The Freudian Doctrine of Man

THE PROTESTANT ETHIC consists of a system of values and sentiments that translates into action as individual enterprise. These values and sentiments undoubtedly were, as Max Weber claimed, historically related to Protestantism; and it was Luther's break with the Church that signaled the liberation of man from traditional authority and from the authority of tradition. Incorporated in the Protestant ethic, however, is the idea that man is a creature of reason; and this idea, as distinct from the ethic, was a product of philosophy rather than theology.

The theology of Luther provided every individual with an innate guide to moral conduct—his conscience. Since he possesses this personal power to determine for himself what acts are in accordance with God's will, he need not turn to any higher authority for guidance in matters of morality. Ethics as a moral code is, thus, an expression of each individual's conscience. But while conscience may provide the authority for moral conduct, it is no guide to the more crass and practical affairs of life—to earning a living, to exploring the world, to cultivating the soil, to healing the body's ills. The medieval view had been that the individual was to be guided in such pragmatic matters, even as in matters of morality, by tradition as represented by the authority of the Church. The philosophical idea that man possesses reason and can be guided by the evidence of his senses in all practical affairs freed man from reliance upon traditional practices and provided the Protestant ethic with a rationale for the individual self-confidence that enables men of enterprise to ignore the authority of the past and follow the dictates of their own judgment.

The roots of this new philosophical idea of man reached well back into the Middle Ages, when here and there an extraordinary man had succeeded in breaking to some extent from the mental restraints of Church dogma and had endeavored to explore some aspect of the world about him through his own senses. The practice had been stanchly opposed by Church authorities, if only because sense perceptions were seldom compatible with Church dogmas; but it had been stimulated by rediscovery of the knowledge of the ancients, and it had been supported by secular princes who became patrons of early would-be scientists as a means of bringing discredit upon Church authorities. By the time of the Reformation a goodly body of new, if rather uncertain, knowledge about the world and its place in the heavens and about man and his organic structure had been accumulated, and the idea of empirical exploration of natural phenomena was thoroughly established. In breaking the hold of the Church over men's consciences, the Reformation also loosened the theological bonds on men's minds; and before long scientists of the Protestant persuasion were unhampered in their search for knowledge by religious restraints.

Meanwhile, a philosophical justification for science had evolved. Sir Francis Bacon was, perhaps, its first great advocate, and throughout the sixteenth and seventeenth centuries philosophers struggled to define and refine the concept. The problem faced by the philosophers of science was that of demonstrating to their own satisfaction that the evidence of an individual's sense perceptions is valid and may be used as the basis for formulating actions, however contradictory to traditional understandings, to the authority of the Church, or —later—to the authority of kings and princes. To this end they set up the postulate that man is by nature a creature of reason and that failure to act reasonably is the result of ignorance. Ignorance is to be overcome by scientific examination of the universe, which yields knowledge—as distinct from superstition and unfounded belief; and when provided with the appropriate knowledge, reasonable man conducts himself in a reasoned fashion.

The philosophers of science were never very clear about what is meant by "reason." It was thought to be an ability possessed by all men, although possibly in varying degrees; it was considered to be innate; and it was eventually deemed that this ability, rather than the possession of a soul, most distinguishes man from the lower animals. Because he has this unique ability to reason, man is able to calculate the consequences of any contemplated action in advance, to compare the consequences of two or more alternative courses of action, and then to select that one which will most fully satisfy his desires. And when because of inadequate knowledge he is unable to calculate in advance the consequences of an act, he may apply his reason to the discovery of the conditions—the "laws"—determining those consequences and then be guided accordingly. The systematic discovery of the laws affecting man is science; and through science man can, and in time will, solve all his problems and thereby achieve the perfect society.

This philosophical doctrine was not, as has since become evident, entirely scientific. For one thing, it assumed that since some few men—the scientists—were exploring some small segments of the universe rationally and in terms of sense perceptions, all men could and would do so. For another, the philosophers of science vastly underestimated the complexity of reasoning—of what we now term "creative thinking" (the kind of thinking that makes man able to construct electronic computers but that such devices cannot do). All men can, and all constantly do, rationalize their conduct—i.e., find justifications for what they do. But rational thought is not, as the philosophers of science seem to have believed, a highly mechanical and exact procedure; it is, rather, a trial-and-error process that sometimes, but not invariably, leads to achievement.

The significance of the doctrine of man as a creature of reason stems, not from the fact that it contained an element of validity, but rather from the fact that it created and maintained the social fiction that *all* men are rational. During a period in which an exceptional proportion of men—compared to other times and places— were striving to be enterprising, and thus were calculating in the conduct of their practical affairs, the idea that man is by nature a rational creature was an encouragement and a reassurance. It lent the supportive powers of faith to endeavors that were, by their very nature, inherently discouraging and often ultimately unrewarding. Thus it became the rationale for the Protestant ethic; and by the latter part of the eighteenth century it was, in fact, an integral part of the ethic.

Revolt from Reason

The nineteenth century produced some few men who arrived, by reasoning, at the conclusion that man is an irrational creature. And they arrived at this conclusion by the same procedure that the philosophers of science had followed—by generalizing from a part to the whole. Thus the French sociologist Durkheim concluded from the observation that the highly specialized worker unknowingly contributes his small bit to that of many other specialized workers to produce the "whole"—the total goods and services of society —that the individual workers are directed by a supraindividual, "collective" mind. And from the fact that mobs had run at random through the streets of Paris during the Revolution, the social psychologist Le Bon concluded that the individual is always and everywhere subject to "crowd-mindedness."

Toward the close of the nineteenth century academic psychology had, particularly in America, severed its historical attachment to philosophy and in the process temporarily abandoned the attempt to explain all human behavior in terms of one principle. To William James, perhaps the outstanding psychologist of the time, some conduct was rationally arrived at, some was but the repetition of acquired habit, and some—such as the infant's sucking at its mother's breast—was instinctive. Such eclecticism provided the basis for the development of a true science of psychology, since it freed, at least to an unprecedented extent, the minds of psychologists from the preconceptions of dogma, including the dogma that man is by nature a rational animal. Within a matter of years, however, many psychologists were abandoning the scientific pursuit of an understanding of man and taking refuge in new dogma. Apparently few men can for long face the uncertainty and the recurrent disappointments of innovative endeavor, scientific or otherwise. Most men, even many of those who are ostensibly dedicated to the search for knowledge, as are scientists, are prone to fall back at the first opportunity upon the comforting certainty of authority. In the case of scientists, authority is usually the dogma of some exceptionally enterprising fellow scientist; and the history of every science is littered with the bones of dogmas that were for a time widely and enthusiastically acclaimed by the less enterprising members of the discipline.

The layman may think that scientists are a breed apart; and the fact that the pure scientist struggles in incomprehensible and apparently impractical realms and passively accepts his lowly social estate lends support to this assumption. But scientists are also human and, being human, exceedingly variable; as a class they may be considerably more innovative than any other class of men in contemporary society, but as individuals they range inevitably from the very bright to the humdrum, from the industrious to the indifferent, from the leader to the follower. Scientific knowledge does not, therefore, grow by steady and continuous accretions. Each special field of the sciences, in fact each special area in each field, is subject to erratic advances and retreats. From time to time an enterprising scientist will make what he considers an important discovery, which may or may not eventually become integrated into the body of established scientific knowledge. But also from time to time an idea—a hypothesis or perhaps a tentative conclusion—will become the center of a vogue, a scientific fashion; and many other scientists will rush to acclaim it as the final truth, or, at the very least, the key to the ultimate truth.

One such fashion swept through the ranks of psychologists and gained many adherents from sociology and political science following the publication of William McDougall's *Social Psychology* in 1908. McDougall took the then generally held view that *some* of the behavior of man is instinctive, and developed it into the doctrine that all human conduct is the expression of one or another of the instincts with which man is equipped upon coming into this world. In this view, men may think up reasons—explanations—for the various things that they do; but the fact is that they are impelled from birth to death by biologically determined drives into the courses of action that they take. There is, therefore, nothing reasonable, nothing calculating, about human conduct. Freedom is an illusion; thought is but a mental pacifier; and society is but the sum of the instinctive actions of the individual members. Such being the case, the explanation for conduct and for society is to be found in the identification of the specific instincts that motivate men to action; and since instincts can be known only through their expression, the identification of actions constitutes an explanation of them. For more than fifteen years this circular interpretation of human conduct was the dominant vogue in psychology and sociology; and the many disciples of McDougall had a field day classifying and naming the forms of conduct under the illusion that they were thereby explaining them.

McDougallian instinctivism provided an exciting break with the old and by then traditional idea that man is rational, and it had the virtue of dogmatic simplicity—of seeming to explain everything in terms that even the dullest scholar could comprehend. But it was perhaps too simple to wear well, lacking as it did a mysticality that would enable successive generations of scholars to maintain the illusion that through paraphrasing the dogma they were enlarging upon a vital truth. Instinctivism did not go entirely out of fashion until the mid-1920's, when an equally dogmatic if ultimately more fruitful vogue, behaviorism, rose to replace it. Meanwhile, instinctivism had been fused with and transformed by the Freudian doctrine of man.

Sigmund Freud was a product of the nineteenth century who had the unusual distinction of providing the twentieth century with a new and very radical idea of man, and of living to see that idea rise to a position of dominance in the thought of Western peoples. It may well be that, in the further perspective of time, Freud will be acclaimed as the intellectual father of Western society, even as Marx is now being credited with having provided the theoretical basis for Russian and Asian communism. No man is indispensable; the course of recent social history would no doubt have been much the same had there been no Napoleon, no Bismarck, no Hitler, no Roosevelt; others would have taken their place in the events of their times. Had Marx remained within the confines of academic philosophy, as he had intended, the Russian Revolution might have been delayed by a day or two, and it would certainly have had to find some other ideological inspiration; but there is every reason to suppose that Russia and China would still be trying to find an easy short-cut to an industrial utopia. And had Freud stayed with the practice of medicine, the condition of contemporary Western society would no doubt be but little different from what it is. Someone else would presumably have provided a usable and durable alternative to the Freudian doctrine of man.

It so happened, however, that Marx did devise a rationale for communism and Freud did originate an idea of man that has become a justification for many of the changes being worked in our society. Both men exemplified in high degree the Protestant ethic, for they were men of enterprise and they applied themselves to the rational explanation of man and society. In so doing, they personally demonstrated that men can live up to the standards of the Protestant ethic and that men can be highly innovative. And in the end, each came up with a doctrine that is inimical to individual enterprise. To Marx, men of enterprise are the villains of history—the capitalistic exploiters of the downtrodden, productive masses. To Freud, on the other hand, men of enterprise are neither villains nor heroes—they are neurotics.

Sex and the Psyche

Freud's doctrine evolved over many years, and elements of it, often conflicting one with another, are embodied in uncounted documents. He remained, over those many years, remarkably innovative and did not hesitate to abandon a prior interpretation in favor of a new and more interesting one. Moreover, Freud wrote with zest and considerable poetic license. As a result of all these factors, Freud's writings have little more internal consistency than does the Old Testament; anything that may be said about Freud's ideas can be contradicted by citations from Freud; and no one has yet been able to interpret Freud in a way that is acceptable to all Freudians.* What follows is a lay version of the conceptual frame-

---

* A comparative study of the currently dominant interpretations has been made by Ruth L. Munroe and reported in *Schools of Psychoanalytic Thought* (New York: The Dryden Press, Inc., 1955). The brief analysis of Freudianism given here follows mainly that of Horace M. Kallen, "Psychoanalysis," *Encyclo-*

work upon which Freud strung his many and often contradictory analyses.

Freud began his medical career conventionally enough. His preliminary training was in chemistry, botany, and physiology; and he started his professional practice as a neurologist. Shortly after he had been appointed to a chair of neuropathology at the University of Vienna, he went to Paris to study under Charcot the use of hypnosis as a means of probing into the secret recesses of the human mind. There he came to believe that sex is the unconscious but prime factor in neuroses. To this one postulate he remained true throughout his life; and upon this postulate he gradually, and quite haphazardly, erected his doctrine of man.

Freud's efforts to elicit from his neurotic patients evidence that their mental problems were at basis sexual led him to evolve over the years an ingenious and self-validating concept of the structure of the individual's psyche. Man comes into this world, Freud concluded, biologically equipped to live in a never-never land. Something, apparently, had gone wrong with the evolutionary process. For rather than being the biologically best adapted to survive under the conditions of life in this world, man is by all odds the worst prepared to do so. It is a miracle, which Freud never attempts to explain, that for countless generations men have been surviving and in the process developing the complex social systems that, according to Freud, are the total negation of man's natural needs and inclinations. What sort of never-never land the human individual is biologically prepared to live in is by no means clear. Freud does not define it, and his comments upon society as actually known to man are all derogatory.

At birth, then, the human animal is a wondrously complex organic machine designed to lead a life that will be denied to him. So from birth to death the individual is engaged in a continuing and irresolvable conflict with the world about him. Of course, he is not

pedia of the Social Sciences. Kallen's discussion, written before the Freudian invasion of the social sciences, is undoubtedly the most objective, unbiased treatment of the subject available. One of the many orthodox treatments of Freudianism is provided by Calvin S. Hall in _A Primer of Freudian Psychology_ (Cleveland: The World Publishing Company, 1954).

consciously aware of that conflict. Otherwise he would destroy himself, or alternatively destroy the society that prevents him from realizing his true self. Since he rarely does either, the Freudian premise that man is by nature antisocial was neither demonstrable nor self-sufficient. But by a most ingenious series of secondary premises, Freud resolved these difficulties to his satisfaction and that of his countless followers. These premises, laid one upon the other, constitute the structural core of the Freudian doctrine.

The aboriginal psyche, that with which the infant is biologically equipped, is a pleasure-seeking, pain-avoiding constellation of unconscious drives and urges, whose being and striving are thus governed by the "pleasure principle." Various and distinguishable though they are, they fall ultimately into two contradictory modes of instinctual propulsion. One is Eros, or "the libido," the sexual urge. It is neither exclusively male nor female; for the human infant, having two parents, inherits sexuality from both. The other driving force is the death or destructive instinct. These two instincts are "active in every particle of living substance, though in unequal proportions." They are fused together in such a way that Eros dominates, at least until in the end death resolves life.

The womb is the perfect environment for man, for here there is total adjustment and all is pleasure and there are no pains. Birth is a shock, a traumatic experience, for with birth the infant enters upon a world of pain and consciousness. At birth, or possibly before that event, the libido becomes integrated or organized; and to this entity Freud gives the term "id."

As the world imposes itself upon the unwilling, intransigent id, two additions to—some would say "modifications of"—the id develop. The first of these is the ego, the second the superego. The ego is that part, phase, or level of the growing infant's self which is composed of the infant's perceptual responses to the human beings around him (consciousness) and of his unconscious ideas received from his id. The latter are responsible for the fact that during infancy the libido is expressed and some at least of its needs satisfied through autoerotism, the particular nature of which depends upon whether the infant is anal erotic or oral erotic. (Freud seemed confident that the infant would be one or the other, but did not attempt to explain why the one or the other. As will be demonstrated later, the anal-oral aspect of Freud's infantile theory has been made the basis for dogmatic interpretations of national character and dogmas regarding desirable child care.)

Along about the fifth year the child shifts from anal or oral eroticism to the alloerotic stage, in which the genitals take precedence as erogenous zones. Now the libido secures its expression in masturbation, penis or clitoris exhibition and comparison, and erotic fantasy. It is during this early genital period that the Oedipus and castration complexes become manifest. Freud considered that the discovery of the Oedipus and castration complexes was his greatest achievement, and the concepts do in fact demonstrate Freud's amazing innovative genius.*

The Oedipus and castration complexes are, according to Freud, universal. The individual is not born with these complexes, but they are inevitable products of the inescapable conflict between the individual and the world in which he must live. They come about in something of the following ways: In boys, the Oedipus complex comes first as an unconscious incestuous love of the mother, with corresponding feelings of rivalry and hostility toward the father. The complex consists, then, of socially inadmissible and hence repressed sexual attraction to the mother and sexual antagonism toward the father, both of whom the boy must, according to social convention, love in a filial way. The internalized, but unconscious, conflict between these libidinous urges and social requirements is, in Freud's view, the cause of much otherwise inexplicable behavior of man. The id, which seemingly comprehends what is occurring, recognizes that the id of the father is aware that his son is a potential competitor for his wife's sexual favors and becomes fearful that the father, to protect his sexual prerogatives, will deprive his son of his penis. That fear is the castration complex. Just how the son unconsciously knows what the father

* A systematic, if that is the proper term, analysis of Freud's concept of the libido is offered by Richard Sterba in *Introduction to the Psychoanalytic Theory of the Libido* (New York: Nervous and Mental Diseases Monograph, 1942). Patrick Mullahy discusses the Oedipus complex in *Oedipus Myth and Complex* (New York: Hermitage House, 1949).

himself does not consciously know is one of the many mysteries of the Freudian doctrine, a mystery that can, the layman will be told, be known only to those who have been properly inducted into the mysteries of Freudianism.

The Oedipus and castration complexes develop in reverse order in girls. The girl tends to interpret her lack of a penis as a punishment inflicted upon her by the mother—she has been, in effect, pre-castrated. So she turns against her mother, and this antagonism is intensified when she becomes incestuously attracted to her father and thus a rival of her mother. All of this, of course, is unconscious, unknown to the ego.

Both sexes form their superegos first as transformations of the Oedipus and castration complexes. The superego is largely unconscious and independent of and inaccessible to the conscious ego, although an outgrowth and modification of this ego. And unlike the ego, the superego is in contact with the id. Functionally, then, the superego acts as a sort of psychic censor, protecting the ego from knowledge of the id's socially inacceptable urges and preventing the Oedipus and castration complexes from either entering into the ego or being manifest directly in action. It is, presumably, through the efficient intervention of the superego that so very few children engage in incestuous relations with mother or father, or murder or otherwise evidence through direct action their antagonism and fear of the other parent, and that fathers rarely if ever castrate their sons. But all this is accomplished at a heavy cost; for although the superego usually prevents the individual from violating sexual and other social taboos and makes the ego think that in following the socially prescribed forms of action—filial love, etc.—the ego is sincere, the real conflicts are only submerged and never resolved. The child, and later the adult, is at constant war with himself and with the world about him.

The process of personality formation does not end with the establishment of the superego, for the three psychic systems of which the personality is now composed—the id, the ego, and the superego—are dynamic. The subsequent life history of the individual consists, however, only of modifications of these three systems and their changing, but unceasing, conflicts. There are crises in this life process, of which that of puberty is the most difficult; but even during the comparatively calm periods between critical phases of life the internal equilibrium of the individual is always precarious. At best, the id, the ego, and the superego can maintain an uneasy truce. Even then, the ego must maintain itself against undue pressure from the id and repressions by the superego. And always the system as a whole is subject to the unwanted, and for the most part intolerable, demands of the external world. Freud does not wonder, then, that many an individual breaks down from the strain of trying to live in a society for which he was not biologically designed and to keep his conscious self from realizing that he is engaged in a futile and unrewarding struggle from which only death will give release.

Freud's concept of the nature and structure of the human psyche is original with Freud. Unlike most new ideas, his concept was not a synthesis of pre-existing elements. The idea of instincts was, it is true, an old one; but in the traditional view instincts are social and they are expressed directly in action. To Freud, on the other hand, the instinctive equipment of man is contrasocial and never gains free expression. Freud's idea of the superego does have some resemblance to the old lay concept of conscience; and the idea of the ego as the conscious awareness of self is also an old one. But in Freud's hands the superego becomes a bewilderingly complicated and elusive psychic entity that is unknown to the conscious self, with the result that no man can say of it: "I am sorely tempted, but my superego forbids." And the ego of Freud is also so diffused and so subjected to the counterpressures of the id and the superego that it cannot possibly be understood in traditional terms.

Freud is not so original, however, when he infers from his psychic system that nothing a man does is what it seems to be. This cabalistic principle, followed invariably by Freud and his disciples, may be a logical correlate of the Freudian view of man, but it is a very old one. All, or nearly all, primitive systems of magic and witchcraft have operated upon the assumption that the evident is never the real and that only those—the magic men—who know the secret art of reading signs (or omens) can peer behind the obvious to ascertain the truth. Thus in some primitive systems of thought, the cause of a man's actions is not his own volition but some spell—usually evil—cast surreptitiously by another. Should he, therefore, kill his wife, he would almost automatically be absolved from guilt, and the local magic man would be called in to ascertain who cast the spell that caused the husband to act in the way that he did. The cabalistic principle is everywhere applied to the interpretation of religious documents; and on the grounds that what is written is not literal truth but anagogical, priests can maintain a monopoly over the hidden truth and are enabled to interpret documents in any way that suits their convenience.

Freud did not, one may suppose, intend to inaugurate a new system of cabalistic authority. In fact, he was much opposed to all traditional forms of authority, and he specifically decried religion as the "universal obsessional neurosis of humanity." Nevertheless, he adhered to the principle that what a man does is not what it seems, and he used his idiosyncratic concept of the human psyche as a scheme by which to read behind the obvious to ascertain the Freudian truth—i.e., the anagogical meaning, or motivation, behind the most commonplace act. It is for this reason that Freudian interpretations of human conduct are so contrary to sense perceptions and so incomprehensible to the layman. Consider, for example, the now-famous sexual symbolization so recurrent in Freudian writing, old and new. To the layman, the chalk in the schoolmaster's hand, the cane carried by the elder, the candy stick sucked by the child, the flagpole in the public square, and the campanile on the university campus may seem to be, respectively, a writing device, a support for feeble limbs, a sweet, a means of displaying the national flag, and a bell tower. But these are only the ostensible functions of these devices; the real function is erotic, and for those who use or see these devices they serve as penis symbols.

Sexual symbolism, both of the penis and the clitoris, comes about as a consequence of one of the seventeen mechanisms that Freud discerned whereby the urges of the id are discharged through substitute channels that are acceptable to the ego because they are not recognized as such. These seventeen mechanisms, ranging from "fixation" to "rationalization," encompass almost everything that any man—or woman—may do. And since the id is in large part sexual, almost everything that a man or woman may do becomes in the Freudian interpretation a disguised and distorted sexual act. No man can, in the Freudian view, know himself, but he might perhaps operate upon the Freudian principle that most of what he does has hidden sexual meaning and absolve himself from the necessity of doing these things by taking his id to the nearest bordello. But should he take such direct action, it would follow, in the Freudian view, that he had "transferred" to the prostitute of his choice his unconscious love of his mother, sister, or even daughter. For the principle still applies that nothing is what it appears to be, and only one skilled in the application of the Freudian system can ascertain the truth.

Psychoanalysis and the Spread of the Ism

For some ten years after his return to Vienna from study in Paris, Freud worked alone and unacclaimed. During this period he seems to have formulated the core ideas of his interpretive system and to have demonstrated to his own satisfaction that his analytical procedure was effective—or at any event more effective than any antecedent method—in the treatment of neurotic patients. About 1906, he was joined by a number of young enthusiasts, two of whom, Adler and Jung, eventually evolved competitive systems of interpretation and set up their own schools of thought. Many of this original coterie were to become lifelong disciples of Freud.* They and the men whom they recruited may have added little but confusion to Freudian theory, but most of them have been indefatigable advocates of Freudianism and loyal admirers of Freud as the discoverer of a new and universal truth.

The early history of Freudianism followed a course familiar to the student of messianic movements, religious and otherwise. The fame of the man himself was diffused more rapidly than the ideas

* Of this group, perhaps the most devoted and noted is the late Ernest Jones, who became the official biographer of Freud and the Freudian movement (*The Life and Work of Sigmund Freud*, Vol. I: 1856-1900, Vol. II: 1901-1909, Vol. III: 1919-1939. New York: Basic Books, Inc., 1953, 1955, 1957). For contrast, there is the critical, hence quite unofficial, biography, *Freud: His Life and Mind*, by H. W. Puner (New York: Grosset & Dunlap, Inc., 1947).

he represented; and as he gained followers—lay and professional—
they imputed to him powers which he himself never thought to
claim. By the early 1920's the more unrestrained among his followers had generated a charismatic image of Freud the man, and
the excitement, although limited and localized, had reached the
intensity of a true mass movement. Meanwhile, the organizational
apparatus for the systematic promotion of Freudianism had begun
to evolve, starting with the formation of the International Congress
of Psychoanalysis in 1908; and by the end of World War I psychoanalysis was a medically recognized if not highly regarded method
of psychotherapy.

Freud himself did little to encourage the charismatic aspects of
the Freudian movement; and lay interest in Freud soon receded,
to be replaced among the lunatic fringe by a variety of other, short-
lived cultistic ways to personal or social salvation. As the general
popularity of the Freudian movement declined, the importance to
it of the sober and solid disciples of Freud increased. From the
outset, most of the men who came to study under Freud had been,
like Freud himself, trained in medicine. They tended, therefore,
to bring to the movement something of the dignity and prestige of
the medical profession. Since they were Doctors of Medicine before
they became Freudians, and since they did not abandon their
status of physician in assuming that of Freudian psychoanalyst,
they gave to the practice and advocacy of Freudianism the traditional authority of medicine.

Freud was not himself convinced that the art of psychoanalysis
should be monopolized by physicians, or even that a medical training was a desirable prerequisite to indoctrination in the Freudian
system. Just why he took this position is not clear. Possibly he
feared that limitation of the practice of psychoanalysis to physicians
would unduly retard the spread and application of his ideas.
Actually, it is now evident, the association of Freudianism with
medicine was a historical accident of the greatest significance for
Freudianism. It has meant that the Freudian doctrine has come
into wide acceptance slowly and solidly, and come in, as it were,
by the front door rather than the rear. Thus had it not been for the
fact that the Freudian doctrine was sponsored by men of medicine,

the claim that it is "scientific" would no doubt have long since been brushed aside. And had not an increasing number of medical men come to accept and then to advocate the doctrine, there is little likelihood that it would ever have gained widespread acceptance among psychologists, anthropologists, social psychologists, political scientists, and sociologists. Nor could it have won so many devoted followers from members of the "helping professions"—the social workers, criminologists, child psychologists, counselors, and others.

It is not difficult to understand why the medical profession welcomed, at first grudgingly and in time quite enthusiastically, the psychoanalysts' claim of ability to treat neurotic patients successfully. Most physicians and surgeons are, by training and temperament, interested mainly in critical diseases. To them, the critically ill patient is a challenge, and to save such a patient is personally gratifying as well as professionally profitable. By contrast, the patient with a common cold, who will recover in due course and for whom little can be done anyway, is a bore and a distraction. Even more irritating is the patient who has no ascertainable symptoms of a pathological condition—the hypochondriac with his everlasting complaints of imaginary ills, the constitutional inferior who comes to the physician for reassurance when what he really needs is a mother to hold him in her arms, and the neurotic. When used by the ordinary physician, the term "neurotic" is one of contempt; for a physician is by necessity physically durable and psychologically tough. He may have considerable sympathy for the really sick patient; but he is very likely to feel, and possibly not without justification, that the neurotic is a weakling who takes up his time when worthy sick patients should be having attention.

The emergence, then, of a class of physicians who were willing to specialize in the treatment of neurotics and who, moreover, possessed firm faith in their ability to probe into and then resolve the psychological difficulties of the neurotic fulfilled a vital professional function. The availability of psychoanalysts, who as members of the medical profession were presumably beyond reproach, enabled the general practitioner and the diagnostician to refer his neurotic patients to Dr. So-and-so with a reasonably clear conscience. Because the psychoanalysts served this function, rather than for any regard for the doctrine that they represented, the medical profession here and in England gradually recognized psychoanalysis—especially that of the Freudian variety—as a respectable and responsible medical specialty. By 1930, the field was definitely established, and the teaching of psychoanalysis was being introduced into the curriculum of the more advanced American medical schools. A decade later, the Jungians and Adlerians had been all but purged from the ranks of the psychoanalysts, and the position of the field had become impregnable.*

The Insidious Invasion

In the normal course of events, any minority that is on the ascendancy within a social population struggles noisily and more or less belligerently to gain attention and acceptance; and once it has achieved a secure position, the members of the group—and the organizations representing it—relax and take their status within the society for granted. Christian Science, for example, was aggressively promoted for the first few decades following its establishment; but for the past quarter century or so its proponents have conducted themselves with quiet dignity. For some reason, Freudianism has not followed this characteristic pattern. The doctrine has undergone some modifications, mainly in the direction of making a unilateral compromise with the "environmental" social psychologists. But maturity and professional acceptance have not dimmed the promotional ardor of the disciples of Freud. Some among them are always ready to claim that Freudianism contains the key to an understanding of whatever problem happens to be newsworthy —the latest nasty crime, divorce, juvenile delinquency, the low quality of television programs, the rise or decline of dictators, or the continuing trend toward larger automobiles. Some, more re-

* Ernest Jones (in *The Life and Work of Sigmund Freud, Vol. III: The Last Phase, 1919-1939.* New York: Basic Books, Inc., 1957) relates the exceptional popularity of psychoanalysis in the United States to the fact that a very large number of Freud-trained physicians came here during the 1930's as refugees from Nazi persecution. Jones seems rather resentful of the fact that these refugees often established large and highly lucrative practices through the exploitation of Freud's theories while Freud himself lived out his last years in straitened economic circumstances.

sponsible perhaps, produce a steady stream of articles, books, or public lectures in which they interpret, in somewhat Freudian terms, the social past, the present, or the future.

Whether because of or in spite of its having been constantly and continually advocated, Freudianism has during recent years gained numbers of adherents from the ranks of psychology, social psychology, anthropology, and sociology, and even a few from economics, political science, and history.* The Freudian invasion has no doubt been most marked in psychology. Through the 1920's and well into the following decade, academic psychologists avoided Freudian theories like the plague. This was the period in psychology of behaviorism, which was gradually tempered but not displaced by Gestaltism. The idea then prevailed that the inner life of the individual was, from the scientific point of view, a variable that "intervened" between stimulus and response; and, in accordance with the scientific principle that only that which can be sense perceived constitutes data for science, psychologists refused to be concerned with the hidden motives and emotions of man.

In the years immediately following World War II, however, Freudianism came to be adopted by an increasing proportion of psychologists; and the current domination of academic psychology by Freudianism provides the economic determinists with a sorry case in support of their theory of social change. By the end of the war the demand for psychiatrists far exceeded the supply of professionally trained men; and the rapid expansion of veterans' hospitals necessitated a far greater future number of trained psychiatrists than the existing medical schools could possibly supply. Public moneys were, therefore, made available to numbers of uni-

---

* The books that seem to have been most influential in this invasion of the social sciences, books that offered a "revision" of Freudian doctrine, changing it little but making it appear more palatable to social scientists, are: Karen Horney, *The Neurotic Personality of Our Times* (New York: W. W. Norton & Company, Inc., 1937) and *New Ways in Psychoanalysis* (New York: W. W. Norton & Company, Inc., 1939); Abram Kardiner, *et al., The Individual and His Society* (New York: Columbia University Press, 1939); and E. Fromm, *Escape from Freedom* (New York: Rinehart & Company, Inc., 1941). Arnold W. Green ("Sociological Analyses of Horney and Fromm," *American Journal of Sociology,* Vol. 51, pp. 533-554, 1946) has demonstrated that neo-Freudianism is just Freudian doctrine dressed up in modern clothes.

versities for the establishment of training programs in clinical psychology, a field that had been given only casual support by the academic psychologists. Now, abruptly, those psychologists who were or who could claim to be clinicians were in great demand as teachers, and many of the more ambitious of the young men going into psychology found it to their great financial advantage—current and future—to specialize in the clinical field. The fact that "clinical psychology" was hardly more than a name proved no great deterrent. Freud, it was conveniently recalled, had favored lay, as distinct from medically trained, analysts; and the psychoanalytic approach to mental illness was already established and acceptable to the medical profession. Thus the clinicians, who took over Rorschach's ink blots, Murray's T.A.T., and other procedures that are supposed to provide inferential evidence on the state of the subject's unconscious, but who did not presume to take over the psychoanalyst's couch, were able to become preaching and practicing Freudians without encroaching upon the psychoanalyst's preserves.

It would be an exaggeration to say that Freudian doctrine has completely conquered academic psychology. The inroads of the doctrine have, however, forced the remaining non-Freudian psychologists to distinguish themselves from their Freudian fellows, usually by the designation "experimental psychologists," and to keep their opinions of Freudianism largely to themselves. The current journal literature of psychology does not resound with Freudian charge and anti-Freudian countercharge; rather, each sect goes its way in pretended disregard of the other. And since non-Freudian psychology is by far the older sect, the current silent truce suggests that the Freudians have won, or have at least come to stay.*

The Freudian invasion of contemporary social psychology and sociology has been less spectacular and considerably less forthright. Freudian concepts have seeped into these disciplines in fragments

* One academic psychologist who is not intimidated by his Freudian colleagues is J. A. Gengerelli. His article, "Psychoanalysis: Dogma or Discipline?" (*Saturday Review*, March 23, 1957, p. 9 ff.), is one of the few recent attacks by a professional and academically recognized psychologist. It is also one of the most considered and at the same time trenchant criticisms of Freudian dogma extant. But it is to be observed that this criticism was published in a lay rather than a psychological journal.

and, often, have been camouflaged by the use of non-Freudian terms. The result is a partial retreat from the behavioristic orientation that dominated these fields from about 1925 to 1945 to a modified version of the kind of instinctivism that was popular in the years just preceding 1925. In this version, the antisocial character of man's presumed instincts is not stressed, but it is frequently assumed and stated that man comes into this world with a variety of psychological needs that can be fulfilled only under special social circumstances. Thus the small-group approach in social psychology stresses the desirability of a "democratic atmosphere" in the individual's work, study, and other life circumstances on the grounds that "autocratic" authority violates the innate need for self-fulfillment, self-expression, and self-determination. Those social psychologists who are much concerned with the "tension-producing" conditions of modern life—and who purport to be able to explain everything from divorce to war in accordance with their tensional system of interpretation—likewise assume that there is a common if not universal conflict between the individual's innate psychological needs and the social demands made upon him.

The Freudian influence in sociology is most evident in those borderline fields that deal with social problems of one sort or another; the pure sociologists—those who deal with the structures and processes of society per se—have for the most part ignored the widespread trend toward Freudianism. Nevertheless, the most prolific modern sociological theorist, Talcott Parsons, delves directly into Freudian metapsychology for his explanations whenever he has occasion to refer to the individual bases of the social structures that are his prime concern.

Of all the social scientists, it has undoubtedly been the anthropologists, or the more unrestrained of the anthropologists, who have most assiduously cultivated the Freudian doctrine during recent years. There will be occasion later to consider in some detail their remarkable contributions to the popularization of Freudian ideas; and at this point the general tendency need only be suggested by saying that some anthropologists have undertaken to analyze and interpret the character of national populations in terms of Freud's anal-oral typology, which yields up such astounding discoveries as that the American people are victims of an oral-mammalian fixation, while others have applied the Freudian theory of personality development to the thesis that modern man, unlike his primitive contemporary, is unstable, insecure, and persistently maladjusted.

It is not at all difficult to document the growing reliance on the Freudian doctrine in the presumably scientific fields of psychology, social psychology, and anthropology. The strong influence it exerts in psychiatry is also easy to demonstrate. The extent to which it has invaded the lay mind can, however, be gauged only by indirection. The constantly increasing stream of popular books and articles by Freudians, the increasingly Freudian orientation of popular writers on child care and marriage counseling, the prevalence of watered-down Freudianism in the popular drama and fiction, and the newsworthiness of the wildest of psychoanalytic speculations regarding crimes in particular or crime in general, war, peace, and the latest fashion in women's clothes, all suggest that Freudian ideas are on the ascendancy. This conclusion is bolstered by the observation that such sounding boards of public opinion as the clergy and the educators have, as groups, either made their peace with Freudianism or climbed up on the band wagon. "It would be difficult," concludes a non-Freudian psychologist reluctantly, "to overestimate the impact of Freud's thought on the thinking of our times, especially among the classes which may be considered as supplying the intellectual leadership for the nation." *

Theory or Theology?

There is a strong temptation, which many critics of Freudianism have been unable to avoid, to treat the doctrine as a religious

---

* J. A. Gengerelli, *op. cit.*

The influence of Freudianism upon literature and the arts is obvious and has come to be accepted. But it is something of a shock to discover that psychoanalysis is now being resorted to by some writers as a means of liberating their presumably latent literary talents from the socially established repressions that prevent them from writing salable manuscripts. According to Robert L. Shayon ("A Small Frequency for the Muse," *Saturday Review*, May 18, 1957, p. 35), there is at least one psychoanalyst in New York City who specializes in writer-patients. Next, perhaps, we shall have specialists to psychoanalyze the readers who have become mentally disturbed through reading too many psychoanalytic novels.

phenomenon. Freud does seem to have followed, unconsciously no doubt, theological precedents in the development of his system. There is, for example, the tracing of all phenomena to one unitary ultimate cause—for Freud, nature. Nature, as represented by the libido, is comparable in Freud's analysis to God's will in Christian and other monistic religious ideologies. Everything stems from it; it is the initial source of all human conduct. It is Cause. And although the outward manifestations of the libido are incomprehensible to men, Freud and his disciples have been enabled to probe behind the incomprehensible and ascertain the true, the libidinous, cause of what man does. In religion, this claimed power is supposed to be a divine grant; in Freudianism, it is claimed to be a scientific discovery. Operationally, however, the religious and the Freudian methods of discerning the truth differ not at all; both follow a prescribed formula—the "system" of interpretation—and both produce revealed, as distinct from self-evident, truths.

The difference between revealed and self-evident truths is that the latter are subject to confirmation by comparative sense perception. Thus if one astronomer claims the discovery of a new star, he gives its position in the heavens; and other astronomers may, if they wish, see for themselves whether a star formerly unknown is located in the place specified. If an endocrinologist concluded from experiments on rats that a certain gland has a certain function, others may remove the same gland from rats and see whether its absence does have the claimed consequences. Revealed truths, on the other hand, are not secured through sense perceptions; and they cannot be verified. They are *inferred;* and it is the person who makes the inference who determines, consciously or not, what is revealed.* We all do this sort of thing in a random and rather conscious way when we infer our friends' motives from their behavior; the theologians and the Freudians do it in a somewhat formalized and possibly unconscious way when they "read" the

* In an attempt to meet this criticism, Freudian "experimenters" have resorted to projective tests under the impression that what is recorded on paper is *ipso facto* objective data and can therefore be used for comparative purposes. Zygmunt A. Piotrowski has recently elevated projective testing to a doctrine and provided it with the impressive name "Perceptanalysis" (*Perceptanalysis.* New York: The Macmillan Company, 1957).

will of God or the libidinous causes that are supposed to lie behind human actions.

Freud claimed, and no doubt believed, that his system of meta-psychology had been discovered by the scientific method. His disciples claim, even to this day, that it is scientific; and now that Freudianism has received the sanction of the medical profession, and many recognized scientists have been converted to Freudian-ism, that claim carries with it considerable authority. The weight of authority is not, however, scientific validation of the claim to being scientific. The weight of authority is the kind of evidence that makes up the data of opinion polls; but the fact that this or that many people believe that the world is flat does not make the world flat.

The evidence that Freudian doctrine is contrascientific, and to this extent comparable to a religion, is contained in the Freudian method of validating the system through which truth is revealed. That method consists of "proving" the validity of the system by the truths revealed; and should any question arise as to the validity of the revealed truths, the Freudian procedure is to refer back to the infallibility of the interpretative system.* Logicians call this a "logic-proof" system, since in effect it goes round and round without getting anywhere and cannot be broken into at any point. The most complex and durable system of self-validation was that de-vised by St. Thomas Aquinas. After nine centuries of use and abuse it still serves the Roman Church as a rationalistic system by which the authority of the Church is justified and the validity of its re-vealed truths are demonstrated. The essential difference between the Roman theological method of going behind the evident to God's will and the Freudian method of reading into the evident a libidi-

---

* In this connection, Freud himself has said: "The teachings of psychoanalysis are based upon an incalculable number of observations and experiences, and no one who has not repeated those observations upon himself or upon others is in a position to arrive at an independent judgment of it." (*An Outline of Psychoanalysis.* New York: W. W. Norton & Company, Inc., 1944, p. 9.) One of his disciples goes even further, making the traditional priestly claim to monopoly over God's wisdom: "Nobody can really understand what it [psycho-analysis] is all about without having been psychoanalyzed." (G. Roheim, ed., *Psychoanalysis and the Social Sciences.* New York: International Universities Press, Inc., 1948, p. 32.)

nous cause is that the Church has never claimed that its procedure is scientific. The Church, unlike Freud and his disciples, is content to rest its case on faith—which is, of course, where it belongs.

A further temptation to treat Freudianism as a religion lies in the fact that Freudians profess to an omniscience that is, to the scientific mind, simply frightening. Thus Freud himself did not hesitate to psychoanalyze Moses, dead these many centuries, if, in fact, he was ever more than an ancient Hebrew legendary figure. He also felt competent to make a psychoanalytic study of primitive man, arriving at fundamental truths that field anthropologists had somehow overlooked. The more ambitious of his disciples have rewritten a good deal of human history in the Freudian image; they have, of course, reinterpreted a great many of the current events of their day —political, international, etc.—in accordance with Freudian principles; and not a few of them have even ventured to peer into the social future through the time-dissolving powers of the Freudian system. Such boldness and such self-confidence are no doubt to be commended; but they stem from faith, not from knowledge.

There are, moreover, some suggestive parallels between Freudianism and Christianity as a specific religious ideology. Some fairly leap to the mind, and should not need mentioning. One that has generally been overlooked is the marked similarity between the Christian concept of the Holy Trinity and the Freudian theory of the trinitarian nature of the human psyche. It is not only that both systems divide the whole into three parts—that might be a simple coincidence—but that the parts have somewhat similar functions in both systems of thought. Thus the Freudian id is father of the self; and, like God, the id is never known directly. The Freudian ego is largely known to consciousness; and of the Holy Trinity the one part known directly by man is the Son, who came, and suffered, and so on. In both systems the functions of the third part, the Holy Ghost and the superego, are the same. They strengthen, they comfort, they protect.

Finally, the history of Freudianism is in many respects comparable to that of the rise and establishment of new religions. It has its prophet, its dedicated disciples, its organizational representation and closed body of practitioners, and its fiery opponents. The attacks on Freudianism have, with some notable exceptions, been vitriolic, as dogmatic as Freudianism itself, and have usually reflected faith in some equally closed system of thought. Jung and Adler, students of Freud, inaugurated such attacks as they evolved competitive psychoanalytic systems. Of the two recent full-dress assaults upon Freudian dogma, one is in support of Catholic theology and the other of a cultistic version of behaviorism.* Moreover, Freudianism has been denounced, at one time or another, in all the derogatory terms usually reserved for religious disputation. It has even been decried as the New Judaism and damned as an erudite version of whore-house philosophy. Perhaps a case of sorts can be made for the claim that Freudianism is a new version of Judaistic doctrine; for Jehovah was a god of wrath, and he made life something of an ordeal for man, as in Freudianism nature makes social life an onerous burden. To label Freudian doctrine an erudite version of whore-house philosophy is, however, only name calling, a prime example of the scurrilous art of establishing guilt by invidious association; for there is no firmer basis for the comparison than that both Freudian analysts and prostitutes are occupationally disposed to view man in terms of sex alone.

---

* The former is *Errors of Psychotherapy,* by Sebastian de Grazia (New York: Doubleday & Company, Inc., 1952); the latter, *The Case against Psychoanalysis,* by Andrew Salter (New York: Henry Holt & Co., Inc., 1952). Both are intemperate and reminiscent of the religious controversies of an earlier day; but both authors do, at times, strike telling logical and factual blows at the pretensions, scientific and therapeutic, of Freudianism.

Some of the best nondisputatious criticism of Freudianism is to be found in the writings of Kenneth Burke, especially in *Permanence and Change: An Anatomy of Purpose* (New York: New Republic, Inc., 1935) and *A Grammar of Motives* (New York: Prentice-Hall, Inc., 1945). Two recent criticisms of Freudianism, both relatively objective, are: *Induced Delusions,* by Coyne H. Campbell (Chicago: Regent House, 1958) and *The Case History of Sigmund Freud,* by Maurice Natenberg (Chicago: Regent House, 1958).

Like de Grazia and Salter, Burke, Campbell, and Natenberg object to Freudianism on the very sound grounds that the dogma violates sense perceptions and is therefore contrascientific. A different approach to Freudianism, one that is more in accord with that taken in the present work, is provided by Philip Rieff in *Freud: The Mind of the Moralist* (New York: The Viking Press, 1959). For Rieff, the important matter is not the truth or falsity of the Freudian concept but the moral implications of its acceptance.

Doctrine of Despair

In spite of the many parallels between Freudianism and religion, the Freudian doctrine is in function if not in form the antithesis of a religion. Every true religion serves two major and interrelated social functions. It exercises control over the conduct of the individual members of the society, and it provides the individual with assurance that life—however difficult—is worth living. Freudianism does neither. It is a doctrine of social irresponsibility and personal despair.

Freud's concern, both as a therapist and as a theorist, was with the individual. His data, if so they may be described, were dredged up from the hypothesized unconscious of his neurotic patients; moreover, he delved into this unconscious with a preconceived notion of what he would find there. Both what he looked for and what he found were inevitably biased in favor of the individual and against society. The patients saw themselves as victims of society; they were poor, misunderstood, mistreated creatures in search of someone who could comprehend their troubles and sympathize with them. Such are the common characteristics of neurotics. They are people who have failed, to a significant degree, to make their peace with society; and they believe that society has failed them. Never, in the mind of the neurotic, has he failed society.

What Freud secured from his patients might justly have been used to demonstrate how the neurotic individual regards himself and his relation to society. Freud used it, however, as evidence in favor of his humanistic but completely unrealistic idea that the individual is inevitably and inescapably repressed by the inhuman dictates of organized social life. Freud, like his patients, believed that they were victims of social circumstances; and, like them, he was in all respects antagonistic toward society. So strong, apparently, was that antagonism that Freud never pondered the question: If man is by nature contrasocial, how can it be that men have evolved the social systems by which man lives?

Unlike Marx, who also hated society—but the society of his times rather than society in general—Freud did not counsel general revolt from social restraints. Nevertheless, he implied the wisdom and justice of individual evasion of those restraints by designating (as have all psychoanalysts since) social repression as the cause of the difficulties experienced by his patients. And if he did not directly advise the patient to evade the authority of the feared and hated parent or desert the intolerable wife, his doctrine certainly does nothing to foster submission to the requirements of society and everything to cast society into disrepute.

Neither Freud nor his doctrine sanctions individual acceptance of social dictates, as does every true religion. On the other hand, Freudianism does not offer hope that the dictates of society can be entirely and for long escaped. Conflict between the individual and his society is regarded as inevitable. The effects of that conflict upon the individual may be modulated by one or more of the defensive mechanisms discovered by Freud; but they only displace or shift the onus for the conflict, they do not resolve it. So in Freudianism, as in medieval Christianity, life is a time of trial and tribulation to be borne with what fortitude the individual can muster; and Freud believed that the individual can muster very little fortitude.

In medieval Christianity, unlike Freudianism, this unhappy life is, however, a prelude to paradise. All men need do is submit to the indignities, the inequities, the impoverishments that God has in his wisdom ordained for man in this life, and he will be rewarded, upon death, with everlasting happiness. Those who accept the Freudian doctrine can find in it no such consolation for the wretched life they must lead. Freud's ultimate cause, Nature, is without purpose; we are born, we suffer, and at length we die. After death there is nothing, as before life there was nothing. All that can be said in favor of death is that it releases us from life; and of life there is nothing to be said except that it eventually ends in death.

Never has a doctrine of man that is so morbid, so discouraging, so without hope or confidence, and so lacking in inspiration been so widely acclaimed. Thus the puzzle is not so much how Freud came to devise his pessimistic metapsychological system as why that system should have gained such wide popular acceptance. The roles played in this by his disciples and by the halo prestige of medicine have been indicated. But they are hardly sufficient to explain why a doctrine of despair has become a major, if not yet the major, philosophy of our times. Some of Freud's critics have thought that the popularity of Freudianism stems from its preoccupation with sex; and it has been remarked that, although Freud did not discover the causative basis for human action, he did succeed in deifying the lowest common denominator.

The ancient Greeks deified sex in the person of Aphrodite; but she was a happy and playful goddess, not a grim and destroying force. Moreover, the Greeks had many other gods. To Freud, sex was all, or almost all. It is doubtful, however, that Freud's engrossment with sex explains, even in part, the popularity of the Freudian doctrine. The explanation lies, as will be shown in due course, in the fact that Freud's idea of man has acquired functional value; it has, in recent years, given men a justification for some of the more significant of the changes that they have been working in our society. And in so doing, it has no doubt contributed its force to the other forces that have been inciting these changes.

3

The Freudian Ethic

THERE IS NO scientific evidence to support the Freudian idea that man is born with biologically provided urges, needs, or interests that set him at odds with the society in which he lives; there is no real reason to suppose that sex is the dominant, if submerged, force in the life of the individual; there is no reason, aside from Freud's assurances, to think that what a man does is not what it seems to be; and there is no evidence, aside from that adduced by Freud and his disciples in accordance with their interpretative system, that the child inevitably—or even ever—develops an Oedipus complex, followed by a castration complex or penis envy, and that he thereafter goes fumbling and stumbling through life with the balance between his id, his ego, and his superego ever precarious and ever subject to jeopardy. There is not even any scientific evidence that the concepts of id, ego, and superego represent actual components of the individual's psyche.

Neither is there any scientific evidence that man possesses a soul. Nor is there any scientific reason for believing that there is a life after death. Nor is there any scientific method of validating the scientists' assumption that there is order in the universe. Nonetheless, men have acted and still do act as though they have souls and a future life and as though the world about them is governed by laws of nature or of God. And by so acting they render these various ideas socially valid.

There are limits to the process of socially validating social ideas, beliefs, assumptions, etc. So far, all the wishful thinking of the Jehovah's Witnesses has not brought to pass the battle of Armageddon; the date is repeatedly pushed further into the future. But, within limits, the world is for man what he socially defines it to be; and men have historically defined their world in a great and wide variety of ways. They have also defined themselves and their relations to the world in highly divergent ways. The Protestant ethic is one such self-definition. It is an unusual one, probably without historical precedent, limited to some of the peoples of the West over the past three centuries or so, and now apparently on the wane. As man's idea of what he is (or, more properly, his ideal of what he can and should be), the Protestant ethic is socially valid only to the extent that man through his conduct makes it so. It involves the assumption that man is inherently an independent and sturdy creature, and should therefore conduct himself with courage and be industrious and self-reliant and in all respects responsible for his acts. There is no doubt that men can be highly industrious, and that they can be relatively self-reliant and responsible. Countless men have conformed in considerable degree to the dictates of the Protestant ethic. But they have done so because they were trained to it and socially encouraged to conform to it, not because it is in any sense "natural" for men to be enterprising.

And so the fact that the Freudian doctrine of man is unscientific has no real social significance. What is socially significant is whether man can and will give it social validity. The Marxian doctrine of social evolution was not, as Marx and all his disciples since have believed, derived from the empirical study of social history. Like Freud's doctrine of man, it was imposed upon facts, not deduced from them. Marxianism is, therefore, unscientific in the same sense that Freudianism is unscientific. Nevertheless, a great many men have for well over half a century been exceedingly busy in trying to give some social validity to Marxianism; and while they are still far from the Marxian goal of the prosperous, classless utopia that Marx was confident would shortly follow the proletarian revolution, they are still presumably—or at least according to their claims—struggling to that end.

Marxianism is a doctrine of social destiny in which the individual member of society plays the role of a passive functionary. Marx's goal was the welfare of the individual, but he saw the means to that welfare in the reshaping of society. As a consequence, his doctrine concerns society rather than men in society, and his only treatment of men as such is to attack as "capitalistic exploiters" the enterprising men of his day. In the Communist Manifesto, he does, it is true, glorify those particular men of enterprise who will strike off their chains and lead the mass of workers in the revolt against their masters. But such leadership will be a temporary, transitional thing; and once the communistic society is established, it will become self-perpetuating, a vast social organism, the individual cells of which will thrive from participation in the whole but will not actively influence the character of that whole. Marx's attack upon capitalists may be taken as a rejection of the Protestant ethic; but Marx does not provide a substitute ethic or an idea of man upon which such a substitute might be evolved.

The efforts to validate the Marxian doctrine have, however, produced an ethic of sorts. In fact, one may perceive two rather contradictory ethics operative in contemporary Russia. Following, perhaps, upon the example of the Old Bolsheviks, the political elite seem to esteem as suitable for themselves the personal qualities of physical courage, physical strength and endurance, and insensitivity to the welfare of others (justified, of course, on the grounds of a higher value). They are not, in practice at least, men of enterprise; for their efforts are mainly devoted to rising within the organizational system, or at least staying alive as members of that system. In a crass and crude sort of way, the current political elite of Russia would seem to fit Whyte's definition of the organization man.*

The mass of the Russian people, including apparently artists, scientists, and technicians, are officially required to conform to a rather Spartan ideal of man. The individual must be sturdy and enduring; and he must passively and uncomplainingly—in fact, even enthusiastically—fulfill meticulously whatever duties the society imposes on him and accept as a just reward whatever the society may concede to him. He must not, obviously, be in any way individually enterprising; and should he display signs of individual deviation, he will be promptly damned as a traitor to the system. No one will suppose that either the Russian elite or the Russian masses fully

* William H. Whyte, Jr., *The Organization Man* (New York: Simon and Schuster, Inc., 1956).

live up to these official ideals. But that the Russians have been evolving a sort of dual system of ethics does seem indicated from the rather limited evidence presently available to us. Such being the case, the general sequence of recent historical developments in Russia and the other Communist lands has been the acceptance of a doctrine of social revolt and social reconstruction, followed by efforts to validate that doctrine, which have resulted in the subsequent emergence of one or more new ethics.

By contrast, the general sequence of recent developments in the West, and specifically in America, has been almost the reverse and has tended to parallel the developments by which capitalistic society evolved. Freud presented to Western peoples a new and very radical idea of the nature of man, an idea of man that is in all respects the antithesis of that which was advanced by Luther; and to some extent the role of Freud in the twentieth century has been comparable to the role that Luther played in the emergence of the Protestant ethic. For upon the Freudian doctrine of man there has developed a new ethic, and this new ethic is being propagated by Freud's disciples in much the same way that the Protestant clergymen sanctioned and disseminated the Protestant ethic. And although the Freudian doctrine of man is hardly half a century old and the Freudian ethic somewhat less than this, already this new ethic is gaining considerable organizational representation and being made the justification for various changes in our social order. It is such social validation of the Freudian doctrine that gives to Freudianism its great significance. To question its scientific validity becomes, therefore, irrelevant. Freudianism, like Marxianism, is or will become just as valid as men make it.

Clinical Myopia

The premise upon which the Protestant ethic evolved was the secular supplement to Luther's insistence that the individual human being has a conscience, which can and should be his guide to conduct—the idea that he is capable of independent, rational conduct. This idea was embodied, nearly three centuries later, in the Declaration of Independence as the self-evident truths "that all men are created equal; that they are endowed by their Creator with certain inalienable rights; that among these are life, liberty, and the pursuit of happiness." That Declaration and the political Constitution that was designed to implement it were devised by men of enterprise in order to free men of enterprise from the constraints of a government that still had its roots in the authoritarian tradition of the Middle Ages. These documents, like the Mayflower Compact that had so long preceded them, were attempts to give political sanction to the Protestant ethic. And for a century and a half many, but far from all, of the changes that were worked in American society were in accord with the spirit if not the letter of these testaments to the value and validity of the Protestant ethic.

The rise of Freudian doctrine as the prevailing concept of the nature of man is at once a measure of the decline of the Protestant ethic and a denial of the idea that man is a creature of reason. Freud's idea of man is one that in many respects resembles that which prevailed through the Middle Ages and which was sanctioned by the medieval Church. In the Freudian concept, man is not born free with the right to pursue life, liberty, and happiness; he is shackled by biological urges that can never be freely expressed and that set him in constant and grievous conflict with his society. Life for him must be an unhappy and unending struggle to reconcile, both within himself and between himself and others, forces that are inherently antagonistic. Freud does not say, in the theological manner, that man fell from Grace and must therefore suffer in this life. But he does come to much the same concept of man: that man is by nature (or at least by virtue of the inevitable conflict between man's nature and society) a weak and irresolute creature without the stamina to endure the stresses and strains of living, and who cannot therefore hope to enjoy life on this earth.

There has been interminable debate concerning why Freud devised the particular doctrine that goes under his name. His disciples take the understandable but scientifically untenable position that Freud simply discovered by scientific means the truth about man; his opponents lean to the view that the Freudian doctrine of man is at best a delusion of Freud's and may have been a calculated method of winning him enduring prestige as the founder of a metaphysical cult. Far more tenable, if still unprovable, is the hypothesis that Freud, proceeding in accordance with the intellectual standards of the late nineteenth century, simply invented the various concepts—libido, id, ego, superego, Oedipus complex, etc.—that together make up his doctrine in an honest endeavor to comprehend the still largely incomprehensible behavior of neurotic people. At any event, it does seem evident that his idea of the nature and capabilities of man was derived directly from too long and unmitigated exposure to people, his patients, who were incapable of managing their personal affairs, people who did not, for whatever reasons, conform even in outline to the Protestant ethic.

In a sense, Freud's major error lay in assuming that the people who came to him for treatment were representative of mankind in general. For the very fact that his patients came to him for "mental" treatment is *ipso facto* evidence that they were not—unless, indeed, we wish to assume that all men are at all times in need of psychiatric aid. Had Freud been content to accept his explanatory system as a therapeutic rationale for use in the treatment of neurotics, and had his converts also adhered to this view, a quite different result might have obtained. But almost from the outset of his work, Freud insisted that he was interested in developing—or "discovering"—the laws governing all human conduct, not just those that govern, or fail to govern, the conduct of psychologically abnormal individuals.

The atypical character of the people from whom Freud derived his doctrine of man would seem to explain his conviction that men are inherently unstable; and one must assume that his preoccupation with sex, a fixation that is close to monomaniacal, was a function either of his own personality or of those of the patients who came under his observation. The latter assumption is most acceptable, for even the most ardent anti-Freudian must admit that Freud's treatment of sex was aseptic rather than pornographic; and there is some factual basis for this assumption. Most of Freud's patients were not only neurotic but also neurotic middle- and upper-middle-class Viennese Jews. They were not, therefore, even a representative sample of neurotics.

Vienna in the time of Freud, if not since, was the pretentious, cosmopolitan center of an empire that had all but vanished. It was a once-great city in reduced circumstances, a city that had lost many of its economic and political functions and was—to some extent at least—living on its glamorous past. In sociological terms, it was a highly disorganized and demoralized community; in lay terms, it was a city of sin. Apparently the fashion in Vienna at that time was for men and women of means to engage in elaborate, perhaps even highly ritualized, extramarital sexual play. And while keeping up with this fashion may not have bothered greatly the moral consciences of Catholic Austro-Hungarians, who had long been noted for their adaptability, it undoubtedly ran counter to the strict and rigid moral code of bourgeois Jews. It may well be, there-fore, that Freud's patients were atypical neurotics, *i.e.*, their mental distress was commonly occasioned by the opposition between their training in sexual morality and the social pressures that demanded violation of that morality. This interpretation of Freud's preoccupa-tion with sex is not, of course, acceptable to Freudians; but it has the dual virtues, over alternative interpretations, of having some factual basis and of shifting the onus for that preoccupation from Freud to his patients.

An Ethic of Negation

Freud's preoccupation with sex has only indirect bearing upon the ethic that is being evolved around his idea of man. His sexual interpretations provide, at most, a rationale for his belief that man is an unstable, insecure, and irresolute creature. To Freud and his disciples, the essentially sexual nature of man is responsible for the fact that he is psychologically unstable, not the other way around; and since he cannot alter either his nature or his society, his instability is inescapable. Because Freudians look upon man's problem in this light, they do not advocate sexual immorality as the means of securing psychological stability. It may be that lay converts to Freudianism have at times used the doctrine as a justi-fication for lecherous conduct, and it is certain that a good deal of outright pornography has been disseminated under the guise of

Freudianism. But such use of the doctrine is a willful perversion of it and does not follow from acceptance of the doctrine itself.

The Freudian ethic, as it will be termed hereafter, is not a code of licentiousness. It does not, in fact, grant to the individual the ability or right to *do* anything. As a code of conduct the Freudian ethic is entirely negative. It is composed of sentiments and attitudes regarding man's capabilities that, if literally applied, would keep him from attempting anything positive, to say nothing of attempting to devise anything new. For it makes the world about him a hostile and inhospitable place, and it makes him a terrified (unconsciously, of course) and reluctant inhabitant of that world. It even goes further; not only is his external world inimical to his psychic welfare, but this world has been "internalized" to the end that a part of himself intimidates the rest. There is therefore no escaping psychic agony. Should he withdraw from the external world, he will still be at odds with himself.

Philosophically, the Freudian ethic is related not only to that of medieval Europe but also to the ethical ideal of the Greek-Roman Stoics. It is like the medieval in that it reduces man to a passive state and unlike it in that it does not provide a higher authority—the Church—to assume responsibility for the individual and guide him in the ways of righteousness. It is like Stoic philosophy in that it is contemptuous of the world of external realities and unlike it in that it does not provide a hope that the individual can ignore the world and thereby achieve peace of mind.

Since the Freudian ethic is still undergoing development and since, further, it is negative rather than positive in character, the ethic is at present more a state of mind than an actual ideal of individual conduct. Some appreciation of this state of mind can, perhaps, be gained from the terminology used by those who subscribe to it. In their discourse there is recurrent reference to guilt feelings, personal insecurity, unstructured personality, instability, "internalization" (of hate, envy, and other destructive emotions), "projection" (of anything from hate to love), frustration, aggressive tendencies, trauma, and the all-inclusive term "tensions." Such terms are used in reference not only to recognizably abnormal individuals but to everyone. Still more revealing is the total absence in the Freudian discourse of such terms, prominent in the Protestant ethic, as self-confidence, personal integrity, self-reliance, responsibility, or such very earthy terms as "moral courage," "intestinal fortitude," or, more vulgarly, "guts."

The elements of the Protestant ethic are fairly easy to describe. For one thing, our language abounds in character-designating terms that reflect this ethic; for another, the ethic is structured and positive, rather than amorphous and negative. What the Freudians hold as ideal is adjustment of the individual to his life circumstances —*i.e.*, the maintenance of a precarious balance between his id, ego, and superego, and between all three of these and external circumstances. This adjustment ideal may, in turn, be designated in a variety of positive terms—contentment, complacency, sense of security, and perhaps even apathy. But when an attempt is made to indicate the personal qualities that contribute to the achievement of this ideal state, it is necessary to resort to description by negation. Thus the Freudian ethic comes out something as follows: absence of strong social motivations (the inescapable urges of the libido are, of course, antisocial drives), lack of constraining or inhibiting social principles, lack of supernaturalistic or other fixed faiths (except, of course, faith in the Freudian version of the self), lack of set goals, lack of any rigorous system of personal-social values and sentiments, and complete absence of any sense of obligation toward others.

The Freudians do not deny that men may possess positive personality attributes of the sort incorporated in the Protestant ethic. But to them, such positive characteristics are either the product of the inevitable clash between the individual and society or the consequence of traumatic experiences that have befallen the individual in the course of that conflict. Whatever their source, they are inimical to the individual's psychic welfare; where they exist, they should be exorcised by psychoanalysis; and to prevent their development, society should be remodeled to accord with the Freudian idea of man. No society can really be good, for everything social is contrary to the psychic welfare of the individual. Society could and should, however, minimize its disutility to the individual. To this end it should avoid inculcating in him any socially prescribed personality attributes—motivations, goals, values, sentiments, or feelings of personal obligation. The individual should not be required or even expected to submit to social authority whatever its character, to accept responsibility for his own or anyone else's welfare, or to be concerned with anything except the preservation of his precarious psychic balance.

In the harsh, unsympathetic terms of the Protestant ethic, the individual who even approximated the Freudian ideal would be a selfish egocentric, an incompetent, a wastrel, an irresponsible, and in general a social parasite unwelcome in the company of respectable men. In the days when men who conformed more or less to the Protestant ethic tended to dominate our society, such an individual would surely have failed in competition with more sturdy men and as an incompetent would have been treated with contempt. But in this age of Freudian enlightenment, such an individual seems to represent the emerging ideal type of man.

Shifting the Blame

The last organized effort to perpetuate the Protestant ethic was made by a religious cult, Christian Science. Support of the Protestant ethic by Christian Science was both fragmentary and rather incidental to its central goal; nevertheless, the fact that it provided any support to the values and sentiments of the Protestant ethic is rather curious since Christian Science and Freudianism have in other respects so very much in common. Both grew out of a concern with mental healing—*i.e.*, with psychotherapy. Both had a background in hypnotism. And both developed into doctrines of universal and all-inclusive truth.

One of the precepts of Christian Science doctrine is that nothing is to be taken at its face value. Thus Christian Science and Freudianism take off on the same contrascientific principle. But at this point they diverge: whereas in Freudianism everything is actually worse than would appear at first glance (*e.g.*, the possessive love of a mother for her daughter is really camouflaged hate), in Christian Science everything is actually much better than it would seem to be. All things that may appear to be unfortunate or evil—sickness, death, and social disasters, including wars and earthquakes—are in reality only illusions created by "error." God, the only reality, is the universal, infinite Principle. Endowed with perfect love, He manifests his spiritual power against the world of error, illusion, or "mortal belief" by conquering sin, disease, and death, both through Christ, who "demonstrated" man's identity with God, and through *Science and Health,* his modern revealed word.

Translated into nonmetaphysical terms, Christian Science doctrine holds that it is failure of the individual's will—of his self-confidence, his moral courage—that leads him into the error of thinking that he is ill or otherwise beset by personal difficulties. (And, likewise, it is similar error on the part of many that leads to war and other social disasters.) Thus in the Christian Science doctrine, unlike the Freudian, the individual, rather than his society, is held responsible for his personal and social misadventures. The individual, as "one-with-God," has the power to avoid such error. When he errs, he is revealing weakness (of the mind, of the spirit), and such weakness is not to be condoned; it is a failure both of self and of God. In effect, then, to be ill or to be beset by difficulties is sinful. It is also quite unnecessary. But, recognizing that people do at times sin, Christian Science provides guidance back to virtue. Either privately, with the guidance of *Science and Health, with a Key to the Scriptures,* or with a qualified practitioner, the distraught individual acknowledges his error and is reassured that having done so—having faced up to the fact that he himself is at fault—he can regain his oneness with God and thereby come again to see the true reality, which is, of course, that his troubles were but an illusion, a result of the error that he has now recognized and through acknowledgment corrected.

Like Christian Science therapy, the psychoanalytic method of treating mentally distressed patients involves allocating responsibility for the distressed condition. But in psychoanalytic therapy, the responsibility is never assigned to the patient himself. Every effort is made to relieve him of any sense of personal guilt. To this end the analyst probes the patient's unconscious, for, of course, the true cause of the mental distress is never evident and is systematically obscured from the patient's ego by his superego. The first rule of psychoanalysis is, therefore, that the patient cannot understand himself. The second rule is that only through the psychoanalytic procedure can evidence concerning the cause of his troubles be dredged up out of the patient's unconscious. And the third rule is that only a psychoanalyst is capable of correctly interpreting this evidence. For the evidence procured through the procedure is abstruse, consisting of vague and random bits of psychic reality that have slipped past the psychic censor either in a moment of abstraction or because they successfully camouflaged their true nature.

The couch, which looms so large in the folklore about psychoanalysis, is intended to enable the patient to relax physically while he pours out, with promptings when necessary, everything that comes to his mind. After a few sessions in the comfort, seclusion, and security of the analyst's office, the barriers—or inhibitions—that normally intervene between thought and speech are supposed to break down; and it is considered one of the vital arts of the psychoanalyst to bring about this abandonment of normal reticence by serving the patient as a sympathetic and understanding listener, developing his vocabulary of self-revealing terms, and offering positive encouragements to free expression of whatever may cross his mind. This phase of the analysis, which may at times be quite extended, is actually one of training; during it the patient is taught that, contrary to a lifetime of schooling in self-repression, it is right and proper that he talk about himself endlessly and intimately.

It is no doubt something of an accomplishment so to de-socialize an individual that he will reveal his most intimate thoughts. From childhood on, everyone is taught not to do so; the individual learns, over and over, that many of the thoughts that come to mind are simply not said and that in his own self-interest many others should be kept to himself. Moreover, he learns to be sensitive to the opinion of others and to protect their good opinion of him by hiding from them thoughts and feelings that, if known, might rebound to his discredit. This is a major aspect of social role-playing; and it is a prerequisite for the maintenance of amiable relations between people.

So strong are the socially established barriers to free and intimate self-expression that there is never any assurance that they have been effectively breached. The analyst must judge for himself if and when he has accomplished this primary objective; and whatever he may believe about it, the fact is that he can never really know whether he has established complete rapport with a patient or whether he has only taught that patient to play a new role—the role of seeming to be free of constraints on his speech. Perhaps in recognition of this difficulty, psychoanalysts are currently experimenting with hypnosis (abandoned by Freud) in an effort to probe more directly into the unconscious.

Once the patient has learned to talk endlessly and intimately about himself, or learned to pretend that he is doing so, he does just that—session after session, week after week, month after month. A complete analysis may take hundreds of hours, just how many hours seems to depend upon many variables, including no doubt the patience of the analyst and the pocketbook of the patient.

What happens while a patient is pouring out his innermost thoughts is a matter of considerable dispute. Analysts themselves are somewhat divided concerning just what the role of the analyst is; some believe that he can and should be a passive recipient; others incline to the view that he should—and in any event will—provide subtle guidance to the patient's thoughts. It should be evident even to the layman that the analyst must have extraordinary patience, a very high tolerance for verbal meanderings and mawkish self-concern, and firm conviction that the mental welfare of the patient is worth his time and effort and his being interminably bored.

Freud insisted that the self-revelatory aspect of the psychoanalytic procedure was diagnostic rather than therapeutic, and his disciples have generally held to this claim. This position is taken as a defense against the charge that psychoanalysis is just an elaborate and costly version of the age-old confessional. If such were the case, psychoanalysis could not claim any special therapeutic powers. There is certainly a grain of truth in the old saying that confession is good for the soul; and there is reason to believe that, when psychoanalysis does have therapeutic value, it often stems from the sheer relief that some patients feel at having expressed openly in words their secret fears, apprehensions, and less noble feelings and thoughts. Moreover, the attention-providing aspect of the psychoanalytic procedure (as of the confessional and many less formal circumstances) may often provide patients with a gratifying sense of self-importance and to that extent serve a therapeutic function. But the psychoanalysts hold to the view that their probing of the unconscious elicits data different in kind from that which is revealed in the confessional, formal or otherwise, and that it is the interpretation of this data to the patient—rather than its elicitation—that constitutes the therapeutic procedure.

The process of interpretation presumably runs throughout the entire analysis. It is, ordinarily, made piecemeal and gradually, and it involves inducting the patient into the Freudian way of thinking about psychic matters. In effect, then, the patient is gently schooled in Freudian doctrine; or, as non-Freudians would be inclined to say, converted to the Freudian faith. Even in Freudian theory, it is quite essential to therapeutic success that the patient come to accept as valid the Freudian concept of him as a person. He must learn to think of himself as composed of id, ego, and superego; as a victim of the Oedipus, castration, and other complexes; as one whose behavior has obscure implications; as one whose natural self and socially imposed self are unceasingly engaged in an unresolvable conflict; and as one who is, as a consequence, psychologically frail. For only if he does come to see himself in this way will the analyst's interpretation of the causes of his mental distress be acceptable to him. And it is, presumably, through his accepting the analyst's interpretation that he is absolved from the mental consequences of those causes.

Whatever form the interpretation takes, it is certain to be exactly the opposite to that which would be made by a Christian Science practitioner. The latter would place the onus for distress squarely upon the patient himself; the psychoanalyst, on the other hand, strives to relieve the patient of all responsibility for his difficulties and to shift it to society in the person of the patient's mother, father, sibling, husband, wife, son, or daughter, or all these together. For, in accordance with Freudian doctrine, all mental distress arises as a consequence of the repression of the libido and in accordance with the processes earlier described.

In theory, the shift of blame is therapeutic, since it relieves the patient of any sense of personal responsibility, personal inferiority, or guilt. In fact, in providing that shift of blame, the analyst serves as an advocate of the Freudian ethic. For he makes the possession of negative personal qualities a virtue and absolves the patient from adherence to such positive personal characteristics as were honored in the Protestant ethic. If this procedure, which if effective results in making the patient socially irresponsible, were a demonstrably efficacious way of curing mental distress, it might be socially acceptable on the grounds that the end justifies the means. Better, perhaps, to have a socially irresponsible individual wandering his way through life than one who, untreated by the Freudian method, degenerates from a neurotic to a psychotic.

There is, however, no reason to think that psychoanalysis is the ultimate method of treating neurotics, or even that it is the best of the methods that are currently available. It is certainly the favored method in America today, but that is no assurance that it is the best possible method or even a good one. A hundred years ago bleeding and physicking were the favored means of curing physical illnesses. We now know that they killed many and saved none. Psychiatry may, for all we can now know, be in about the same state of development that medicine was in a century ago. At any event, the claim that psychoanalysis is efficacious has not yet been substantiated, and its use is currently based upon faith rather than knowledge. The same may, however, be said of many another psychotherapeutic method; for no one has yet been able to test scientifically the value of any form of mental therapy.

A scientific test of the efficacy of a psychotherapeutic procedure would require a considerable number of patients suffering from the same mental disorder and to the same degree; a knowledge of the normal course of this disorder (or a control group composed of patients suffering from the same disorder but not being treated); and exact measurement of the actual progress of the patients under standardized therapeutic procedure. The evidence so far advanced in support of the psychoanalytic claim to effectiveness meets none of the requirements. It consists of random, unstandardized case reports on patients who are not comparable, who have been treated by methods that are highly individual, without a control group of any sort for comparative purposes, and in which personal judgments rather than objective criteria measure the effects of the therapy upon the patients. It is, therefore, quite understandable that the psychoanalysts who have conducted these studies have been able to confirm their faith in the psychoanalytic process.*

Extensions of the Ethic

Whether the psychoanalytic claim to efficacy in the treatment of mental disturbances is or is not valid is of importance mainly to those unfortunate individuals who seek relief from mental distress. What is socially significant about psychoanalysis is that it is based upon a doctrine of man that is new to our society, and that the psychoanalysts do not confine their "treatment" to the patients who come to them. They, or rather the more articulate among them, advocate the application to all mankind of their view of man and of the values and sentiments that they represent. Whether they can relieve the mental distress of the individual patient remains debatable; there can be no doubt, however, that they have won many adherents to the Freudian doctrine of man or that the Freudian ethic is rapidly displacing our traditional ideals of human character. To what extent the responsibility for the growing acceptance of the

* A few years ago the American Psychiatric Association established a Section to deal with the question of therapeutic effectiveness that, either by intent or accident, has come to represent the psychoanalytic wing of the Association. Under this Section, an investigation is being conducted that can hardly fail to "validate" claims to effectiveness, since the data are being secured by questionnaires in which the practitioner judges for himself the success of his therapy. Psychoanalysts, like other classes of people, vary considerably; and while all of them presumably have greater faith in or hope for the psychoanalytic procedure than any other, some are less than faithful to its tenets. In *Sigmund Freud's Mission* (New York: Harper & Brothers, 1959), Erich Fromm, for example, stresses the messianic nature of Freudianism rather than the therapeutic values of psychoanalysis; and Lawrence S. Kubie ("Some Unsolved Problems of Psychoanalytic Psychotherapy," in *Progress in Psychotherapy*, F. Fromm-Reichmann and J. L. Moreno, eds. New York: Grune & Stratton, Inc., 1956) has cautioned his fellows that they must not assume that their procedure is effective. Nevertheless, most psychoanalysts—like most of the practitioners of any art—do operate on faith and, being faithful, tend to see the therapeutic benefits that psychoanalysis is supposed to produce.

Freudian ethic is attributable to the psychoanalysts is impossible to ascertain. But they have labored with aggressive persistence on its behalf; and it has become the ethic that is most commonly advocated by the intellectual leaders of the United States.

The tender concern of a host of modern writers with the psychological welfare of the working man is inexplicable except as a reflection of the wide acceptance of the Freudian view of man. Half a century ago the concern was with such vital and tangible matters as the material standard of living, the level of health, the freedom from gross exploitation, and the opportunities for the ambitious and competent to rise in the social scale. But today's worriers fret about far more subtle matters. They fear that the modern industrial worker suffers from *anomie*, that his work tasks are ungratifying because they are so very fragmentary and repetitious, that his occupational and other roles are incomplete and ambiguous, and that he lacks a sense of personal importance and of belonging. In sum, they fear that he is unhappy in his job and that he does not secure compensatory gratification during his many leisure hours.*

The idea that modern workers are atypically unhappy because of the nature of modern industrial operations is actually pure assumption. The evidence, when any is advanced, consists of worker-opinion surveys or interview materials. What is thus obtained is then evaluated against nothing more tangible than an idea of perfect contentment. It is held that discontent is a modern condition and, since industrial production is also modern, that modern industry causes modern discontent. No one has run comparative tests of the contentment of nonindustrial workers; it is just taken for granted that the primitive and the peasant are happy because they do not have to work with machines.

In view of the fact that there is no real basis for believing that

---

* It has been demonstrated that the worker is a human being, not a piece of impersonal machinery, and that his work efficiency is closely related to the character of the informal groups to which he belongs in his work relationships and, more distantly, to the social milieu outside his work relationships.

It is a considerable jump, however, from the observation that the modern industrial worker is a human being to the conclusion that he is therefore an atypically unhappy man. That jump has been made by, among many others, Erich Fromm (*The Sane Society*. New York: Rinehart & Company, Inc., 1955).

the modern worker is atypically unhappy and discontented, current worry over the mental welfare of the modern worker is simply a special application of the Freudian view of man as an unsubstantial creature—one who should not be required to suffer the psychological indignities of disciplining himself to labor for forty hours or so a week at workbench or desk in order to earn a livelihood for himself and his family.* On a historically comparative basis, the life of the modern worker is easy and without marked strains. It may be monotonous; but when has work ever been anything but monotonous? It may be confining, but work is by its very nature confining. It is certainly not more demanding of attention and skill than is the craft of the primitive hunter, nor is it as monotonous and physically arduous as the labors of the premodern stonemason or the peasant in his fields; and it is no more socially isolating than is the work of the hunter, the mason, or the agricultural peasant. And it is, on the other hand, far more rewarding than any of these in terms of the material goods and the leisure that it provides.

The adoption of the Freudian image of man has perhaps reached its apex with those who deal, intellectually or therapeutically, not with the working man, but with the man who is no longer able or willing to work. There was a time, not long since, when charitable work consisted mainly of doling out food and cast-off clothing to the indigent or of maintaining bleak establishments in which the aged and infirm could be housed until they finally died. The rationalization of charitable work has largely been accomplished during this present century, and it is a testament to the enterprise of many men and women of good will. But the current elite of the profession of social work, those turned out by the three or four major schools of social welfare, have all been indoctrinated into Freudianism; and they see their clients through the framework of the Freudian doctrine and their task as that of providing the poor, irresolute, insecure, and inherently incompetent creatures put into their care with psychiatric care and guidance.

* The way the Freudian ethic pervades thinking about the worker is perhaps most clearly reflected in the writings of industrial counselors such, for example, as S. G. Law (*Therapy through Interviews*. New York: McGraw-Hill Book Co., 1948).

Many of the schools of social welfare originated as divisions within university departments of sociology, for it was initially assumed that social welfare was to be the practical application to the solution of social problems of the scientific knowledge of society that was being accumulated by sociologists. But the relationship between sociologists and social-welfare people did not last long. The students and practitioners of social welfare were faced with urgent, practical problems, and they were in a hurry to solve them. The sociologists, on the other hand, tended to proceed slowly and cautiously; and, on the whole, the more they learned about society, the less confident they became that such social problems as juvenile delinquency, adult crime, economic dependency, and marital discord can be solved by direct-action programs. Since this position was unpalatable to the social-welfare people, they drifted away from sociology in search of reassurance that welfare projects are as helpful as they would like them to be. And many of them found such reassurance in Freudianism.

Today most of the college and some of the university departments or schools of social welfare teach pragmatic welfare procedures untroubled by regard for the philosophy underlying welfare programs. The public-welfare agencies need people so trained to administer their legislatively designated programs, and the long-run social consequences of such programs is not the concern of either the teachers or the students. On the whole, the products of such schools do good, conscientious—and inherently discouraging— work administering the old-age pension, unemployment-compensation, and other public-welfare programs. Like other bureaucratic functionaries, they do their job because it is their job and keep any doubts that they may have strictly to themselves.

Not so with the major schools of social work and the polished, highly professionalized products that they turn out. Many of the teachers in these schools are dedicated Freudians, and the rest are at least sympathetic toward the Freudian view of man. The students are, as a consequence, indoctrinated rather than simply trained. They are indoctrinated into the theory and practice of what is termed "case work" but is actually a sort of lay psychoanalysis for people who cannot afford the more extended and intimate type of professional analysis.* The people so trained usually secure positions in the private agencies; and since these agencies have been relieved of the major burden of charitable work by the rise of public-welfare organizations, they deal with a highly select clientele in a markedly Freudian manner. The underlying assumption is that whatever may seem to be the matter with the client—poverty, illness, inability to get or hold a job, desertion by husband or wife, abandonment by parents, or the infirmities of old age—the real difficulties lie deep within the client's unconscious. Such being the case, the simple manipulation of environmental factors is obviously futile. What is needed is diagnosis of the underlying psychological causes of the apparent difficulties and therapy to modulate the effect of these causes.

So the really professional social-welfare worker does not trouble herself with crass and practical matters. She (sometimes he) interviews the client over and over. These are "depth" interviews and may run for an hour or two. The reports on these interviews, dictated by the case worker in a sort of free-associational manner, run to many pages. And if the client hangs on long enough, his complete and intimate life history will eventually be assembled and his case will be ready for diagnosis. The character of this diagnosis and of the therapy that will finally be prescribed is predetermined by the doctrine upon which the entire operation is based: the doctrine that man is an unhappy victim of the conflict between his nature and society. His troubles may seem to stem from occupational incompetence, the irresponsibilities of an unfortunate wife, or the physical disabilities that often come with advancing years. But the real trouble lies far deeper: he is psychologically insecure, he suffers from a sense of guilt, he has never outgrown the infantile stage of narcissism.

* Marion K. Sanders ("Social Work: A Profession Chasing Its Tail," *Harper's Magazine*, March, 1957, pp. 56-62) believes that in taking over the Freudian approach social workers have become socially irresponsible. To be irresponsible is, of course, entirely in accordance with the Freudian ethic.

Some appreciation of the extent to which Freudianism has permeated the field of social work can be gained from *Social Work Yearbook: 1957* (New York: National Association of Social Workers, 1957), or any issue of the *Journal of Psychiatric Social Work*.

What the Freudian doctrine has done for the elite of the teachers and practitioners of social welfare is, to put it in their own terms, provide them with a sense of security, absolve them from any sense of guilt, and assure them that they are engaged in meaningful and useful tasks. Sociology could do none of these, for the current findings of sociology do not lend much support to programs of social reformation. By shifting the point of attack from society to the individual and by providing a fixed and certain concept of the individual and his welfare, Freudianism relieves the social-welfare worker of all responsibility to society.

The Freudian orientation of the elite of the social-welfare people is not, perhaps, of great importance in itself. They deal with but a small fraction of the total "case load," most of which is now handled by public agencies. But this elite tends to set the example for all those who labor in the self-designated "helping professions." The hard-working, pragmatic, and overloaded workers in old-age, unemployment, and similar public agencies have neither the time nor the energy to become involved in Freudian circumlocutions. But the Freudian view of man is now dominant with the psychiatric social workers, and it is at least the prevailing view among those social workers and clinical psychologists who deal with juvenile delinquents and adult criminals. The result is a marked tendency, as will be shown in detail later, to look upon criminals—especially young offenders—as the victims and upon society as the evil agency from which the criminals should be protected.

The advocates of the Freudian view of man and of the ethic that stems from that view have recently been augmented by a host of bright young men whose ostensible task is to aid in the shaping of advertising and other promotional endeavors. A generation ago it was the assumption along Madison Avenue that people buy goods for their use or prestige values. Market researchers, as they were then called, endeavored by interview and survey studies to ascertain what people wanted to buy or why they bought what they did buy rather than something else. From such studies the "wants" of men were determined, and the advertising copy writer then slanted his appeals toward the satisfaction of these wants. If it appeared that people wanted economy in their automobiles, he claimed that his car was the most economical; if they seemed to want speed, he claimed the highest speed; etc.

Of recent years, however, market researching has given way to a more complex, impressive, and costly operation called "motivational research." * The motivational researchers proceed on the assumption that people do not know why they buy what they buy; therefore it is futile to ask them what they want to buy or why they bought what they did. One must, they believe, probe behind the obvious to the real—dig down through the public's conscious self to its unconscious motivations. To this end a sample of the population must be subjected to depth interviews, and the interview materials must then be analyzed to determine the hidden, unconscious motives that have been inadvertently revealed. When the psychoanalysts of the public have made their diagnoses, the advertising copy writer, or the political propagandist, can then pitch his appeals to the real rather than the ostensible motives of men.

The motivational researchers have become, it would appear, a considerable power in advertising and related circles. An increasing proportion of advertising is slanted toward such "unconscious" motivations as the need for emotional security, ego gratification, guilt release, and—inevitably—thwarted sexual desires. Whether the new appeals actually fool the buying public is debatable, but the fact that the advertising fraternity believe they do suggests that advertisers have taken over the Freudian idea of man and have made the public in its image.

One might speculate upon the possibility that this most recent vogue for viewing man through the Freudian doctrine is a major stride in the direction of socially validating that doctrine. If the advertisers tell the public, however indirectly, that it is motivated by hidden unconscious forces—to which, of course, all the sensible members of the public will promptly give way—it may not be long before the editors of newspapers and popular magazines will be catering to the unconscious motivations of their advertisers by slanting news, articles, and short stories in the same direction. Thus

* A persuasive analysis of motivational research and its consequences has been made by Vance Packard in *The Hidden Persuaders* (New York: David McKay Company, Inc., 1957).

it may then be only a matter of time before the entire weight of our mass media is devoted to shaping the reading, listening, and viewing publics into conformity with the Freudian idea of man. But such speculation is superfluous; for long since the Freudian idea of man was introduced into the American home and public school, and the process of inducting the young into the Freudian ethic is now well under way.

PART II

PROPAGATION OF THE ETHIC

4

The Permissive Home

ALTHOUGH THE Freudian doctrine is a revolutionary one, it is not a doctrine of revolution. Unlike Marxianism, it has not given ideological sanction to direct and violent assault upon the social *status quo*. It does not, in fact, provide a logical basis for any kind of effort to remodel society. Freud was himself disinterested in society as such, and he treated it as a miserable but inescapable and presumably for the most part unchangeable context that the individual must endure as best he can—with, of course, aid from psychoanalysis. Freud was, for example, as antagonistic to religion, whatever its form, as was Marx; but, unlike Marx, he did not suggest that it might be dispensed with. For Freud there was no good society, past, present, or future.

Freud's disciples have, however, ignored the logical implications of his doctrine and have advocated modification of society to the end that the conflict between the individual and society would be lessened, if not resolved. Such advocacy has not been organized, as was that of Marxianism, and has been neither systematic nor consistent. It has, rather, been "spontaneous" and individualistic, with the result that the attacks upon the social *status quo* have been both segmental and insidious. And for this reason, if no other, the attempts to remodel our society to fit the Freudian image of man have aroused only limited and scattered resistance. It is far too early to say whether these attempts will have enduring consequences; but it does seem likely that the current acceptance of the Freudian doctrine and the current efforts to validate the Freudian ethic profit from the fact that their attack on existing society is only in limited areas and by indirection. For it is clear that social change

81

is always fragmentary, unsystematic, and for the most part inadvertent. Social revolutions and revolutionary mass movements may dramatize the desire for change, but they do not of themselves work significant changes in the existing social system. Those changes, when they come, are produced slowly and piecemeal.

The Freudian social reformers advocate changes favorable to the fulfillment of the Freudian ethic. In so doing, they are themselves actively subscribing to the Protestant ethic; for as advocates of the Freudian ethic they proceed energetically, confidently, and most ingeniously. In this, as in other respects, they differ markedly from the doctrinaire and highly organized prerevolutionary Marxians. They are men (and women) of considerable enterprise; and it is only a logical contradiction that they apply their enterprise to the creation of a world that would preclude enterprise such as their own.

One measure of the energy and ingenuity of the advocates of Freudianism is the extent to which they have attacked the social *status quo* via the grass roots, rather than attempting, in the Russian manner, to impose the desired social reforms upon the members of society by sheer force. In so doing, they have necessarily subscribed to the sociological dictum that society is embodied in the personalities of the members of society and that only as the personality attributes of those members are modified does the society itself undergo significant and durable changes. Thus the advocates of Freudian social reform are proceeding in accordance with a concept of the relations between the individual and society that is definitely anti-Freudian; and to the extent that they succeed in socially validating the Freudian doctrine, they are demonstrating its unscientific character. But this will not, of course, be the first time that scientific knowledge has been put to quite unscientific ends.

A Nation of Weaklings

A considerable number of the advocates of Freudianism have applied themselves, skillfully and with seeming effect, to remodeling the American family system. They do so, presumably, upon the sound sociopsychological assumption that as the twig is bent the tree will tend to grow. They do not, however, urge a particular method of twig bending; on the contrary, they counsel that the twig be nourished with love and affection and permitted to grow in its own sweet way. This counsel stems from a revolutionary concept of the role of the family and an entirely new theory of child psychology that was derived from the Freudian idea of man but that did not become crystallized—or the basis for a cult—until some fifteen years ago.

It had long been assumed—and most sociologists still hold to this assumption—that one of the major functions of any system of family life is to provide for the transmission of the cultural heritage from generation to generation. Two decades ago social psychologists were firm in the belief that the most important phase in the socialization of the individual occurs in and about the home, that what the child is taught—directly and indirectly—by his parents and siblings constitutes the basis upon which all else is superimposed, and that "teaching" consists of complex and subtle procedures through which the attitudes, values, and sentiments of others are transposed to and incorporated into the personality of the child. From this point of view, the home prepares the child for social membership by inducting it into those social standards that are appropriate to one of its age, sex, and social station. And again from this point of view, the good parent is one who inducts his child into the proper standards, rather than some inappropriate ones, and into all the proper standards, rather than just some of them, and who does so in such ways that the child will "internalize" those standards rather than just conform outwardly to them. No one has supposed that to be a good parent in this sense is a particularly simple or easy task, that complete success in socializing the child is ever possible, or that all well-intentioned parents possess the skill and patience necessary to fulfill those intentions. Nor has it been assumed that socialization ends as well as begins in the home; on the contrary, social psychologists have recognized that socialization continues throughout life and have placed much importance upon the role of peer group memberships, interpersonal relationships of school life, and informal associations in occupational and other organizations. They have even granted that formal education and exposure to the mass media

—the newspapers, the motion pictures, the radio, television, etc.—
play some part, if a highly variable one, in developing the
individual's personality.

This view of the socialization process is eclectic and nondoctrinaire
and cannot, therefore, be boiled down into slogan form. It is perhaps for this reason that whenever public interest has swung
momentarily to concern over the welfare of youth, publicists and
other amateurs have been called upon to explain why the young
were misbehaving. They, unlike social psychologists, have been able
to come up with such capsule explanations of juvenile delinquency
as that which was so popular during the 1930's—movies about crime
make children into criminals. And so when the early years of World
War II produced some evidences that American young men were
not quite the heroic material that we had presumed them to be,
the Freudians were provided with an opportunity to develop a new
and doctrinaire concept of the function of the family and the process
by which the child's personality evolves.

That development has a curious history, one that accords with
the old Hegelian concept of thesis, antithesis, and synthesis. The non-
Freudian thesis was that too much mothering makes the boy a
weakling; the Freudian antithesis was the stock view that the boy
is inherently weak; and the final synthesis is the neo-Freudian theory
that the more the child is mothered, the stronger the boy will be.
It came about in the following way:

During the preparatory prelude to American participation in
World War II, political considerations dictated that the young men
being called into military service be treated with unmilitary regard
for their civilian sensitivities. Training camps were made as comfortable and homelike as possible, the draftees were granted frequent leaves from the military establishment, and the practice of
camp following—in which wives and even mothers might trail along
in the wakes of their husbands and sons—was not effectively discouraged. All this was exceedingly irritating to military leaders of
the old, or hard-boiled, school, who continually grumbled about
the way the draftees were being pampered. It was this pampering,
they claimed, that was responsible for the low performance record
of our troops in mock battles, their undisciplined conduct both on

and off the military reservation, and their common failure to acquire the skills, the sentiments, and the hardihood of the good soldier.

The old regulars subscribed to the traditional military view that one can make a competent soldier out of almost anything, provided only that one proceeds in the proper military manner. As they left the training camps to go out to direct the fighting of the war for which they had been preparing, they came to be replaced by younger officers of a new and enlightened school of thought. These new men accepted as normal the methods of military indoctrination that were then in operation, for they had been so indoctrinated themselves; and their complaints were, as a consequence, directed against the human material that was being assembled for them by the draft boards. It was next to impossible, they charged, to make decent soldiers out of the callow youths and flabby young men who were being recruited. The draftees resented discipline; and although they might in time learn the mechanics of soldiering, it was simply impossible to induct them into the code of the good soldier and to inspire in them love of and loyalty to the military way of life.

As the war went on, reports from field commanders lent substance to the complaints of these training officers. The American soldier was not, it seemed, quite the hero that home newspapers made him out to be. In fact, he was often an indifferent fighting man, and he was sometimes actually unreliable. In rear-echelon positions he was apathetic and inefficient; in combat he far too often failed to act aggressively. Indeed, he sometimes seemed to be concerned only with preserving his precious neck.

After the North African fiasco a detailed and fairly impartial study of "battle fatigue" was undertaken.* It revealed that, for whatever reasons, the American soldier was considerably more prone than his British comrade-in-arms to develop under comparable stress conditions such psychogenic disabilities as, for example, gastric ulcer. The only possible conclusion that could be drawn from these findings was that the American soldier had less psychological stamina than the British; and when this was translated into lay language, it came

* R. Grinker and J. Spiegel, *Men Under Stress* (Philadelphia: The Blakiston Company, 1945).

out that the American soldier was, on a comparative basis, something of a coward.

As the war wore on, military concern over the quality of American troops became acute and led, eventually, to a full-dress, scientific study of the morale of American soldiers.* The findings were not reassuring. The American soldier, on the whole, was unhappy with military life and unenthusiastic about fighting. He was cynical regarding the war itself; contemptuous of our announced war aims; convinced that the sacrifices and risks demanded of him were unjust; perpetually dissatisfied with the provisions that the Army made for his physical comfort; distrustful of his officers; and inclined to conspire with his fellows in the avoidance of duty, particularly that which was in any way dangerous to him. He had little of the pride of the professional soldier in his craft; he scoffed at medals and other symbols of military excellence, and his one constant goal was to come out of the war alive. Thus the American soldier was, by and large, a most reluctant dragon.

The evidence of these studies, if not the complaints of the generals, gave rise to the suspicion that there is something about American society that breeds weaklings. The anthropologist Margaret Mead quickly rushed into print with the explanation that it was too much mothering that had brought us to this sorry state. Soon this general thesis was raised to the level of a popular doctrine, momism, by the novelist Philip Wylie. Mom was the viper who, having little better to do with her time and energies, sucked the manhood from her male children, reducing them to total dependence upon her ministrations and rendering them incapable of aggressive, independent action. The young men of America could hardly be expected to go out valiantly to war; after eighteen to twenty years of protective mothering they naturally shrank from the harsh realities of military life. They missed their mothers and their mothers' tender care.

The doctrine of momism survived the winning of the war that had given rise to it. The rapidity with which our victorious military forces were demobilized and, perhaps, the conduct of some of those

* The study referred to is reported in *The American Soldier*, by Samuel A. Stouffer, *et al.* (Princeton, New Jersey: Princeton University Press, Vols. I and II, 1949).

who returned to civilian life may have given some impetus to the perpetuation of the doctrine. At any event, the views of the American people presented by the British anthropologist Geoffrey Gorer provoked more sighs than laughter.* After a casual glance over the American continent, he came up with a Freudian variant of the Wylie thesis. It is not, Gorer said, the viperous character of the individual American mother that is at fault. The real cause of the un-British-like infantilism of the American youth is too-long nursing at the mother's breast, with the end result that the individual comes to make a fetish of mammary glands. Note, for evidence, the typical American fondness for milk and ice cream. And observe, if further evidence is necessary, the American idealization of the female who has bovine breasts.†

For a time after the war there was, then, considerable agreement that American society was being undermined by too much mother— or, at least, too much milk. And campaigning politicians were constrained to skip the traditional reference to American Womanhood, which left them with nothing to revere but God and Country. There was, however, some hopeful speculation that our possession of the atom bomb might more than offset the deterioration of our military manpower; but as the cold war waxed and the Russians achieved the bomb, this consolation waned. And then, with that marvelous inconsistency of which only man of all the animals is capable, the doctrine of momism was largely forgotten as a new and exciting

* *The American People: A Study in National Character* (New York: W. W. Norton & Company, Inc., 1948).

† Recently another British anthropologist has attempted to psychoanalyze the American people and to explain the presumed weakness of the American male. In *The American Woman* (New York: Rinehart & Company, Inc., 1957), Eric John Dingwall offers such entertaining ideas as that American women have feminized their males, as is demonstrated by the fact that the American male wears garments such as the athletic supporter that are in fact symbolic of his quasi castration. This interpretation is, of course, derived from Freud's concept of "penis envy" and constitutes a sort of inversion of his belief that the father unconsciously desires to castrate his son.

Gorer, Dingwall, and a variety of lesser interpreters of the contemporary American scene provide the "antithesis" that was referred to earlier; for, as will shortly become apparent, the Freudian synthesis that is now so popular is a reversal of their position concerning the role of women in the creation of weaklings.

extension of the Freudian doctrine gained popularity with those of our intellectuals and practitioners who concern themselves with the care and feeding of infants.

Everything for Baby

In the latter 1920's and on through the 1930's, the dominant theory of the care and feeding of infants was one that had been derived from behavioristic psychology. In the behavioristic view, all learning is a matter of simple association. To rear an infant into a proper American, it is necessary only so to arrange the circumstances in which he lives that he will associate progressively this with that, and that with whatever constitutes proper American conduct. Thus the bathroom culture in which we Americans take such pride requires that the child be effectively and irrevocably housebroken. The cycle and occasion for the elimination of his body wastes must be geared to the availability of toilets, and he must associate the elimination of such wastes with the toilet as an object; or, as it was usually described, he must be "conditioned" to use the toilet for the purposes for which it was devised. Likewise, the fact that we Americans lead a time-geared life means, among other things, that the child must be conditioned to eat his meals on schedule. The fact that our food, like our automobiles and everything else that is ours, is highly standardized means, further, that the child must develop the standard food preferences. So equipped, he will be able in later life to eat at the designated time the Businessman's Special Lunch along with all the other Rotarians, suffering no ill consequences and undisturbed by a desire to relieve himself.

To this and similar ends, it was widely advised that the infant be placed, immediately he is brought home from the hospital, upon a rigorous feeding schedule and, within a few weeks, set at stated intervals upon his little potty. In these and other ways, the infant should be conditioned to live in a world that demands certain orders of conformity. If he wails, let him. Society does not approve of wailing members. If he is allowed to wail, he will soon be conditioned to not-wailing; for he will discover that wailing brings only discomfort, *i.e.*, he will associate wailing with the fatigue induced by wailing. Since, when he becomes an adult, he will live for the most part in and through impersonal relations with his fellows—with political functionaries, corporation employees, etc.—he should be cared for in infancy and childhood in as mechanical and unsentimental a manner as possible. The infant should not be held, except when it is necessary to minister to his physical needs; and as rapidly as possible he should be made responsible for the details of his own care, feeding his own face, buttoning his own panties, and so on. All this added up to the counsel that the infant should be weaned, literally and figuratively, as soon as that becomes physically and psychologically possible.

To what extent parents followed the counsel of behavioristically oriented pediatricians, child psychologists, and publicists, no one knows. And no one knows what would have been the consequences if everyone had followed the approved program. Most of those who were raised under this ideological creed were, at any event, too young to participate in World War II, and so were not among those who contributed to the view that Americans are a nation of weaklings. In theory, the behavioristic regime should have produced stalwart young men and women, beautifully disciplined, unencumbered by sentimentality, and entirely unafraid as long as their meals came on schedule, bathrooms were periodically available, and trains ran—as American trains are supposed to run—on time. So much for theory.

What is clear is that the early postwar idea that too much mother had demasculinized American youth was in sharp contrast with the prewar view that our children were being brought up on a rigorous and effective schedule, and that both these ideas were totally disregarded by those who subsequently rose to popularity on the pediatric platform of "everything for baby."

The doctrine of everything for baby mushroomed into the status of a cult in a period when our birth rate was rising rapidly and thus at a time when, logically, one would expect the social value imputed to the individual child to have declined. But contrary to logic, the everything-for-baby vogue swept through the ranks of pediatricians, child psychologists, and publicists, and was soon receiving sanction from many academic psychologists and still more anthropologists. At this writing, the latter show signs of wearying of the task; but the damage is done, if damage it is, for the vogue itself is still in full force.

Everything for baby goes under a variety of more or less official names. Some of those who accept the premises upon which the vogue is founded speak, glowingly, of "the child-centered home." Others litter their dialogue with recurring references to "love and affection" or, among themselves, just "L and A." Academicians are prone to dignify the concepts and views included within the vogue with the designation "permissive method." All make much of the need to preserve the infant's sense of security, and all agree that the infant is a very tender bud that must be given hothouse treatment if it is to unfold into the beautiful—if useless—flower that nature has intended. Thus they begin with the Freudian idea that man is inherently fragile and conclude that he should, therefore, be coddled into the negative attributes of the Freudian ethic.

But before examining the concept in detail and exploring its social implications, it may be well to dispose of the historical justification for the concept that is advanced by the more thoughtful of its advocates. They argue that this doctrine of child care is a necessary and most desirable corrective to the authoritarian character of the traditional American family.* The harsh conditions of frontier life in early America may, so the argument runs, have made absolute rule by the father over his children functionally necessary. But the frontier is gone, American society has produced abundance and physical security for all, and the authoritarian family system is as archaic as the Conestoga wagon. In this age of democracy and plenty the family is the last bulwark of autocratic rule, and it has become an instrument of tyranny. Men with no other claim to fame

---

* Various facets of this thesis are provided in *The Authoritarian Personality* (T. W. Adorno, *et al.* New York: Harper & Brothers, 1950). Documentary evidence of the persistence of presumed authoritarianism is offered by W. A. Davis and R. J. Havighurst in *Father of the Man* (Boston: Houghton Mifflin Co., 1947). In commenting upon the Davis and Havighurst findings, John W. M. Whiting and Irvin L. Child (*Child Training and Personality*. New Haven: Yale University Press, 1953, p. 70) remark, "There has been in recent years, of course, a widespread effort to change the practices of the American middle class in this respect." That is, to get parents to raise their children in the new permissive mode.

than the fact that they have fathered their children impose their will, selfishly and usually in terms of antiquated values and sentiments, upon their children.

It is difficult for socially perceptive native Americans of native American parentage to take seriously the claim that the everything-for-baby vogue is a necessary corrective for the traditional authoritarianism of the American family. For the American family can be typified as "authoritarian" only if the standard of comparison used is the ideal permissive home advocated by those who make that claim. By any other standard of comparison—the British middle-class family, that of the peoples of northwestern Europe, even that of France—the American family has been far more matriarchal than patriarchal, and much more democratic than autocratic. Exceptions there have been, of course. The Amish of Pennsylvania, the Proper Bostonians, and the recent immigrants to this country have maintained something of the old autocratic tradition; and no doubt many individual fathers have endeavored to dominate their households. But the idea that the American family has been and in considerable measure still is typically autocratic is a modern myth that must have been foisted upon us by people unacquainted with the subtle and salient characteristics of American society.

The American self-image has for long been conditioned by the evaluations and interpretations of America and the American character that have been made by European writers. One of the first of these interpretations was that made by the French statesman de Tocqueville, who concluded that Americans were living the democratic life that his own countrymen talked so much about. Subsequent observers could find little in American society to commend. The English have been especially critical and still continue to be, as is evidenced by the recent efforts of the British anthropologists Gorer and Dingwall to find psychoanalytic explanations for the assumed weakness of the American male. Why Americans should take the criticisms of Europeans so seriously is difficult to understand, but that they do is quite evident.

The Unbridled Self

The cult of everything for baby is not, as its proponents claim, a necessary corrective for authoritarian rule of children by American parents. It is, rather, an invasion of the traditionally nonauthoritarian family by Freudian-oriented advocates of the Freudian ethic. The value that it purports to achieve, and to which all else—society included—is subordinated, is the mental welfare of the individual. Baby should, indeed must, grow up into a calm, complacent adult, free from the psychological disfigurements of traumatic experiences, and uninhibited in the free expression of his feelings and interests. Phrases such as "full flowering of the child's personality" and "at one with himself" frequently appear in the discourse of those who believe that baby comes first. There is the implication that if baby is permitted to grow up untrammeled by the harsh hand of authority, he will make an acceptable addition to society. No attempt is ever made to reconcile this implication with the Freudian idea that the innate self of the individual is contrasocial in character; yet the everything-for-baby vogue is definitely Freudian, for the permissive milieu that is advocated is supposed to minimize conflict between baby and society by allowing him complete opportunity for self-expression.

The properly permissive mother is one who constantly attends, in the most loving manner possible, to the desires of her child. Permissive treatment is, of course, the direct antithesis to the kind of training regime that was advised by the behaviorists. From the moment he is brought home from the hospital the infant should, according to the permissive school, be the center of domestic life—hence the child-centered home. No demands should be made upon him; every concession should be made to him; and every waking moment of his life should be attended by some adult, preferably his mother.

The magic word in the permissive mode of child rearing is "security." No one has yet made clear exactly what security is, but it is held to be both essential to the welfare of the infant and extremely easy to destroy. To preserve her child's sense of security is the hallowed objective of the permissive mother. At birth, of course, the infant's sense of security was badly strained, for he came out of the comfortable womb reluctantly. Re-establishment and maintenance of his security therefore depend in the first instance upon constant assurance that he is loved, that he is really *wanted*. Just what maternal conduct constitutes evidence of love to the infant is never very clear. But the mother is advised to hold, cuddle, caress, and otherwise relate herself physically to her child and seldom, if ever, leave him alone; in fact, she is advised to do just about everything that the behavioristically oriented pediatricians and child psychologists made taboo and to avoid just about everything that they thought would contribute to his effective social conditioning. Far from preparing the child for the cold and mainly impersonal world of adult life, the permissive school insists that he must be protected from the slightest indication that he is not the center of an adoring and indulgent universe.

No member of the everything-for-baby cult would use the term "indulgence." The child is not to be indulged, naturally. The child is, rather, to be permitted to express himself, to manifest in unrestricted and uninhibited ways his inner nature or, if one prefers, his "personality." There seems to be one general exception to this rule: crying is not self-expression. Crying is, rather, protest behavior, at basis a protest against the very necessity of trying to live in this inhospitable world. Specifically, the wail of the infant or child is an indication that he is being thwarted in his desire to do something, and the proper response to the cry is to identify and remove whatever it is that blocks baby in his efforts to be his lovely little self.

With this one general exception, treating the baby permissively means, on the one hand, encouraging and aiding him to do whatever he happens to try or want to do and, on the other, never attempting to determine what and when he does anything. In practice, this policy must result in a species of unordered chaos in which neither time nor the traditional tastes, values, or standards of adult society play any part.

Like the doctrinaire Freudians, the advocates of the permissive mode of child rearing believe that all the standards of social life contravene nature. This idea, which has been remarked elsewhere, is by no means peculiar to the Freudians and their fellow travelers. It is based upon the naïve assumption that the universe was in truth designed for man's special benefit and that, therefore, such ills as man may suffer arise from his failure to live naturally. Countless special cults have been derived from this single assumption. There are, for example, the back-to-nature farmers who put their faith in compost and insist that the well-manured crop plant has no need for modern insecticides to protect it from plant parasites and diseases. At the other extreme are those who believe that all the physical diseases and disorders of man himself are a consequence of civilization; thus the nudists would cure all our ills by simple removal of civilized clothing, while the food faddists promise the same ends by a reversal to the diet of berries and nuts that they presume man ate before he became civilized.

The advocates of the permissive method of child rearing differ from the food faddists, the nudists, and the organic farmers only in what they single out as the major curse of civilization. They are little concerned with the physical health of the individual, since they believe that most of man's troubles are psychological. They are not much concerned with sex per se. For them the primary sin of society is that it imposes fixed and unnatural standards upon the individual, repressing the natural organic processes and requiring conformity to artificial daily and other life cycles.

For some reason, such "unnatural" procedures as putting shoes on baby or requiring him to live in a house do not distress the members of the permissive school. But any attempt to impose social standards of what, when, and how to eat upon baby is, they are convinced, certain to shatter his sense of security. Ideally, the infant should nurse at his mother's breast, and for as many months or years as he indicates any desire to do so. He should, moreover, be allowed to suck at the breast (or, if he must be bottle-fed, the bottle) whenever he feels like it.

Weaning, whether from breast or bottle, should be a natural process, inaugurated by the child and aided but never initiated by the mother. Weaning is at best a critical period for baby, since weaning constitutes the second major—and, in a sense, final—break with the mother organism. Any sign, however slight, that the mother is anxious to hasten the process will be taken by baby as an indication that he is unwanted, that is, unloved and not held in affection. The result, of course, would be a traumatic experience.

Once baby is safely weaned, he should be enabled and encouraged to explore the culinary resources of the household. And here another tenet of the permissive school becomes operative: the belief that baby comes into this world fully equipped with special, and highly individual, insight into the particular food substances that will provide him with adequate vitamins, minerals, carbohydrates, proteins, fats, etc. The adult, long since indoctrinated into the food preferences of his society, may need the guidance of a highly trained nutritionist to aid him in the selection of a properly balanced diet. He is prone to select his foods in terms of taste, which is no adequate criterion. But baby is not so handicapped. On the contrary, unspoiled by social training, baby will, given the opportunity, pick and choose from all the foods available just the right ones and right amounts to assure him proper nourishment.

The properly permissive mother must apply, as best she can, the same general principles to baby's eliminative processes that she applies to his eating. Ideally, he should be permitted to mess himself freely and wallow in the mess for as long as he may wish. But diapers may be used as a matter of convenience, provided that they are changed only in the most gay and lighthearted manner. A sort of game, casual and happy, should be made of the diaper-changing operation. Otherwise, the infant may discover that his body wastes are offensive and a nuisance to others. And since he does not as yet distinguish between himself and those body wastes, distaste evidenced toward the latter will be taken as distaste toward himself. It is this initial inability of the infant to distinguish between himself and the material by-products of his living that makes the problem of toilet training so difficult to solve.*

---

* And, it should be added, it was Freud who first observed that the infant does not distinguish between himself and his body wastes. On the basis of this observation Freud erected his elaborate interpretation of the nature and development of the "anal" type of personality. Anyone who saves string, paper

From the infant's point of view, the modern flush toilet is a mysterious, noisy, and hence frightening object into which things disappear, never to return. Should he be placed forcibly upon that object, he would immediately assume that he was about to be disposed of; that he would leave, in some horrible, unknown manner, the world with which he has become familiar—and this very prospect would constitute a major, and possibly fatal, blow to his self-confidence. To avoid this hazard, the infant, now become the child, should be permitted to discover, entirely on his own initiative, the nature and mechanics of the toilet. Curiosity will eventually overcome his initial apprehension; and the example of others, especially the mother, will ultimately arouse a desire to sit upon the seat. Not until then should the child, now perhaps become the youth, be introduced to the social practice of using toilets for the disposal of body wastes. And that introduction must be very casual in nature, for there may still be some tendency for the child-youth to think of his excreta as an extension of himself.

Properly permissive parents will presumably remain permissive toward their children as long as they live. Indeed, they will in due course become permissive grandparents, permitting their children to bring up the grandchildren in any manner that they may wish, provided that it is properly permissive. This may lead to various complications, but since pediatricians, child psychologists, and other advocates—as distinct from practitioners—of the permissive mode restrict their attention to children, they properly leave the adult complications to such functionaries as the police, judges, juries, and psychiatrists.

The Romance of the Natural Life

Those who have been brought up to an acceptance, even partial, of the Protestant ethic may find it difficult to believe that anyone, least of all educated professional people, can accept as valid and

---

clips, old rubber bands, the meat left over from dinner, or money, belongs to the anal type; and all such savings are in fact symbolic hoarding of the faeces, stemming from the fact that the individual has not really learned to distinguish himself from his faeces.

desirable the tenets and practices of the everything-for-baby cult. Most of the current books on child rearing are, nevertheless, more rather than less sympathetic toward the permissive mode; and a rather surprising number of otherwise normal people have endeavored to find experimental or other evidences that support the doctrine.*

At one time, for example, the anthropologist Margaret Mead attempted to demonstrate that the human child does actually have some sort of natural ability to pick from available foods those particular ones that will most effectively meet his nutritional needs. The findings were, it is true, distinctly inconclusive, and the experiments themselves of doubtful validity. But before she hurried off on another scientific quest, Mead left behind her the impression that the permissive mother could safely leave to the discretion of her children the determination of their diet. More significant, if only because more enduring, have been the efforts of numerous anthropologists to apply the theory upon which the permissive mode is based to the study of primitive groups. Anthropologists were among the first of the American social scientists who became enamored of the Freudian interpretative system. Their interest led, in the years immediately following World War II, to the emergence of a new field in anthropology that, for no particular reason, took the name "culture and personality." Abram Kardiner, a psychoanalyst, was its father; a few such outstanding professional anthropologists as Ralph Linton and Clyde Kluckhohn became its advocates; and

* The advocates of the permissive mode of child rearing are a most varied lot, although they all have in common faith in the Freudian doctrine—variously interpreted. On the extreme left are such writers as Dorothy Baruch (*One Little Boy.* New York: Julian Press, Inc., 1952) and Erik Erikson (*Childhood and Society.* New York: W. W. Norton & Company, Inc., 1950); about due center are, among others, Bruno Bettelheim (*Love Is Not Enough.* Glencoe, Illinois: The Free Press, 1956), J. J. Honigman (*Culture and Personality.* New York: Harper & Brothers, 1954), and Fritz Redl and David Wineman (*The Aggressive Child.* Glencoe, Illinois: The Free Press, 1957); while the far right, in which permissive counsel is tempered with some consideration for practicality and the interests of society at large, is best represented by Benjamin Spock, whose *Baby and Child Care* (New York: Pocket Books, Inc., 1946) sold more than three million copies in its first edition. The second edition, published in 1957, is considerably less permissive in tone than was the original.

within a decade the anthropological literature was heavy with psychoanalytical terminology.*

Most of the psychoanalyzing of primitive peoples has taken such amorphous directions that it defies analysis. A considerable number of researchers have, however, attempted to apply to the study of primitive societies the specific thesis that children brought up permissively will grow into well-adjusted adults. The effort to test this hypothesis with primitive peoples was evidently inspired by the impression that, on the whole, primitives are happy and well-adjusted human beings. Such being the case, it should be possible to relate the methods of child rearing of primitives with personality adjustment in adult life.

The assumption that primitive peoples are, by and large, well adjusted to their conditions of life has an interesting history. It is quite a modern assumption, and it reflects the modern man's uncertainty regarding himself far more than it does the actual findings of anthropological field workers. During the early phases of the exploration of the world by Western peoples, the native peoples who were encountered were thought of as little better than animals—and in those days the distinction between man and the animals was categorical and very much to the disadvantage of the latter. The idea that the natives are somewhat less than human was no doubt a simple rationalization of the fact that, for various practical reasons, Western peoples were treating them in much the same manner as they did their dogs, pigs, cattle, and horses. They plundered, slaughtered, and enslaved them in the name of God, country, and expediency. But during the nineteenth century the Western view of native peoples changed gradually to one of com-

---

* Abram Kardiner and Ralph Linton, *The Individual and His Society* (New York: Columbia University Press, 1939); Abram Kardiner, *et al.*, *The Psychological Frontiers of Society* (New York: Columbia University Press, 1945); Ralph Linton, *The Cultural Backgrounds of Personality* (New York: Appleton-Century Company, Inc., 1945); Clyde Kluckhohn and H. A. Murray, eds., *Personality in Nature, Society, and Culture* (New York: Alfred A. Knopf, Inc., 1948).

All the above, indeed the entire permissive school, have drawn upon neo-Freudianism rather than the old orthodoxy for their concepts. The authoritative document of neo-Freudianism is Karen Horney's *New Ways in Psychoanalysis* (New York: W. W. Norton & Company, Inc., 1939).

parative benevolence. The American slaves were liberated—on paper; the surviving Indians were granted reservation lands and the right to live—if they could manage it; and missionaries were sent out from all the Western countries to Christianize and so save for the kingdom of God the poor, misguided heathens of the world.

Rousseau had long since idealized the simple, uncivilized life; but it was not until well into the present century that this ideal became, here and there, identified with the actual life of primitive peoples. For there are, in fact, certain inherent difficulties involved. Primitive peoples are, after all, primitives. They live, to put it mildly, close to nature and in ways that are often, to the Western taste, anything but savory. So it was necessary to glamorize primitive peoples and their ways of life before primitive society could be held up as a comparative standard for Western peoples. Just how this glamorization came about is not clear. No doubt romantic novelists and idealizing artists contributed a good deal to the fiction that a South Sea island is a bit of earthly paradise inhabited by lovely, simple, and willing Polynesian maidens; and in time the motion-picture industry began using idealized natives in idealized native habitats as the stock setting for stories of idyllic love. At any event, the concept of the primitive as a simple, happy creature living in lush and lovely circumstances did become widely accepted in Western society; and during the unhappy days of the great depression, when Western society was undergoing acute self-criticism, the evils of modern civilization were often set against the virtues of primitive society. The practice proved a great stimulus to anthropological study and writing, elevated the anthropologists in the eyes of both academicians and the general public, and gave a sort of scientific sanction to the belief that the primitive life is conducive to a happy, carefree, and contented outlook.* It was

---

* More recent study has cast discredit upon the idea that simple peoples are characteristically happy and contented, and that mental stress and break-down are uniquely the products of civilized life. Joseph W. Eaton and Robert J. Weil (*Culture and Mental Disorders: A Comparative Study of the Hutter-ites and Other Populations.* Glencoe, Illinois: The Free Press, 1955) have, for example, demonstrated that the incidence of mental breakdown in one "simple, homogeneous" society is not far different from our own. Nevertheless, the Freudians continue the charge that modern society is atypically hard

during this same period that many Western people took to the woods and bared their skin to the sun under the misapprehension that clothing and cooked foods are the curse of civilization.

The culture-and-personality school of anthropologists took off from the popular view of the primitive; and they endeavored to ascertain what there is about a primitive society that enables its members to grow to adulthood free from the complexes and neuroses that plague modern, civilized peoples. Into this study they took, unfortunately, two preconceptions: the idea that primitives are well adjusted and hence free from complexes, guilt feelings, the sense of insecurity, frustrations, etc.; and the neo-Freudian thesis that the bases of adult personality maladjustments are laid down in infancy and childhood by autocratic mismanagement of the individual's innate biological needs. It is not surprising, therefore, that many of the early, preliminary reports on such studies lent support to the idea that a permissive milieu for children will produce well-adjusted adults. Even scientists are prone to discover what they are looking for, which is the reason why freedom from preconceptions is the first law of the scientific method.

The permissive school of child rearing drew strength from these early and enthusiastic reports, which are still quoted and referred to by current writers representing the permissive school. But as the initial excitement over this newly discovered field of anthropological study passed, anthropologists realized that the initial findings were not so reliable as had first been supposed. On the whole, it did seem true that many primitive peoples treat their children casually, if not permissively. They are often, by Western standards, "permissive" about the two specific matters that loom so large in the thinking of members of the permissive school—weaning and toilet training—although, to any but a hardened anthropologist, the term "indifferent" or "careless" might seem more descriptive of the manner in which many primitives deal with these two matters.

What cast considerable doubt upon the validity of the early reports was the difficulty of demonstrating the assumption that

---

on the individual (*e.g.*, Harry F. Tashman, *Today's Neurotic Family*. New York: New York University Press, 1957); and that idea has by now become firmly established in the folklore of modern society.

adult primitives are well adjusted. Too often for comfort, the field researcher came up against evidence that this or that particular group of primitives was anything but happy and contented; they might be, in fact, as quarrelsome and even drunken a lot as the worst of Western peoples. And depth interviews, a favored method of uncovering deeply seated or unconscious motivations, almost invariably revealed disgruntlements, frustrations, aggressive tendencies, and other indications that the happy primitive was difficult to find. Specious, Freudian-type interpretations of such evidence delayed but could not prevent the growing suspicion that something was very wrong. Those who were loath to reject the assumptions upon which they had undertaken their studies took consolation from the fact that their particular primitive groups were not, after all, representative of pure primitive society, since they had been contaminated through contact with Western peoples. Although, they argued, the children were raised permissively, their perfect little personalities were subsequently disfigured by exposure to civilized values, sentiments, and experiences.

But although scientists are human, they are also, by and large, men of scientific integrity. They do, on occasion, become enthusiastically involved in vogues and may, for a time, proceed with less than full scientific caution; but when and if the evidence runs against them, they usually, however regretfully, abandon a pet theory. By and large, the anthropologists have now renounced the attempt to validate through the study of primitive peoples the neo-Freudian thesis that autocratic—meaning socially determined—training of the infant and the child produces neurotic adults.* The desertion of the anthropologists has so far, however, failed to dampen the enthusiasm of the advocates of the permissive home. They proceed on their socially irresponsible way, propagandizing on behalf of a child-rearing procedure that might produce adults admirably suited to life in an idealized version of the welfare state

---

* One of the leaders in this renouncement is Marvin K. Opler, whose *Culture, Psychiatry and Human Values* (Springfield, Illinois: Charles C. Thomas, Publisher, 1956) promises to end the psychoanalytic excesses of the culture-and-personality school of anthropology and thus render this scientific discipline a major service.

but will certainly ill fit them for living in any actual society that man has yet devised.

Prepared for What?

The advocates of the permissive mode of child rearing are, in effect, attempting to validate the Freudian ethic, although it is doubtful if any of them are aware of or comprehend the social implications of their endeavor. They propose that the infant and child be treated *as though* man were in fact what Freud's fancy made him out to be. They hold, with Freud, that as a consequence of his biological nature, the individual is an exceedingly delicate organism and that any attempt to teach him to behave in accordance with socially designated rules of conduct will make him into a complex-ridden, guilt-ridden neurotic. Unlike Freud, they seem to assume, further, that if the individual is from birth showered with love and affection, granted his slightest whim, and never in any way guided or constrained, he will grow untrammeled into a wholesome maturity, emerging from infancy and childhood like a butterfly from its cocoon to stretch its lovely wings and soar gracefully through life.

How many parents deliberately and successfully follow the counsel of the permissive school is not known. One thing, however, is fairly certain: the parent who does systematically bring up his son or daughter in the permissive way will in due course become as baffled as the anthropologists who attempted to test the permissive theory against the evidence of primitive societies. For although it is possible to indoctrinate the child into the view that he is a fragile creature, the permissive mode of nontraining will not bring forth the expected "full flowering of the personality." The human infant does not come into this world equipped with the seeds of an adult personality. He comes into this world able to learn, as the behaviorists well understood, though they underestimated the complexity of the learning process. What he will learn depends upon his experiences, in which the Freudian mechanism of the traumatic experience plays a rare and trifling part.

The assumption of the permissive school—derived from Freudian doctrine—that the infant arrives with an innate self and wants to express it is, of course, a fallacy. It may be loosely said that the infant wants to live, but this holds true also for puppies, fledglings, and other newborn organisms. It may also be said, again very loosely, that he wants to eat. But the animal wants of the human infant can be satisfied in a great variety of ways, and at the beginning one way is just as good for the infant as another. Thus the infant will be just as well satisfied and perhaps as well nourished at the teat of a goat as at the breast of his mother.

As time goes on and the infant becomes the child, he does indeed have preferences. These preferences—whether for teat or breast, for sleeping in his mother's protective arms or on a pallet on the floor, for toddling aimlessly about the dusty village or playing sedately in the city park—are acquired through experience; none of them is in any sense natural. What preferences, tastes, desires, wishes, interests, values, needs, etc., the child acquires as he grows up—and which all together constitute his self or personality—depends therefore upon the social treatment that has been accorded him, plus, no doubt, the accidents and incidents of his private adventures. This is true whatever the society and whatever the school of child care to which his parents may subscribe.

So it is a major error of the permissive school to think that parents can, and should, let the "innate self" of the child unfold in a favorable—and this seems to mean uncontrolled—environment. The dependent error, fully as serious, is the assumption that, if the child is permitted to express this self on a day-to-day basis throughout infancy and childhood, he will face adult life with a harmoniously structured personality—by which they mean that he will be adequately prepared to meet and surmount the problems of daily life that every individual encounters, whatever his society.

And that, it may be said with great assurance, is exactly what the permissively raised child will be totally unprepared to do. The permissive milieu socializes the child just as surely as does the autocratic one; but what it teaches the child to want, need, expect, etc., is prompt and willing conformity by others to his own whims and fancies. No society, not even our own, is prepared to cater to the infinitely varied and contradictory wants of a multitude of adults brought up in the permissive mode. What is even more important, no society, including our own, can maintain a very high proportion of members who have been inducted into the view that they are inherently frail and must therefore be given all and required to give nothing in return.

A society, whatever its particular forms, is a system of reciprocal relations. A prince, a king, a son of great wealth, or an exceptionally beautiful girl may get much and return little; but most members must give as much as, and many much more than, they receive. This fundamental aspect of social life should be self-evident; yet it is completely ignored by all those—including those of the permissive school—who take their clue from the Freudian doctrine. The permissive mode of child care is, in ideal at least, one in which parents give everything and secure nothing in return, not even obedience. The child so reared will, if the procedure works, want much but be unprepared to give anything—even so little as a pleasant smile—in return.* So it should surprise no one if the permissively untrained child, as he grows toward maturity, finds more and more of his wants denied, becomes more and more frustrated, suffers more and more traumatic experiences, and thus becomes more and more neurotic until, at last, graduating into a full state of psychosis, he withdraws from this horrible world into one of his own creation.

---

* J. A. Gengerelli ("Freudianism: Dogma or Discipline?" *Saturday Review*, March 23, 1957) has described the permissive home and its consequences rather beautifully. He says, in part: "In the vacuum of wills into which he was born and raised, certain attitudes slowly develop on his part. As the years go by he perceives that he is the center of the universe he knows. . . . It is, so to speak, a world without limits, where every situation can be turned to one's liking by 'finding the angle' and pressing the right button. He grows up to think that his opinions, his likes, and his dislikes have a unique value in the world and are binding for those around him, and that, in general, his person embodies a special worth which is part of the public domain. Real *work*—the condition of all true creativity—is never introduced to him. This is an excellent way to develop neurotics, personality problems—and first-rate heels."

5

The Progressive School

COMPULSORY PUBLIC-SCHOOL education shares with baseball, the hot dog, and jazz the distinction of being indigenous to the United States. Until the 1830's, when agitation for a publicly supported school system acquired the fervor of a mass movement in America, formal education was largely a prerogative of the sons of the upper classes, both here and in Europe. Today, it is practically impossible for a child to grow up in America without at least ten thousand hours of exposure to public-school influence, and a high proportion of children will not be released from formal educational direction until they have devoted the equivalent of eight and one-half years of their lives to the classroom. In terms of time, if nothing else, the school is second only to the home as an agency of socialization.

The American public-school system is a monument to American enterprise and a demonstration of the fact that, whether or not faith can move mountains, it can determine the conduct of countless people over long periods of time. The number of people who are currently engaged in providing and consuming the offerings of our public-school system far surpasses the number engaged in any other kind of activity, including the production and distribution (but not, of course, consumption) of food. The provision of public-school education accounts for the major part of local and state taxes; and of all tax expenditures, that for public schools is by far the most popular and least resisted. There can be no doubt that the American people want and are reasonably willing to pay for the present school establishment. To suggest a reduction of current facilities would be, in the popular mind, close to treason; and the campaigning politician is always safe in promising more and better schools.

The public-school system is firmly embedded in American culture, and going to school is a normal and sanctioned aspect of growing up in American society. This is, however, about the only generalization that one can make with confidence about public-school education in America. It is, of course, possible to enumerate the number of quasi-autonomous school districts in the nation; the number and size of primary schools, secondary schools, and publicly supported colleges and universities; the number and powers of the state departments of education, the numbers, ages, sex, and formal educational qualifications of public-school teachers; and the number and size of the teacher-training agencies. But it is not possible to make many generalizations concerning what our public schools are trying to do to the children and youths who come under their jurisdiction, and it is quite impossible to estimate what those schools actually accomplish.

For one thing, the schools in America are remarkably diverse. They range from little shacks to vast, modern factory-type structures; from the disappearing one-room, one-teacher school in which children of all age levels are taught whatever the teacher thinks appropriate to the large, specialized plants in which the teacher is a bureaucratic functionary following prescribed procedures with fixed subjects and students of a single category. The diversity of our schools is in considerable measure a consequence of the fact that they have never been nationalized. From the beginning our public schools developed as grass-roots agencies; and even now they are largely under the control of, and to a considerable extent reflect the values and understandings of, the local populations that they serve. In this respect, public education in America has paralleled Protestant religion. Each school district, like each church congregation, has enjoyed a remarkable degree of local autonomy; and thus the schools have been comparatively free from the standardizing and stabilizing effects of centralized authority.

The fact that our public schools are for the most part maintained by local tax moneys and are to a considerable extent under the jurisdiction of local citizens has many and diverse consequences. It means, on the one hand, that schoolmen have to cater to local prides and prejudices and that they cannot, as would be possible under a centralized system, operate their schools in terms of some constant and uniform ideology. Thus our schools have not become as yet agencies of systematic political indoctrination; they have, rather, continued to change and each somewhat in its own way. The local schoolman, like the Protestant minister, must provide as best he can what the local market demands; and if the offerings of the primary and secondary schools have something of the variety and blandness of the foods in a supermarket, the explanation lies, in considerable measure, in the fact that we have managed to adhere to a remarkable degree to the principle that the public school is of, by, and for the people.

In Europe, the schools, public or private, have always been agencies for the transmission from generation to generation of the more general values and sentiments of the society, or of the class of the society represented by the school. They have therefore been, on the whole, agencies of tradition. This is most evident in the case of church schools of France and Italy, the German Gymnasium, and the private (called "public") schools of Britain. But even the trade and technical schools have in each country provided reinforcement of a traditional way of life, be it that of peasant or of engineer, as well as training in craft or mental skills. Almost from the beginning, however, public-school education in America has been expected to provide the individual with opportunity to surmount his status at birth, to escape or at least improve upon what is traditional for him and for his society. And whatever the deficiencies of public-school education in America, it has been one of the major avenues of individual movement up the class and occupational hierarchy. In this respect, if no other, the school system has contributed to the dynamism of American society.

One of the recent changes in American life that seems likely to reduce the adaptability of American society is the emergence of a philosophy of education that would make the public school a stabilizing agency. For a century and more, our public schools have tended in vague and random ways to honor the Protestant ethic as well as offer opportunity for the lad of enterprise. Critics have often complained that the school misleads the young into thinking that their fate is in their own two hands and that no goal is beyond achievement, with the result that many have been encouraged to set their sights unrealistically high. No doubt it often has, and no doubt also that great ambitions often fall short of fulfillment. But only the faint of heart will thereupon conclude that men should not be ambitious to accomplish anything and that the public schools should not encourage the young into thinking that they can through their own efforts get ahead in the world. Yet this is now the prevailing philosophy among the high priests of education; and if they get their way, the public schools will join with the permissive homes in inducting the youth of America into the negative attributes of the Freudian ethic.

The Educationists

The demand for free schools for free men seems to have sprung initially from the desire of women in the newly settled and still very wild West—the Ohio country—to provide their sons with the civilizing influence of the classroom. It is no doubt indicative of this desire that the McGuffey Readers, on which successive generations of Western lads were subsequently reared, contained little more than snatches of poetry and high-brow literature interspersed with moral homilies and moralistic anecdotes. As the free-school movement spread eastward, however, it acquired highly vocal advocates and, perhaps inevitably, an elaborate rationale. The proponents of publicly supported schools were soon claiming that the schools would, in a generation or two, be the cure for every recognized social ill; and that the schools would, moreover, in the course of time, cost the taxpayer nothing, since the educated boys would grow up to be reasonable and honest men and the need for public support of jails, prisons, poor farms, and homes for the aged indigent would thus be eliminated.

Public-school education for all (all males, that is) would, further, purify both local and national politics. An ignorant man is susceptible to persuasion by false political prophets and may even succumb to bribery. For he does not realize that his personal welfare is ultimately dependent upon the welfare of the nation. The educated man, on the other hand, will vote wisely and well. He will not fall under the control of political spellbinders, and he most certainly will not sell his vote for cash or get drunk on the free whisky given out by dishonest candidates and vote while under its influence.

Such was the promise of the public-school movement. For half a century the believers waited for the school to produce its miracle. Some of the early eagerness of parents—or at least mothers—to have their sons educated seems to have waned through that half century; at any event, the growing tendency for boys to avoid free schooling gave rise to a second wave of reformism. It was not that the schools had failed; rather, the people had failed the schools. The cure was simple—and political. Make education compulsory as well as free. Since this new movement coincided with that of feminism, the compulsory school attendance legislation that was gradually passed encompassed girls as well as boys. And in the course of time, the years of legally required schooling have steadily been increased, presumably on the principle that where moderation fails, excess may succeed. For not even compulsory free education brought the expected decline in the need for jails, prisons, and public agencies for the care of the indigent, or the anticipated improvement in political morality.

From the very outset, the establishment and development of public schools were hampered by a shortage of men of learning to serve as teachers. American society was then, as it still is, oriented toward practical matters rather than scholarship; and the few institutions of higher learning then extant were more interested in giving the sons of the wealthy a genteel polish than in creating an intellectual class. Moreover, although Americans expected much from their public schools, they were not prepared to grant to the teachers of their young a living wage and a respected status. So it often happened that the brightest and most advanced student in a school became the teacher until he, like his predecessor, could find more promising and profitable employment.

American ingenuity to a degree solved the teacher shortage, not by elevating the status of teachers to a point where the occupation would attract and hold ambitious and competent young men, but by developing a recruitment and training system. The "normal school," patterned somewhat after the French *école normale,* tempted ambitious but impoverished young men into the teaching profession by the promise of free higher education; usually these were small schools that, unlike many of the competing church schools, were located in towns to the end that the student might live economically at home. The growth of normal schools led quite naturally to the development in state universities of departments of education in which to train teachers of teachers; and while these departments were of necessity originally staffed with philosophers, men of letters, and scientists of one sort and another, they turned out professional pedagogues who in a short time took over the entire operation. By the end of the century the normal schools were on the way out, and the university departments of education were becoming teacher-training schools staffed by graduates of the schools. Other graduates of these schools were finding employment, and a degree of power, in the state teacher-accrediting and other school-administrative agencies that had arisen to aid local officials in the establishment and maintenance of primary and secondary schools. The end result of these and other related developments has been the creation of a fairly closed system of teacher recruitment, training, and accrediting that is impervious to correction from without and that generates only nominal self-criticism within its own ranks.*

Today, American schoolmen, who like to describe themselves as "educationists," are not unlike a traditional priesthood. They have a priestly zest for the fulfillment of supraindividual values, priestly confidence in the efficacy of their good works, and unbounded faith in the supremacy of their own rituals and ceremonials. It is impossible to question the sincerity and personal integrity of the good educator. He may conceivably be misguided, but he is certainly not crass or venal; and on the whole, he and his fellows manage to inspire their students with the ideals and values of serving mankind through public-school education.

Prior to the development of a cadre of professional educators—

---

* An official version of this development is provided by Edgar B. Wesley in *NEA: The First Hundred Years* (New York: Harper & Brothers, 1957). It details the growth and functions of the National Education Association.

i.e., professionalized teachers of teachers—the public schools were inclined to proceed upon the principle that education was an end in itself. They taught, of course, the tool subjects—reading, writing, and arithmetic; but even these tended to be treated as ends in themselves. What the student was required to read, in addition to the moral precepts provided by McGuffey's and other Readers, was mainly classical in orientation. But with the growth of public colleges and universities, which were established by politicians for practical purposes, there came a gradual reorientation of the high-school curriculum toward the sciences and such practical arts as mathematics, drawing, composition, etc. Through the same period it was discovered that the public schools could be used as agencies for propaganda; the moral precepts of the old Readers were replaced by political chauvinism masquerading as History, by the fine arts pretending to be Culture, and by a series of short-lived reformistic programs that ranged from fresh air at any price to down with the Demon Rum. Since about 1910 the vocational movement has steadily gained momentum, and our better high schools can now turn out everything from aircraft mechanics to beauticians.

Meanwhile, the emergence of schools of education and professional educators led, perhaps inevitably, to a search for a *raison d'être*. The extreme claims of the original advocates of public-school education had not stood the test of time and could not therefore be used in their old form. But the educators found ample and convincing justification in the theory of the evolutionary sociologist Lester F. Ward. Society advances, he believed, as the mass of men behave more rationally; and they become more rational simply as they acquire more knowledge. *Ergo*, by making knowledge available to every child, the public school is working improvements in the social order.

The idea that public-school education is the *modus operandi* of social progress dominated educational philosophy for thirty years or more. Under this philosophy the goal of the school was social reform, and the education of the student was seen as a means to this end. It was during this period that the professional educators discovered, in addition to Ward's evolutionary philosophy, that the school is an "agency of society"; and for a time educators drew heavily on the findings and views of American sociologists. They did not, however, implement their philosophical goal by teaching teachers to transmit knowledge to public-school students. They became, rather, so preoccupied with the techniques of pedagogy that they largely and often totally ignored the fact that pedagogical techniques are means to an end rather than an end in themselves.

Thus there came about an isolation of the professional educators from the sources of human knowledge—science and the humanities—that is now so complete that in every university the school of education—its faculty, and its students—is viewed with a mixture of anger and contempt by the scientists and humanists. The number of courses that are offered in the teachers' colleges and schools of education on how to teach is unbelievable to the outsider and is equaled only by the number of courses on how to administer teachers. As a consequence of this professional detachment from content, the undergraduate student earns his degree and his teaching credential by taking innumerable courses in pedagogy and only a small handful of courses, and those usually of the most elementary sort, that provide him with something to teach. At the graduate level, the student—who is usually preparing himself for an administrative post—repeats all the undergraduate courses in pedagogy, at a slightly higher level, and supplements them with course after course on the administration of teachers, school buildings, operative personnel, and so on.

The fact that schools of education devote themselves to pedagogy and administration, to the practical exclusion of all else, has provoked sharp criticism from those who believe that educational institutions should educate and that education consists of training in our symbolic heritage. Over and over it has been demonstrated that the majority of high-school graduates are barely literate, that they are hardly aware of the natural or political geography of the world in which they live, and that their knowledge of history begins with Washington—who founded our country—and ends with Lincoln —who freed the slaves.

There is undoubtedly justification for the charge that the public-school system provides almost nothing for the mind.* It is quite possible for a student to graduate from high school incapable of writing a meaningful sentence, unable to comprehend anything written above the level of the advertisement and the comic strip, unprepared to handle simple fractions, and almost totally unacquainted with the literary, scientific, and historical heritage of his society. But it may very well be that the current low level of academic standards in our public schools is an inevitable consequence of the attempt to educate, forcibly and at public expense, every child born into our society. For that attempt is based upon the assumption that all men are or can be made equal by education and that equality is socially desirable.

The truth is, however, that society is everywhere the negation of equality. Every form of organization—tribal, familial, corporate, national, etc.—exists through a differentiation of men. In the first place, social organization necessitates a categorical distinction between those who belong and those outside the organizational sphere; in the second place, such organization provides different functional roles for the members of the organization. The Joneses are Joneses, not Smiths or Browns; and the Joneses themselves are unequal, one being father, another mother, and so on. What compulsory public-school education was supposed to do was eliminate intellectual inequalities in American society, to make all men—and later, women —scholars. What it has, perforce, come to do is strive to prevent any individual from rising above the intellectual mediocrity of the majority. Since it cannot make intellectuals of the entire American

---

* Such is the central thesis of all the recent attacks upon the present state of education. Leading these attacks is historian Arthur Bestor (*Educational Wastelands: The Retreat from Learning in Our Public Schools.* Urbana: University of Illinois Press, 1953; *Restoration of Learning.* New York: Alfred A. Knopf, Inc., 1955; and numerous articles including "What Went Wrong with U.S. Schools?" *United States News and World Report,* January 24, 1958). Hilda Neatby has reported critically on education in Canada in *So Little for the Mind* (Toronto: Clark Irwin, 1953). Albert Lynd, a very vocal businessman, has decried the movement with all the adjectives at his command, and not a few telling facts, in *Quackery in the Public Schools* (Boston: Little Brown & Co., 1953). William H. Whyte, Jr., considers current educational practices one of the factors that is making for what he calls the organization man (*The Organization Man.* New York: Simon and Schuster, Inc., 1956).

population, it endeavors, quite without conscious intent, to prevent potential intellectuals from distinguishing themselves from their fellows.

Pedagogical Gadgetry

The charge that the American public-school system provides little for the mind does, however, seem a bit beside the point. In spite of our school system, past and present, a considerable number of bright and highly motivated children do manage to acquire considerable formal education. The social need for truly educated men is small at best, and our modern technology has so subdivided work and other tasks that the ordinary individual needs little formal knowledge to perform efficiently. Moreover, technological changes—ranging in character from television on the one hand to the IBM machine on the other—have largely relieved the individual of the need to read, write, or compute. And the modern mass media have, in theory at least, relieved the individual of any responsibility for thinking about such major matters as national policy, the respective merits of milk and beer, and the role of cigarettes in lung cancer.

All the great civilizations of the past have been developed and maintained with no more than a small class of formally educated members. We are, perhaps, exceptionally dependent upon the continuing services of highly trained scientists and technicians; but we do not need a social population composed largely of humanists, mathematicians, scientists, etc. The failure of our school system to produce mass intellectuality may be amusing, pathetic, and even ludicrous; but it is in no way crucial. So those who charge the professional educators with failure to fulfill their function—i.e., teach teachers to transmit knowledge—do so on the basis of an educational philosophy that the educators themselves have by now completely abandoned.

The idea that the public school is the primary agency of social progress went out of fashion among professional educators slowly and rather imperceptibly. They never, in fact, overtly and officially abandoned this original position; and whenever it seems expedient to do so, they revive the old thesis that public-school education is the means through which significant social reforms are accomplished. Such claims are, however, for public consumption. Among themselves, and when opportunity offers in public, they almost to a man subscribe to the philosophy of what is fatuously termed "progressive" education. It is this philosophy and what stems from it, rather than the failure of the public school to turn out intellectuals, that should occasion alarm. For the progressive school, like the permissive family, is dedicated to the proposition that the psychological welfare of the individual is the highest value and that the function of the school is to foster self-expression and aid in the development of personality.

The progressive movement in education is usually traced to, or blamed upon, the philosopher John Dewey. About the turn of the century Dewey and some other scholars established an experimental school at the University of Chicago in the hope of discovering more effective methods of teaching small children. The experiment was short-lived, but Dewey went on to become the philosopher for educators. He had one outstanding qualification for this role: even among philosophers he was noted for his tortuous way of communicating his views. As a consequence, what he wrote about education is at once so abstract and so deviously expressed that it can be used to sanctify any educational principle or practice.

Presumably, but by no means certainly, Dewey was primarily concerned with how things were taught rather than with what was being taught. He objected to the traditional pedagogy, which consisted, for the most part, of routine drill in spelling, word definition, sentence parsing, rules of grammar, the multiplication table, etc. In his view, intellectual drill is a parallel to military drill. It establishes fixed patterns of response but little comprehension. Moreover, it deadens rather than stimulates student interest in intellectual matters. If the student really learns anything, it is because he wants to do so and is provided with the opportunity to do so. The function of the teacher, therefore, should be not to teach, but to generate motivation and make knowledge available.

The idea that children learn best what they want to learn is psychologically sound; and it is undoubtedly true that the old traditional method of drill was pedagogically effective only in the establishment of such basic routine skills as spelling, sentence construction, reading, and computation. The child who is forced to memorize large chunks of poetry, to bound the forty-eight states, or to name the past Presidents of the United States may be on the way to winning a television jackpot, but he is not acquiring a comprehension of poetry, geography, politics, or history.

In principle, then, Dewey's progressive idea that education should consist of more than simple verbal drill has much to commend it. In practice, however, progressive education has often taken the form of some trivial pedagogical gadget that is all the rage among schoolmen for a few years, only to be abandoned in favor of another, equally silly procedure. Thus at one time the truly progressive educator advocated, and his disciples endeavored to apply, the project method of teaching. This procedure was based upon the assumption that learning proceeds from the known to the unknown. If, therefore, one desires to teach a class to spell "cat," one should begin by presenting them with an actual cat; the cat, presumably already known to them, is the project around which a variety of learning problems can be constructed—how to spell the word "cat," how to read the word "cat," and so on. The cat project can then lead by gradual stages—e.g., to milk, milk bottle, dairy—to "cow"; and after four or five decades of this, the children will be able to spell and read many of the more common nouns in our language.

The project method has appeared and reappeared, under different names, in educational dogma for thirty years and more. Between vogues for some variant of the project method there have appeared such other progressive pedagogical fads as that of teaching from the whole (the *Gestalt*) to the parts. In this procedure the child is not taught first the alphabet, then to recognize the combinations of letters by which we notate the basic sounds of our language, and thence to learn words as combinations of these syllables, and so finally to construct sentences. One begins with the sentence—or, for that matter, the entire book. Once the child comprehends the whole, it is no problem at all for him to understand the parts, words, and finally letters. And, likewise, in the teaching of arithmetic. One begins with the theory of least squares and works down to digits.

The pedagogical gadgetry advocated by the self-styled progressive educators has had an indeterminate effect upon actual school practices and has tended to be self-liquidating—if for no other reason than that the methods cannot be put into operation on a mass basis. Unfortunately, the same cannot be said for the philosophical orientation of the progressive educators. The new orientation, never explicit, involves a tacit abandonment of the idea that the school should be an agent of society and instrumental in the improvement of society and an acceptance of the antithetical view that the proper educational goal is "the integration and development of the whole individual into a well-rounded human being." Translated, this means that the public-school system should be concerned solely with the psychological welfare of the individual.

For the Placid Life

The modern progressive educator is not necessarily a disciple of Freud or a lay practitioner of psychoanalysis. He may not even be aware of the relation between his ideas of the child and what should be done with him and the ethical values and concepts that stem from the Freudian theory of human conduct. Nonetheless, the modern progressive educator accepts a philosophy of education that, if fully realized and actually effective, would produce high-school graduates totally incapable of living in society and prepared only to spend the rest of their lives on the analyst's couch. They would be passive, uncompetitive, unambitious, irresponsible, egocentric, and—of course—wondrously adjusted to doing nothing at all.

The progressive educators have come to the acceptance, if not overt acknowledgment, of the Freudian view of man and to the promotion of the Freudian ethic by easy and almost imperceptible stages. And, unlike the advocates of the permissive home who loudly and even proudly proclaim their attachment to Freudianism, the progressive educators do not acknowledge their debt to Freud. Recognizing, perhaps, the dangers of open advocacy of any clearly stated doctrine, they do not even offer their current philosophical position for critical public examination. It is transmitted via the classroom to their students, sometimes directly but more often by vague indirection.

The historical convolution by which the progressive educators have come to an acceptance of the Freudian view of man and of the Freudian ethic suggests, although it certainly does not prove, that acceptance may have been thrust upon them by considerations of political expediency. For although the professional educators are, as was indicated earlier, almost completely isolated from the intellectual currents of American society, they are to some extent dependent upon the continued good will of the general public as represented by the members of local school boards. This being so, the climate of opinion among professional educators may be taken as a fair criterion of public sentiment regarding education; in sum, as the nation goes, so go the educators. They are currently going strongly in the direction of Freudianism, which is possibly one of the most significant indications of the general drift of American society.

The adoption of the Freudian ethic as an educational goal seems to have started in a small and insidious way with the discovery, made early in the 1930's, that the public-school system was inadvertently subjecting the youth of America to the antiquated values and practices of interpersonal competition. The traditional examination procedure sets each student against all the others, and all students individually and collectively against the teacher. It makes education a competitive struggle for superiority, publicly stigmatizing those who fail and holding up for special and favorable attention those who are atypically industrious or bright, or simply better prepared at the outset. As a consequence, the social climate of the classroom is tense and combative; and the general atmosphere is one of hate, apprehension, and uncertainty.

The initial criticism of the competitive milieu provided by the classroom centered about the presumed adverse effects of this social climate on student learning. The charge was freely made that the standard examination and grading system diverted student attention from learning to getting grades, *i.e.*, it made high grades rather than the acquisition of knowledge the goal of the student. Here the educators were on fairly solid ground. The examination-grading system no doubt does tend to make learning a means to an end rather than an end in itself. Every competent teacher is aware of this tendency, and many of them consider it a grave disadvantage of the examination-grading procedure. But no one has yet come up with a satisfactory alternative; and that proposed by the progressive educators—the simple abandonment of examinations and grades—is not a solution to the problem but an evasion of it.

Perhaps because they were faced with an unsolvable pedagogical problem, the progressive educators were soon off in full cry in another direction. The economic distress of the times had given rise to the slogan, "Educate for the Good Society." It seemed clear that a society in which, by Presidential count, one third of the people are ill fed, ill housed, and ill tempered was anything but good; it seemed equally clear that a really good society would consist of people who, besides being well fed and well housed, lived together in harmony. Our failure in the latter respect was, the progressive educators decided, traceable to the competitive characteristics instilled in the members of our society by the competitive milieu provided children in the existing educational system. To bring about the good society, they concluded, it would be necessary only to eliminate competition from the classroom and bring up a generation of adults who were noncompetitive. Thus they detached themselves, categorically and perhaps irrevocably, from support of the Protestant ethic.

The idea that to be good a society must be composed of congenial, placid, uncompetitive individuals is by no means new. Since at least the time of Sir Thomas More, the utopians have portrayed the good life as one of calm, unhurried, and unselfish activity. Even Marx anticipated that the communistic society would, after the initial, tutorial period, become stabilized at a condition of complete social equilibrium in which each individual would fulfill his designated social role without thought of self-gain and in the interests of the general welfare.* There would be no competition between

---

* Marx was primarily concerned with the social fulfillment of the individual's economic needs. Currently the utopians are inclined to see the psychic welfare of the individual as the primary goal of the good society, a practice

individuals and no rewards for superior performance; and, since government would have withered away, presumably there would be no punishments for failure to contribute to the general welfare. Just what would motivate men to rise in the morning and get on about their work the utopians—including Marx—never bothered to explain. Not hunger; for in Utopia there is no hunger. Not the want of more or better clothes, or houses, or automobiles; for in Utopia everyone has everything he desires. And not, most certainly, the urge to outdo his fellows; for the citizens of Utopia are always altruistically concerned with the welfare of others to the end that no one of them would even think of striving to excel in any activity. It might appear to the nonutopian that under these conditions little actual work would be done and that this little would be performed in a most casual and unenterprising manner. For to work hard, or to display enterprise, would be most unkind to one's fellows. It would, in fact, be unthinkably competitive.

The progressive educators were no more concerned with how the noncompetitive society would produce the necessities of life than Marx and other utopianists had been. They simply assumed that, since our traditionally competitive system was failing to produce all that men desired, competition was the cause of the inadequacy and no-competition was its cure. As it turned out, we did not have to wait upon the rearing—in a reformed school system—of a new generation of noncompetitive adults for the solution to our economic ills. The various political panaceas administered by the Roosevelt administration, the inherent recuperative powers of our system itself, or the approach of another world war—opinions differ—gradually brought the economic machine back into high gear and deprived the educators of an opportunity to test out their theory.

Democracy in the Schoolroom

Through the war years the progressive educators devoted their efforts to "educating for survival," and they were thereby diverted

that seems to reflect the acceptance of the Freudian idea of man. Such is clearly the case with utopian-Freudian Erich Fromm (*The Sane Society*. New York: Rinehart & Company, Inc., 1955).

from their long-term objective. They did not resume it at the conclusion of the war, perhaps because they assumed that, the war well won and the Four Freedoms universally established, there was no further need for building the good society. Or they may have sensed that in an era of rising economic activity there was little public interest in the proposal to bring about the good society by educational means. Whatever the reason, they abandoned the good society and turned their attention to the production of the desirable individual; and in so doing they completed their ideological journey into the land of Freud. For the "desirable individual" does not differ materially from his predecessor, the citizen of the good society. He is still noncompetitive; but whereas the value of noncompetitive characteristics was once for the good of society, it has now become for the good of the individual. And so at this point the goals of progressive education and those of the Freudian ethic become indistinguishable. The new goal of progressive education is personality integration or "adjustment," which is just a non-Freudian way of saying the achievement of a reasonable balance within the individual of the forces of the id, the ego, and the super-ego. To that end the child must, decreed the progressive educators, be protected from the stresses and strains of participation in a competitive educational milieu.

The prime requisite for a truly progressive school is, therefore, complete freedom for the individual child to follow his personal inclinations—if he has any. The classroom situation must not in any way be "structured." There should be no program or schedule of joint work; for any such program or schedule will necessarily constrain the individual child, with results not unlike those that are produced when an infant is forced to abide by a feeding schedule. There must, of course, be no measuring of student accomplishment. On the contrary, everything that a child does—or does not do—should receive the approval, and even praise, of the teacher. In this way the development of competitive attributes will be avoided and, quite as important, the child will not be stigmatized as a failure simply because he accomplishes nothing. The stigma of failure, or the threat thereof, is not an encouragement to achievement, as was so long believed. It is, rather, one of the major causes of maladjustment in adult life. It may impress upon the student that he is incompetent, it may establish blocking, and it may in these or other ways assure that he will be frustrated in his adult roles. And it is such individual frustration, as all modern psychologists recognize, that leads to strikes, riots, murder, and even wars.[*]

The truly progressive school must, further, provide a completely democratic atmosphere. This means, in the first instance, that the teacher must not in any way be autocratic. She must not be a disciplinarian; she must not make learning assignments; she must not dictate class procedure. She may suggest general lines of activities that her students might find interesting, but she should never require that they engage in any specific activity—or, for that matter, any activity at all. She may offer to aid them, individually or collectively, in accomplishing whatever they may decide to do; but she must never impress her help upon them. Her role in the classroom is that of benefactor, not that of supervisor; she is, therefore, to be a sort of foster mother operating on the permissive principle. In this way she will supplement the mothers of her students—and correct for the adverse effects of mothers who are not properly permissive; and the school itself will serve as an extension of the home. Home and school will then be in harmony; and each child will progress, almost without break, from home into school and through school.

The provision of a completely democratic atmosphere in the classroom means, further, that the pupils—if the old-fashioned term "pupil" is still permissible—themselves determine what they shall do and how they shall go about doing it. For collective self-determination is the essence of the democratic method; and just as in adult life we determine the course of the ship of state by voting, so in the classroom the pupils should jointly determine their activities. That there is some contradiction between letting each pupil go his independent way—which is the prime requisite for truly progressive education—and that of having the pupils collectively decide what they will do, has occasionally been recognized. But it is thought

---

[*] This thesis was borrowed directly from the Freudians. The basic work is *Frustration and Aggression*, by John Dollard, *et. al.* (New Haven: Yale University Press, 1939). A more recent and very popular version of the thesis is provided by D. Krech and R. S. Crutchfield in *Theory and Problems of Social Psychology* (New York: McGraw-Hill Book Co., 1949).

that the democratic method provides the fullest possible scope for individual self-determination and at the same time results in group, as distinct from purely individual, forms of action. Thus the pupil can eat his cake and the school can have it, too.

The advantages claimed for the nonauthoritarian, completely democratic method of educating the youth of America are many and quite varied, and sometimes they are also contradictory. Those of the progressive school of education who are still so unprogressive that they cling to the idea that education is a process of inculcating knowledge and developing mental abilities take their cue from some experimental studies of "democratic" and "autocratic" leadership made by Kurt Lewin and his disciples.* Lewin, a psychologist, was unalterably opposed to political dictatorship, which is not difficult to understand in view of the fact that he was a refugee from Nazi persecution. As a scientist, he was not content to say that dictatorship is bad and let it go at that. To fulfill the scientist's code, he had to demonstrate that dictatorship does not work, or, at least, does not produce as effective group action as does leadership that is democratic in character. A series of ingenious experiments, in which the performance of paired groups operating under autocratic and democratic leadership was studied, led him to conclude that the democratic mode of leadership is conducive to higher individual motivation and, thence, to greater group effort and efficiency. The studies have lately been criticized as providing highly artificial test circumstances, as involving unclear and probably unrealistic concepts of democratic and autocratic forms of leadership, and as using for the test purposes forms of group action that loaded the experiments in favor of the so-called democratic mode of leadership. This latter is perhaps the most serious of the charges against these studies. It should be obvious that children will play a game of baseball that they have jointly decided upon with more enthusiasm than one of tit-tat-toe that has been imposed upon them by "autocratic" leader-

---

* The initial reports on these studies were made by Kurt Lewin and R. Lippitt, "An Experimental Approach to the Study of Autocracy and Democracy: A Preliminary Note" (*Sociometry*, Vol. 1, pp. 292-300, 1938); and by Kurt Lewin, R. Lippitt, and R. K. White, "Patterns of Aggressive Behavior in Experimentally Created 'Social Climates'" (*Journal of Social Psychology*, Vol. 10, pp. 271-299, 1939).

ship. On the other hand, it does not follow that the crew of an anti-aircraft rocket launcher will fire faster and more accurately at a target that they have, through joint discussion, selected than at one designated for them by higher authority.

The Lewin studies have, however, been seized upon by the rear guard of the progressive movement in education as proving that students will learn more rapidly in an atmosphere of classroom democracy than they will if the teacher, acting as an autocrat, assigns learning tasks and directs them. But all this has been of slight concern to the *avant garde* of the same movement—those who believe that the sole function of the school is to aid the individual child in integrating his personality. For them, the virtue of the democratic method is not that it fosters learning but that it discourages interpersonal competition, provides each pupil with an opportunity for self-expression without at the same time resulting in differentiation among the various pupils, and prevents anyone—pupil or teacher —from exercising authority. Under these conditions, so they contend, the individual child is free from constraint and is therefore free to develop his personality fully, without danger of acquiring in the process any such frustrating characteristics as the desire to excel, scholastically or otherwise.

Permissive, If Not Progressive

The actual impact of the current version of the progressive movement upon educational practices is impossible to estimate. Here and there a specific school, usually private but sometimes public, openly prides itself on being progressive. In such a school considerable effort is made to achieve and then maintain the democratic atmosphere, to avoid anything that smacks of competition, and to protect the pupil from stress or strain of any sort. In practice this means no specific work assignments, no designated classroom procedures, no examinations, no grades, and, inevitably, no education.

The public schools for the most part, however, still go through the motions of the old-fashioned pedagogy. The teacher calls her class to attention, she makes study assignments, she calls for recitations, and, occasionally, she gives examinations. At the end of the semester she distributes grades among her students and wishes them good-by and good luck before turning her attention to the next batch of children. The philosophy of the progressive movement is given considerable lip service by public-school administrators and even teachers; but the sheer impracticability of operating in the progressive manner, if nothing else, has prevented the school from practicing what the progressive educators preach. To do so would require a host of teachers trained into an acceptance of the progressive philosophy, a sufficient number of them so that each would be responsible for no more than fifteen or twenty pupils. For a democratic atmosphere in the classroom, whatever it may mean, cannot possibly be maintained on a mass and routine basis. And there is no host of trained teachers for this purpose; on the contrary, the postwar baby boom has strained our educational facilities to the utmost, and the supply of teachers—progressive or traditional—has not begun to keep up with the demand. As a consequence, the school administrator has been hard pressed to staff his crowded classrooms, and the trend toward progressive education therefore comes at a most inappropriate moment.

Originally the local control exercised over school administrators came via the lay school board—usually prominent local business and professional men. But, by an accident of history, the schools of America are now more or less under the jurisdiction of those mothers of school children who have a keen and vocal interest in the education of their children. The accident was perpetrated by the school administrators themselves, who thereby largely abdicated from the role of educational authority. On the assumption that it would tend to strengthen their hand and somewhat offset the powers of the school board, they encouraged the Parent-Teachers movement. They saw the P.T.A. as a convenient grass-roots organization through which they could secure popular support for demands for more and better schools, more and better paid administrators, etc. Instead, P.T.A. meetings have generally become a forum in which those mothers who have the time, energy, and interest to concern themselves with school matters tell the educators what they want and how to go about providing it.

In many places, it would seem, the mothers of school children have demanded that the school provide their children with a progressive education. It is not clear whether this demand means that the professional educators have sold their progressive philosophy to such mothers or that, having adopted the permissive doctrine of child rearing, the mothers simply want the school to be an institutional extension of the child-centered home. But it has certainly posed many practical school administrators with a dilemma: in the midst of a critical teacher shortage they are expected to adopt a pedagogical procedure that requires two or three times the normal proportion of teachers. They have not, of course, been able to escape this dilemma; but they have evolved a sort of Everyman's version of progressive education that, while it may satisfy no one, at least enables them to claim that their schools are progressive.

The new—or should we say "practical"—version of progressive education accepts the basic assumption that the individual is a very delicate creature of which very little can be expected. It takes, or pretends to take, the integration of the individual's personality as the educational goal, and it makes courses on social adjustment and school "activity" programs the means to the fulfillment of this goal. The courses that have of late years been introduced into the school curriculum, particularly that of the high school, on the grounds that they facilitate student social adjustment range from instruction on applying make-up and conversing on the telephone to slightly disguised versions of the popular concept of the art of winning friends.* To the extent that the school administrator has introduced such courses, however unwillingly, he has of necessity displaced parts of the more traditional curriculum. And since courses of this sort can have little if any content, they provide students with undemanding ways to fill out their course load; thus their inclusion in the school curriculum automatically lowers the minimum standards of the school. In this respect, if no other, the courses on social ad-

---

* This statement may seem an exaggeration, and one wishes that it were. But the long list of fanciful courses advocated in a recent teachers' manual, the product of six years' labor by some one hundred professional educators, reveals all too clearly the educators' preoccupation with student adjustment (Paul F. Pierce, ed., *Source Materials of the Educational Program: A Guidebook of Living and Learning Experiences.* Chicago: The Chicago Public Schools, 1957).

justment do contribute to making the school permissive if not progressive.

The second concession to the demand for progressiveness in education, that of encouraging activity programs, is just a dressed-up extension of the old school playground. The "activities" range from directing traffic at school crossings and putting on student plays to running student "government." Some of them are slightly avocational, many of them are simply recreational, and still others are supposed to be youthful versions of normal adult forms of social participation. Most of them are, no doubt, harmless avenues for the dispersion of youthful energies; and some of them may even have some socializing value. But they are all essentially play, and they tend to intrude more and more upon the classroom time of both teacher and student. While it is no doubt true that all work and no play makes for a rather grim and unsociable person, it is also true that all play and no work makes for an irresponsible, however sociable, one.

It may well be, as Whyte and others have observed, that success in our society has become increasingly a matter of playing the organizational game, *i.e.*, of subordinating oneself to the rules, informal as well as formal, of the business or other organization through which one secures one's livelihood. But "playing the game" is not just play; it demands of the individual that he subordinate himself to forces, personal in origin, over which he himself has no control and that he do so diligently and tenaciously. The kind of adjustment contemplated, and quite possibly fostered, by both the school courses on social adjustment and the activity programs is of quite a different order. It is intended to liberate the individual from restraints, to enable him to adjust "spontaneously" to others, and to equip him to play through life.

The Child's-eye View

The average public school is far from fulfilling the ideal of the progressive educators, but it is certainly moving in that general direction. The result, if this trend should continue, is not likely to be the creation of future generations of relaxed, uncompetitive adults, living together in peace and plenty, but, rather, the creation of a population of indolent, undisciplined, unprincipled, and incompetent people quarreling in random and fretful ways over the diminishing fruits of a dying social system.

For the real significance of progressive education—theoretical or practical—is that it strives to validate the Freudian idea that man is a fragile creature from whom very little can be demanded without jeopardizing his mental stability. To the extent that the public school proceeds upon the assumption that the child must be treated "democratically," must be given freedom to express his personality, and must be encouraged to play spontaneously with his fellows, it cannot require that he learn anything specific, it cannot discipline him into accepting responsibility for his own actions, and it cannot hold him accountable for failure to conform to normal standards of social conduct.

Any child who is permitted to follow his own whims and fancies through years of public schooling can hardly fail to acquire, from this experience if no other, an idea of himself and of his society that is in one way or another distinctly contrasocial. The effects of such schooling will of course depend upon the child himself, upon what he is when the school begins its contribution to the development of his personality. No doubt the sturdy little product of a demanding but considerate and affectionate home, the lad who has already acquired the beginnings of a character conforming more or less to the Protestant ethic, can take what positive offerings the school may still provide and come out unswayed by the pampering to which he has been exposed. The school will not have exploited fully his abilities and his drive to accomplishment, but at least it will not have reduced him to the level of mediocrity which is its unofficial goal. Others, less prepared by prior training to survive under organized adversity, will not fare so well. They will come, to some degree or other, to see themselves as the school defines them or to see in the school proof positive that they can get away with anything—anything short of murder, and perhaps even that.

The child, of which there is many a one in our society, who has acquired his conception of himself and of his relations to others in the rough and tumble of an underprivileged home and the city streets is not likely to take over for himself the progressive school's definition of him as a fragile creature who needs permissive nourishing. He is, rather, likely to interpret the "democrat" atmosphere of the classroom, the freedom from adult supervision, and the stress upon social adjustment as evidence that society is weak and he is strong. For here the assertive, competitive drives acquired at home and in the streets can be expressed without meeting the resistance to which he has been accustomed. He will presumably find in his new freedom, in the absence of restraints, and in the failure of adults to punish him for willful acts, reinforcement of the gangland code that only weaklings submit to adult authority and the wise guy can do what he wishes with impunity.

The child of the slums, the city streets, or the demoralized home is, thus, not at all likely to be inducted into the negative values and attributes of the Freudian ethic by the progressive school. On the contrary, the progressive school may inadvertently intensify whatever positive qualities, such as strong motivation and an active concern with his personal welfare, he may have brought with him to the school. At the same time, the progressive school will no doubt quite as inadvertently indoctrinate him in the Freudian thesis that society is inherently opposed to the individual and invariably at war with him. And superimposed upon this view of himself and society will be the understandable conviction that in this war he can, and will, come out the victor. So while an inadequate home and a very adequate, but antisocial, gang life may bear the main responsibility for the development of his personality, the public school, if it is in any measure "progressive," will do nothing to correct for them and will in fact further what they have already begun.

6

The Adjustment Motif

IN ACCORDANCE with the Protestant ethic, nineteenth-century Americans were ostensibly oriented individually and collectively toward achievement. Not all of them were, of course, but achievement was the standard; and whether achievement was measured in crass or in idealistic terms—in money or in religious, scientific, or some other form of endeavor—a man was judged largely by what he accomplished during the course of his lifetime. To be rich or learned was, on the whole, less important than to have become rich or learned; and so the scion of wealth was honored less than the man who had started with nothing and won wealth through his own efforts; and the politician born in a log cabin could garner more votes than the one born on Beacon Hill. And so, too, the home, the school, the church, and countless publicists from Horatio Alger to Horace Greeley tended to glorify a life of accomplishment and to encourage the child and youth to strike out for himself. This, it was then said, is the land of boundless opportunities; and anyone who fails to take advantage of them has only himself to blame.

Within this present century the achievement motif—or, as the anthropologists would designate it, "cultural theme"—has given way to a new motif, one that is logically and historically related to the rise of the Freudian ethic. This new motif, which usually goes under the appellation "adjustment," is one aspect of the current stress upon individual security; and it is a major if not entirely dominant motif in American society today. Many of the recent developments in American government, business, academic, and other aspects of social life are directed toward the elimination of individual misadventure. That they also, and quite inevitably, lead to the elimination of

130

opportunities for individual adventure—and possible achievement—
is either ignored or else considered unimportant.

Adjustment is the *sine qua non* of all those who accept the Freudian doctrine of man and sanction training into the negative attributes
of the Freudian ethic.* The psychoanalytic process is supposed
to bring about an adjustment of the mentally distraught person
to the forces and circumstances that have induced distress. The
advocates of the permissive home and the progressive school believe that the child who is brought up permissively and progressively
will become a well-adjusted adult. Vocational counselors guide
their clients into those occupations in which they will be best adjusted. Marriage counselors endeavor to adjust the husband to the
wife and the wife to the husband. College and university admissions
officers favor the high-school graduate who is rated well adjusted by
his teachers and principal. And the personnel directors of large industrial and business enterprises often consider social adjustment the
major criterion in the selection of new employees.

To the psychoanalysts, permissive psychologists, progressive
educators, counselors, guiders, and other agents of the new American
motif, adjustment is not a process but a value. To them the ideal
individual is the one who is content to accept things as they are,
who is uncritical, who is undisturbed by contradictions in the
world about him, who never resents, rebels against, or becomes
indignant over anything he may encounter. Such an individual is
well adjusted, and to be so adjusted is the highest good. From
their point of view, no one should, then, exert himself in the effort
to shape external circumstances to his own ends, for any such
endeavor would involve stress and strain and mental disturbance.
In effect, they adhere to the idea of nothing risked, nothing lost.

---

* It is rather interesting that the most vigorous opponent of the adjustment
motif should have been the psychoanalyst Robert Lindner (*Prescription for
Rebellion*. New York: Rinehart & Company, Inc., 1953; and *Must You Conform?* New York: Rinehart & Company, Inc., 1956), for the adjustment motif
has a close affinity both historically and ideologically to Freudianism. Lindner,
nevertheless, held that the basic fault of modern society is its preoccupation
with adjustment. As an alternative he offered a theory based upon the idea that
the individual should rebel from the pressures to conformity; in effect, if
not in terms, he advocated a return to the Protestant ethic.

The well-adjusted individual is represented as poised and serene, unencumbered by any doubts or uncertainties. He is an extrovert who sails imperturbably through life with no ups or downs. He is the American boy as we would no doubt like to have him, and at his side is the American girl as he would no doubt like to have her. They play their happy way through childhood, they pass through adolescence without anxiety, they marry without hesitation, and then quite effortlessly and without a qualm they settle down in a fine suburban home to bring up their many children in the permissive way and in due course send them off for a progressive schooling.

All this would be very well if it were possible, but it is no more than an idle dream. In real life, whatever the society, every individual encounters a wide variety of difficulties, the mundane misadventures inherent in living. Their specific nature and the definitions made of them vary somewhat from society to society and from individual to individual, but no society can possibly protect any individual from experiencing some of them. Sickness, injury, bereavement, and the infirmities of old age are among the most obvious and inescapable of these. Personal disappointments are less obvious and perhaps somewhat less inevitable; but no society can protect the individual from all chance of misadventure in courtship, in marriage, and in parenthood. And until now, and as far into the future as we can foresee, no society can fully protect him from natural calamities—fire, flood, earthquake, etc.—or insure him against the personal disaster that follows upon war or riots or variations in the tempo and direction of economic and political activities.

Learning Without Living

The adherents to the cult of adjustment picture the well-adjusted individual in utopian terms; but they seem to recognize that his life will be considerably less than utopian, for they would prepare him for and guide him through the problems of living in accordance with a theory that is, to say the least, peculiar to themselves. The theory seems to have been derived, by analogy, from the observation that, other things being equal, the physically sturdy body is more resistant to disease than is the one weakened by malnutrition, physical hardship, extreme mental stress, or prior illness. To the extent, definitely limited, that current physical health is correlated with future health, there is good reason to advocate and if possible achieve high standards of housing, nutrition, sanitation, and the other circumstances and practices that seem to be conducive to good health.

Similarly, on the grounds that the mentally sturdy person is better able to adjust to the problems of living, the adherents to the cult of adjustment contend that the individual should be protected in infancy, childhood, and youth from mental stress. But since they assume, in accordance with the Freudian idea of man, that any misadventure will have psychologically injurious consequences, this amounts to bringing up the individual in as close to a social vacuum as it is possible to provide. In this view, an experience such as being spanked or futilely endeavoring to get the jam jar off a high shelf is not a learning experience but a traumatic one. They equate any such experience, that is to say, with undernourishment and exposure to disease.

If the home and the school are successful in protecting the individual from misadventure, as defined above, he will, in this view, grow up to be a well-adjusted human being. He will be free from inhibitions, frustrations, apprehensions, and other barriers to easy adjustment; and he will therefore be able to meet the challenge of adult life with confidence and assurance. Since he has never experienced failure, he will be free from fear of failure. Since he has always known success in the protected world of home and school, he will be prepared to succeed when it at long last becomes necessary for him to adjust to real-life circumstances.

All this is based on the idea that the better adjusted the individual, the better able he will be to surmount difficulties; but all this ignores the fact that the effective way to learn to live is by living, not by avoiding life until maturity. Ideally, the home and the school should provide the child and youth with a small-scale and modulated replica of the larger society in which he will ultimately live.* In such a

* There is, in fact, a school of sociology that holds to the view that normally the family and other small groupings are microcosms of the society. G. Gur-

home and school the child would gradually learn through experience how to deal with the various adventures and misadventures of adult life. Only through experience with problems can he learn to solve problems; only through experience with difficulties can he learn to meet and surmount them.

It is no doubt true that some kinds of misadventures during childhood or youth may malprepare the individual for adult life. The child who is subject to overly severe punishments may have his spirit broken, as the dog fancier would say, especially if those punishments are administered erratically. The child who is nagged—or guided— into meticulous adherence to adult ideas of what is right and proper may be malprepared for the hurly-burly of life outside the home. The child who is caught between the cross fire of parental incompatibility may develop a duality of self, an ambivalence toward external circumstances, that may make him timid and uncertain throughout his life. Certainly no special benefits can accrue to the child or youth who is subjected to major disasters, natural or social. The idea that hardship, physical or social, is hardening has only limited validity; at some point hardship becomes weakening rather than strengthening. But the fact that extreme or critical experiences may have adverse consequences to the developing personality does not mean that freedom from all experience with the problems of living is the ideal preparation for adult life. After all, freedom from all experience would simply mean no preparation for the problems of living.

The more sophisticated of those who believe that the best preparation for life is no-preparation will argue that it is impossible to anticipate the specific conditions to which the child will be required to adjust when he reaches adulthood. Ours is a variegated and everchanging society; thus what is expedient for one person may not

---

vitch (*Sociometry in France and the United States.* New York: Beacon House, 1950) has developed this view into what he calls "microsociology." C. H. Cooley long ago advanced the same view in his *Social Organization* (New York: Charles Scribner's Sons, 1909), and there is much evidence in support of it. What the advocates of the permissive home and progressive school propose is to make both home and school as unlike the world outside them as possible. They are to be social hothouses in preparation for the cold and windy world of adult life.

be for another, and what is expedient today may be antiquated to-morrow. The best, and the correct, thing to do is prepare him for the unpredictable conditions with which he will in time be required to deal by keeping him adjusted, and, hence, "adjustable," not by inducting him into predetermined patterns of conduct. This justi-fication for the permissive and progressive mode of nonpreparation avoids the simple error of those who hold directly to the Freudian view of man, and it has in fact a good deal to commend it.

But by keeping the individual adjustable the adherents to the cult of adjustment do not mean training him to adapt to the contra-dictory and often changing circumstances that he will meet as he goes through life in an active and enterprising manner. On the contrary, they would have him deal with these circumstances pas-sively—i.e., in whatever way is least disturbing psychologically. And they assume that the individual who has been brought up in the properly permissive and progressive manner will be so free of complexes, frustrations, guilt feelings, and other inhibitions to spontaneous action that he can without thought or effort conform to the requirements of any circumstance that he may encounter.

The kind of passive conformity that is currently being advocated as adjustment is, in theory, entirely a function of forces external to the individual. The well-adjusted individual is in no sense a deter-minant of the actions that constitute adjustment. He might perhaps be described analogously as a half-inflated ball, so nearly empty of character that he can fit himself into any circumstance in which he finds himself. For to achieve adjustment in the modern manner, the individual must accept and subscribe to the values, sentiments, wishes, and demands of the people to whom at any moment he is adjusting. He must merge or blend into the company of his fellows, whoever they may be and whatever they may represent.

In the popular version of adjustment, the individual makes him-self a sycophant: he smiles on everyone, he agrees with everyone, he flatters everyone, and he avoids giving the slightest indication that he himself has any personal opinions on anything or, in fact, any personal values and sentiments of any sort. He must not, there-fore, be a man in his own right, conducting himself in the manner that he himself considers proper. He must, rather, be a mirror held up to the view of others, reflecting them so that they may bask in the sight of their own images. For the goal, the end to which the individual should aspire, is the approval of his fellows; and that approval can be bought only through catering to their vanity.

The popular concept of the adjustment motif may be crass and superficial. It has, however, sold fabulously in book and lecture form for many years, and the demand for counsel of this sort shows no signs of abating. Apparently there are people who feel socially isolated and, having tried such simple cures as breath purification and body ablutions, turn in desperation to the counsel of lay psychologists for assurance that there is nothing wrong with them that a course on how to be obsequious will not correct.

The Course of Least Effort

The serious devotees to the cult of passive adjustment will depreciate the importance in adjustment of such devices as the winning smile and flattering attention. To them, adjustment is a very complex condition at which the individual arrives by incorporating his self with the selves of others. And it is at this point that the concept of adjustment and the progressive school's stress upon the maintenance of a "democratic atmosphere" converge to produce a remarkable synthesis. Adjustment, we are given to understand, is not really a process of individual subordination to the group—of simply accepting as one's own and acting upon the values, sentiments, opinions, etc., of others.* True adjustment consists of federating one's self with others in such a way that all the advantages of belonging to and participating in a group are secured without loss of one's personal identity. When all the members of the group are adjusted each to the others in this way, the result is a social coalition rather than a coalescence. The distinction is, of course, a rather fine one; but upon it would seem to depend the peace of

* David Riesman (*The Lonely Crowd.* New Haven: Yale University Press, 1950) concludes, however, that this is the kind of adjustment that is becoming normative in America. The "typical" modern American tends, in Riesman's terms, to be "other-directed."

mind of those who advocate providing the child with a permissive home and a progressive school.

It will be recalled that the immediate professed goals of permissive child rearing and progressive education are to protect the child and youth from the psychologically scarifying consequences of trauma and to enable him to realize the fullest development of his inner self. To these ends, the child and youth is to be freed from social constraints, absolved from discipline of any order, encouraged but never directed or judged, and so on. Much of this is directly in accord with a literal interpretation of the Freudian doctrine and provides a sort of household and schoolroom version of the therapy provided mentally disturbed patients by the psychoanalysts. But while the psychoanalyst can prescribe for his patients almost anything that he deems advisable, since his professional status absolves him from responsibility for everything but his patient's welfare, parents and teachers and others who deal with the young are at least somewhat hampered by practical considerations, if not by a sense of social responsibility. The mother who permits her son to do anything that occurs to him around the home simply cannot permit him to defecate in the public streets or sample the foods displayed in the delicatessen, and the teacher who encourages her pupils to let their minds wander at will dare not let them wander with the same freedom across the highway on their way home.

The cult of adjustment provides permissive parents and progressive educators with a rationale for the fact that children who have been brought up to be in every conceivable respect unprepared to conform to social demands do for the most part eventually leave home and school for playground and other nonpermissive and nonprogressive realms of society; and in these realms they must, if they are to gain social acceptance, play and work and live in accordance with standards of conduct that are not of their own making. To the child or youth who has been for years assured by his parents and his teachers that he is free to satisfy all the demands of his personality, irrespective of the desires and demands of others, it might be something of a shock—i.e., a traumatic experience—to discover that his playmates and, later on, his co-workers have no regard whatever for his personal needs, his personal views, or his personal desires in any matter. It will probably in no way cushion this shock for him to be told, by parent or teacher, that true adjustment does not involve a loss of "self." But, presumably, this idea consoles the parents and the teachers, who might otherwise be faced with the realization that they have malprepared him for the commonplace demands of social life.

Should the child who has been brought up permissively and educated progressively follow the precepts of the cult, he will in fact, as distinct from the theory, be forced to subordinate his highly developed sense of personal importance to the will of others. It may upon occasion be possible for the members of a family to come to some joint decision regarding a family enterprise, with the result that the individual members can adhere to that decision without painful loss of "self." It may also be possible in the school-room for numbers of pupils to decide in a properly democratic manner what they shall jointly do, to the end that each asserts himself a little prior to conforming to the dictates of the group. In every society, however undemocratic in theory, there are circumstances in which the individual does express himself in and through group activities. But these are mainly recreational circumstances—the discussion around the campfire, the gossiping, the singing, the dancing, the playing of games, the activity that is undertaken as an end in itself. Any group activity that is, by contrast, a means to an end—the gathering or growing of food, the raising of babies, the building of houses, and so on *ad infinitum*—must be organized; and that means member conformity either to traditional procedures or to individual leadership or, and most commonly perhaps, to an admixture of both. And under such circumstances adjustment means conforming.

But it need not mean that passive, supine kind of conformity that, in spite of their talk about the preservation of "self," the modern advocates of adjustment envisage. For although they depreciate the popular school of adjustment, they are agreed with it in principle. They do not advocate such adjustment devices as the fawning smile and the insipid compliment; but they hold that the well-adjusted individual is one who in the company of his fellows does not assert himself, distinguish himself, or otherwise evidence initiative.

To do so might, they fear, invoke disapproval from one's fellows, which would have devastating psychological consequences. The adjusted individual is, rather, one who has succeeded in so blending into the group membership that he is a perfect representation of the group ethos. (Always remembering, of course, that he does not thereby lose his personal identity, since he has contributed to the formation of that ethos.)

Dutifully followed, the counsel of adjustment will result, in every social circumstance, in the individual's taking the course of least effort. Should he find himself among teetotalers, he will sip his tea with evident approval. Should circumstances put him in the company of heavy drinkers, he will manfully accept every drink that comes his way. Should his dinner companions turn out to be Democrats, he will be a stanch Democrat; should they be Republicans, Socialists, Communists, or just good Lutherans, he will be equally at home. With those whose views and values he does not already know, he will wait quietly until a consensus has emerged; then, and only then, will he express himself—that is to say, he will express as his the ideas and sentiments of the group. What he is to do when he finds himself among people who do not agree—say, when some of them want to go slumming and the others vote for the local art gallery—is not clear. Presumably, however, he counts heads and agrees with the majority.

Counseling and Guidance

The cult of adjustment is more than an intellectual exercise by which the unsociable products of the permissive home and the progressive school are theoretically reconciled to the necessity of living in society. It is the ideological base for a number of socially sanctioned practices in which people are actually encouraged to follow, in some one or many respects, the course of least effort.

The most numerous and active advocates of adjustment via the course of least effort are the student counselors, who are now an established part of the administrative apparatus of most large high schools and of many colleges and universities. The development of student counseling and guidance as a special branch of educational administration began innocently enough some twenty-five years ago in the practice, common to the larger high schools, of assigning one member of the faculty the task of advising students on personal and academic matters. This relieved the busy principal of direct responsibility for deciding what to do with problem students—that is, those who distinguished themselves by deviating from the normal patterns of behavior in social, moral, or intellectual matters. But what began as a practical division of administrative labor rapidly evolved into a system of psychotherapeutic practice that has now spread from the high schools through the institutions of higher learning and on into business and industry.

A generation ago the school counselor was a more or less fatherly fellow who listened with what patience he could muster to the juvenile troubles and uncertainties of those who came to him and, when the necessity arose, suggested some common-sense course of action. The value of his counsel depended entirely upon his personal knowledge and understanding of young people and their problems, and his counsel no doubt tended to reflect his own values and sentiments. But it at least had the virtue of being personal, hence variable; and being variable, there was some chance that it might occasionally be good advice. All that is now changed. The modern school counselor is a professional, trained more or less thoroughly into one or the other of the two currently orthodox—and quite contradictory—procedures. To the extent that he follows one or the other of these sanctioned procedures, nothing is left to chance; the validity of his counsel is entirely dependent upon the validity of the procedure.

One of these counseling procedures was fathered by the psychologist Carl Rogers.* Adherents to it describe themselves as "non-directive" counselors. They take as their basic assumption a rather contra-Freudian view of man; man is, they assume, inherently good and capable of achieving adequate social adjustment. His troubles, if he has any, stem from blockings that have been established in

---

* His *Counseling and Psychotherapy, Newer Concepts in Practice* (Boston: Houghton Mifflin Co., 1942) provides the original full statement of this school. Rogers' later work, *Client-centered Therapy* (Boston: Houghton Mifflin Co., 1951), is the current bible of the nondirective counselors.

his personality by social misadventures. If these blockings, or obstacles, are removed, he will more or less automatically work out
effective adjustments. It is the function of the counselor to free the
client—the Rogerians avoid the idea of mental illness by describing
those who come to them as clients rather than patients—from the
built-in obstacles—fear, dread, apprehension—to the end that he
may realize his true self. He is not, therefore, to be directed into
any given course of action—e.g., into preparing himself for this
occupation or that one, into going to this university or that college,
or into taking as his wife this woman or that one. Rather, the client
is encouraged to talk on any subject that comes to mind. And anything that he may say in the course of such "free associational" out-
pouring is treated sympathetically by the counselor. Through this
sympathetic reception the client is, according to Rogerian theory,
reassured that what he is—his true self—is right and can be and
should be expressed in action.

The opponents of nondirective counseling, and that currently
includes most of those who operate in the "scientific" mode, claim
that the procedure is in fact not nondirective; they contemptuously
describe it as the "Uh, huh!" method, arguing that the counselor
does provide direction through sanctioning some of the self-expres-
sions of the client, if only by grunts, and rejecting others, possibly
only by gesture. In this they are no doubt correct, for it would seem
next to impossible to listen sympathetically to the rambling out-
pourings of a client for many hours and in the process establish
the rapport that is deemed necessary without communicating with
that client. Indeed, unless the counselor does respond to what the
client says, he might as well be a tape recorder; and if he does
respond to the client's inevitably confused and conflicting statements, he can hardly do so without indicating, however subtly,
his personal evaluations of them.

It is at least a reasonable assumption that when the Rogerian
procedure of counseling is effective it aids the individual in following
some personal inclination that has been blocked by extraneous
considerations. Thus the lad who is seemingly uncertain whether
he should make a career of art or advertising may really want to
go into art but be constrained from doing so by the fact that his

father wants him to join him in advertising. By encouraging the lad to talk himself into following his personal preference, the counselor may be doing him and, possibly, society a good turn, although the father may suffer grievous disappointment. But when, as must often be the case, the "extraneous considerations" are in the nature of what is commonly termed "conscience," the results of such counseling may be quite otherwise. Here, and in all comparable personal dilemmas, the nondirective procedure is simply guidance into the course of least effort.

Nondirective counseling is a time-consuming procedure and cannot be applied systematically in the mass operation that often, of necessity, obtains in student counseling and guidance in high schools and colleges. Consequently, the most popular procedure is the one that is known as directive counseling. The practitioners of this persuasion are for the most part products of the same schools of education that teach teachers and school administrators to be "progressive." Unlike the Rogerians, they are open in their acceptance of the thesis that proper counseling consists in guiding the individual into that path which will be easiest for him to follow.* Thus, to the extent that they are effective, they give representation to the Freudian ethic and serve as opponents of the idea that life should consist of active endeavor.

Adherents to the directive school of counseling and guidance like to think of themselves as scientifically oriented, if not actually scientists. The justification for this view of themselves is the fact that they utilize "scientifically" devised tests that provide quantitative data which may be applied in a rigorously logical manner to the solution of the student's problem. They are, in their view, social navigators, charting a course for the troubled student over known

---

* The major schools of education teach guidance at the graduate level as a special educational field. This field now has its technical journal, *Personnel and Guidance Journal*, a cadre of professional specialists, and some more or less standard texts, of which H. B. McDaniel's *Guidance in the Modern School* (New York: The Dryden Press, Inc., 1950), L. L. Chisholm's *Guiding Youth in the Secondary Schools* (New York: Columbia University Press, 1956), and Herbert Sanderson's *Basic Concepts in Vocational Guidance* (New York: Mc-Graw-Hill Book Co., 1956) are representative.

seas with the aid of the latest navigational instruments. The Rogerians, by contrast, use the antiquated method of dead reckoning: they sail by the stars and the currents in unknown seas toward unidentified objectives.

The instruments relied upon by the scientific counselors are paper-and-pencil, question-and-answer devices that are historically related to the intelligence tests that were so popular, and so reverenced, a quarter century ago. These modern tests are assumed to measure in a quantitative fashion such complex qualities of the student's personality as his sociability, his occupational or other interests, his motivations, his emotional stability, etc. Each of the authorized tests has been devised by one or a number of psychologists and tested on a mass basis to determine its internal consistency and its statistical validity. Tests are also tested against one another. Few of the tests can, however, be verified in terms of the actual personality qualities that they profess to measure; they are what is technically known as "operationally valid"—*i.e.*, they validly measure whatever they measure.

The inherent limitations of tests of this sort are many and well known. Perhaps the most severe limitation stems from the uncertain relation between response to a verbal question and to the real-life circumstance that that question symbolizes. Everyone knows that there is no necessary relation between speech and conduct, and all sophisticated people recognize that they cannot accurately forecast what they themselves will do when they encounter some future (currently hypothesized) life circumstance. Nevertheless, the paper-and-pencil tests of personality are predicated upon the assumption that there is a reasonably constant relationship between the answers to questions and conduct, expressive of specific personality attributes, in social situations. That this assumption is unwarranted seems to bother neither the test constructors nor the test users.

Counselors of strongly Freudian leanings, however, usually place greater reliance upon another type of test, that which consists of such things as irregular blot or cloud forms which the person being tested is required to identify or interpret. His interpretations of these meaningless forms are supposed to be "projections" and, hence, revelations of his unconscious motives, desires, frustrations, or whatnot. The projective type of test is thought to probe deeper into the personality than the simple question-and-answer type. It certainly gives the counselor greater latitude in making his interpretations, for the projective test is a sort of short-form version of Freudian dream analysis.

The student who comes or is sent to a counselor with a problem— whether to prepare himself to enter college or not, whether (having arrived at college) to major in English or physics—is given one or a number of tests in order to ascertain his psychological composition. This is usually described as his "potentialities." Having thus ascertained the student's potentialities, the counselor can then predict the probable long-run consequences of the student's following this or that alternative course of action. The determination of the various alternatives open to the student is accomplished by "structuring" the student's problem, and this is considered to be a relatively simple matter. In the case of the high-school boy who wonders whether he should prepare to go on to college, there are, one can see, but two alternatives: to do so or to make his high-school education terminal. A really complex student problem, such as that posed by a boy who is preparing for college but wants to get married before completing high school, might possibly structure out into three or even four alternatives, e.g., to postpone marriage, to marry and drop his intention of going to college, to marry and continue preparation for college.

The layman might be inclined to think that the problem of structuring any human quandary into two or three finite alternatives would be quite insurmountable. Is, he might ask, preparing or not preparing for college a problem with just two alternatives? Is not-preparing a single entity? Certainly the consequences of terminating formal education with high school are not the same for all students, either occupationally or otherwise. And if the student is wondering whether to go on to college, does not the question arise, to go on to what college? And to what course of study in that college? There are well over four hundred colleges in the United States, no two quite alike and some of them markedly different from others; and each college offers a wide variety of subject matter. Surely, then, the consequences of going to college will depend not alone upon the student but also upon the particular college that he happens to go to and what he does when he gets there. The actual alternatives open to the student who is debating whether to take a college pre- paratory course or not must run closer to two thousand than just two. And the factors, each subject to wide variation, that are relevant to a decision of whether to get married while still in high school must be infinitely greater.

But the confusion and indecision of the layman would stem from the fact that he sees the trees rather than the forest; he thinks life is complex, bewildering, and chaotic—and for him it usually is— because he is untrained in the understandings and methods of the science of counseling and guidance. This science brings order out of confusion; it finds the pattern in apparent discord; and it locates what is essential in the clutter of trivia. So with his so-called scien- tific tests the student counselor ascertains the relevant personality characteristics of the problem student; and with his scientific knowledge of society he structures the student's problem; and then it is but a simple matter to determine which of the available alter- natives the student will be advised to follow. It is, in fact, just a matter of guiding the square peg into the square hole and the round peg into the round hole.

It is true that the folklore of another day did have it that a man's reach should exceed his grasp, that if nothing is ventured nothing can be gained, and that it is better to have lived and lost than never to have lived at all. But modern scientific realism teaches us quite otherwise: all things are relative; there are no absolutes; good and bad, right and wrong, sin and virtue are but matters of social definition; and the definitions vary between societies and change through time. So the counselor need not ponder over such folk questions as right or wrong, whither and why. He knows that the true goal of life is adjustment; hence he aids the student to find that one of the alternatives which he can follow with the greatest confidence and the least effort. Any other choice would be con- traindicated, for it would involve unnecessary risk and subject the individual to undesirable stress and strain and the grave hazard of frustration.

The goal firmly in mind, the professional student counselor reads his test results, structures the student's problem, and renders his decision. The means he uses may seem to some quite fallible; but there can be no doubt about the end in view. It is to guide the student into doing what comes easiest for him.* Thus the "scientific" counselors, like their nondirective counterparts, provide guidance into that course which promises to be least eventful. It may lead nowhere; it may promise nothing. But it is the proper course, for it is the way to adjustment.

Coddling on the Campus

Students who have been brought up in permissive homes and have wandered through progressive schools will not, of course, need the counsel of least effort. They will no doubt be experts at doing what comes easiest to them. The most that they will need is official reassurance that what they will do is what they should do. Whether the student who has not had these advantages in childhood and who has inadvertently acquired a desire to attempt something venturesome will follow the counsel of least effort is perhaps doubtful. He will be given such counsel, should he seek it; but the counselor can hardly be held responsible if a boy or girl is, as the Rogerians would describe it, blocked by ideals and aspirations from becoming his true self. Apparently a considerable proportion of high-school students do suffer, in spite of all the efforts

* Some of the professional guidance people who write for their colleagues do at least intimate that the course of least effort is not invariably the desirable one. Few, however, take a firm stand against the prevailing practice of adjusting the individual by guiding him into the course of least effort. Of these few, J. R. Seeley has perhaps been the most outspoken ("Guidance: A Plea for Abandonment," *Personnel and Guidance Journal,* May, 1956). Seeley seems to believe that there is occurring a renaissance of the Protestant ethic in America and that it is again possible for the individual to take on responsibility for his own conduct. He advocates, therefore, guidance not necessarily into the course of greatest effort but into that course which holds the greatest potentialities for the individual. He would like to "call a halt to the epidemic process of adjustment," for he views passive adaptation as a kind of death.

on their behalf, from blockings of this sort. And evidently the blocking ideals and aspirations coerce many such high-school students to undertake, unwisely in the view of counselors, a college education. At any event, it has been found necessary to extend the school counseling and guidance program to our institutions of higher learning.

In theory the counselors and testing agencies with which most American colleges and universities are now equipped are merely fulfilling on a formal and systematic basis the various advisory functions that were formerly provided by student deans, faculty advisers, and the local padre. Actually, however, they have assumed a variety of new functions, such as ascertaining through tests what particular subject the student will find easiest as a major and what vocational career will be the least demanding in view of his interests, emotional make-up, and existing skills. Thus the student who has been carefully wet-nursed through primary school and gently escorted through high school and on into college may be absolved from making any important decision for himself—until, at least, that day on which he is awarded his diploma, told that the future is his for the making, and then ushered out into the larger world.

As professional counselors have become entrenched in our colleges and universities, they have come to advocate a host of devices and procedures that they claim aid the student in adjusting to college life. They have also played some part in the development of selective procedures for college entrance that heavily stress the "social adjustment" of the applicant. Practices vary, particularly between universities, but there is a marked and a growing tendency to consider the ratings by the high-school teacher and principal of the social adjustment of an applicant as important selective criteria. Other things being more or less equal, the applicant who is judged well adjusted will be favored over the one who is scored poorly adjusted or maladjusted. If low adjustment ratings mean that the applicant is untrustworthy, lacking in moral character, disinterested in academic endeavor and easily distracted from academic work (thus maladjusted to the academic life per se), or excessively egocentric, refusal to admit such an applicant to college or university is certainly indicated. He would probably do neither himself nor the institution any good by enrolling as a student. If, further, high adjustment ratings mean that the applicant is intellectually industrious, competent in the fulfillment of intellectual tasks, motivated toward intellectual achievement, etc., then it should profit both the applicant and the institution to accept him as a student. No doubt both low and high adjustment ratings do often mean these various things.

But there is reason to think that teachers and high-school principals too often reflect the special values and attitudes of the cult of adjustment in making their ratings of high-school graduates. When they do so, they give the advantage of a "well-adjusted" rating to the applicant who has distinguished himself by participating in all the right social activities of the high school, who has conducted himself in such ways that he has earned the reputation of being well liked, and who has never disgraced himself in the eyes of adjustment-oriented teachers by deviating from the normal patterns of behavior. Such an applicant should have a good chance of becoming a political leader on the college campus; but there is no assurance that he will also contribute to its intellectual life.

The philosophers of higher education recurrently plead for higher academic standards, for the provision of special educational opportunities for the exceptional student, and for more effective methods of assuring that highly motivated and intellectually promising high-school students be encouraged to go on to college. And there are, of course, many devices, such as scholarship prizes for the exceptional student, that are directed toward such ends. But there is also a growing tendency for the colleges and some universities to favor, however unintentionally, the high-school or preparatory-school graduate who has distinguished himself mainly by making himself socially acceptable to his peers and superiors. He may also be bright and highly motivated; but he is far more likely to be an intellectual mediocrity.

There have long been some American colleges that take special pride in providing the student with such a fine moral atmosphere that parents can send in their sons and daughters in full confidence that they will be graduated four years later with their bodies unsullied and their minds untouched. One may feel that the parents who do so are rather naïve about their children and that the claims of such schools are more wishful than realistic; nevertheless, in these schools the student is usually given a great deal of personal attention by the members of the faculty and their wives, courses are given a marked moralistic slant, and everything possible is done to assure that nothing dangerously exciting or informing happens on or about the campus. The professional counselors and guiders, concerned no doubt with those students who have never been free from quasi-parental protection and are therefore unable to adjust to life in a traditional college or university, are striving to bring all institutions of higher learning into accord with the coddling colleges. They strongly favor more synthetic course offerings—the "survey" or general course that covers so much that it touches on nothing at all and can, therefore, be passed by any student, however dull or disinterested.* They urge that teaching be more intimate and personalized, and they sponsor other educational procedures derived from primary- and secondary-school experience that are supposed to eliminate the pain of acquiring an education.

College and university teachers have long complained that students come to them from the public high schools poorly equipped to do advanced work. Even when, as is the case with the better private institutions, those accepted as freshmen are boys and girls who have distinguished themselves academically—as well as otherwise—in high school, they are often unskilled in the basic tool subjects and incapable of studying on their own initiative. As a consequence, they must be provided in college and university with some

---

* The colleges usually describe such synthetic offerings as "survey courses," at least implying that after such a preliminary survey the student will go on to intensive study of the various areas covered in the course. In universities, however, the general practice is to dignify such offerings by calling them "integrated courses" and claiming for them the virtue of being interdisciplinary.

Of them, Adolph S. Tomars has commented: "Many such courses are inter-disciplinary only in the nominal sense that several disciplines are taught in one course, possibly on the theory that if four instructors, each teaching a discipline in which he is competent, cannot provide integration, it may somehow be achieved by one instructor teaching four disciplines in three of which he is incompetent." (*Modern Sociological Theory*, Howard Becker and Alvin Boskoff, eds. New York: The Dryden Press, Inc., 1957, p. 502).

training in reading and writing and, for those who propose to major in the sciences, arithmetic. Moreover, they cannot be treated as mature students for at least the first year or two; they must be fed intellectual materials in small and specific doses. The result is that a good deal of the teaching in colleges and universities is not higher education at all; it is, in terms either of content or method, or both, simply secondary training that is provided in institutions of higher learning.

On the whole, the American college and only to a somewhat lesser extent the American university adjusts itself to the limited capabilities of the entering student rather than requiring him to adjust to it. He is, as a consequence, provided with slightly advanced versions of the kinds of courses to which he was subjected in high school. For the first year or two he may, therefore, drift through a variety of "core" courses, survey courses, review courses, and even remedial reading courses. He may even find advanced versions of the social living courses that he probably took while in high school. Many colleges, for example, offer a course on how to be a college student.* And many universities as well as colleges are now offering courses on marriage and family living. The development of marriage courses has been especially profitable to those sociologists who specialize in the study of the family, although it has no doubt been some strain on their intellectual integrity to write textbooks on marriage that purport to tell the student how to proceed through courtship, how to select a wife or husband, and then how to live happily ever after. But courses on marriage are very popular, and the man who can write a how-to text with an air of scientific authoritarianism can look forward to large royalty checks to supplement his meager academic income. Now that an increasing number of stu-

---

* One of the standard and more successful of the texts for such courses is *Getting the Most Out of College,* by M. E. Bennett and M. Lewin (New York: McGraw-Hill Book Co., 1957). It is supposed, by its publishers, to provide the student with an orientation to the college campus and community, the faculty, and the student body; to facilitate participation in college life, the development of effective leadership and "followership" techniques, the achievement of personal adjustment, etc. A random selection of chapter and section titles suggests the intellectual level of the book: "Let's Get Oriented," "A Home Away from Home," "Teachers Are People," "What Makes a Big Wheel?" "To Join or Not to Join?" and so on.

dents are entering college with wife or husband already in hand, it is probable that the marriage course will be supplemented by one on prenatal care, and then it will be only a matter of time until the college curriculum provides the student with formal instruction on how to bring up baby.

Not all the foregoing developments in college and university course offerings can be traced, even indirectly, to the professional counselors. But the counselors are in considerable measure responsible for the establishment of various institutional arrangements that are supposed to reduce the shock to the student of leaving behind his familiar high school and home and entering the world of college or university. Of these, an increasingly popular device is the dreary procedure of taking the entering freshman through a preplanned and intensive indoctrination routine—although it is not, of course, called this. In this program, which in the current military manner might be termed "Operation Homecoming," the student is taken by the hand and led for a number of days about the campus, told the more desirable of the campus myths and legends, introduced to his new classmates, given a fatherly welcome by at least one of the high officials of the institution, and shown how humble and kindly are the members of the faculty under whom he will presumably study. The goal of the entire operation is so to reduce the gap between high school and college that the student can make the transition without effort—without, that is, having to meet actively a new kind of social environment. In June he is a carefree and well-adjusted high-school boy; in the fall he becomes, simply through the passage of time, an equally carefree and well-adjusted college freshman.

Should this goal be actually achieved, going to college would, of course, cease to be an event—to say nothing of an adventure—in the student's life. And being in college would inevitably cease to be an educational experience. For by then the college would just be an extension of the high school, the high school of the primary school, and the primary school of the home. And by then, one would think, the cult of adjustment would have become obsolete. For if the home is properly permissive, it is but an extension of the womb; so from birth through college no adjustments would be demanded of the individual. All adjustments would be made to him.

Adjustment, Not Enterprise

Perhaps the professional advocates of adjustment foresee that, if they are fully successful in the schools, their services as counselors will no longer be necessary. Their invasion of business and industry does, at any event, provide a hedge against this eventuality. It is a fairly recent move and has so far made limited headway, if only because American business and industry are the major citadels of the Protestant ethic, the one remaining aspect of our society in which individual enterprise is often welcomed and even rewarded. There are today, however, sponsors of the cult of adjustment, usually in the person of an academically trained personnel manager, in many of the larger business and industrial organizations.*

It has for some time been assumed, and actively propagated by men of humanistic inclination, that the happy worker is the efficient one. Armed with this assumption, efficiency engineers, industrial psychologists, and more recently industrial sociologists have induced major employers of labor to try first this and then that means of making workers happy. For a time it was believed that the physical comfort of the worker was the way to his happiness and, hence, to high man-hour productivity. So the physical conditions of the plant or office were remodeled to fit the worker; benches and desks were cut to his measurement, better lighting was provided, and modern plumbing was installed in washrooms. This trend culminated, in the more progressive plants and offices, in air conditioning, pastel-tinted walls, and soft music. Meanwhile, the idea developed that what really makes a worker happy is to be accepted and admired by his fellows, his wife, his children, and the neighbors down the street. As a consequence, the really advanced personnel manager is much concerned with the social adjustment of those whom he employs,

* A definitive statement of the philosophy of adjustment as it is being adopted in business and industry is provided by Lynde C. Steckler, who for many years has served as a counsulting psychologist to industry, in *Problems of Human Adjustment* (New York: Harper & Brothers, 2nd ed., 1956).

preferring to hire a married man with children and a sunny disposition rather than one who is dour and lean and ill disposed toward family life. And over the working force the really advanced personnel manager hovers, like a motherly hen, trying to breathe life into his claim that they are just one happy—if industrial—family.

That the happy working man is necessarily the efficient worker is still an assumption hard to prove, and whether the various efforts that are made to bring happiness to the worker actually do so is still anybody's guess. On the whole, professional labor leaders are contemptuous of the physical- and social-welfare devices of employers. They prefer to believe that the happiest worker is the best paid one, although few of them would go so far as to claim that the best paid worker is necessarily the most efficient one. At any event, no one should object to the efforts made by employers to provide workers with pleasant working conditions. They may not pay off in increased productivity; but they are certainly a contribution to the physical comfort and aesthetic satisfaction of modern man.

One might enter an objection, however, to the idea that what makes for a good worker also makes for a good superior. The worker, whether white or blue collar, need not and indeed in most instances should not be enterprising; in modern large-scale business and industry, work tasks are highly routinized, and all that is required of the worker is that he follow the routine prescribed for him by the organization for so many hours a day. But in so far as the organization as a whole is competing with other comparable organizations, its long-range survival depends upon enterprising management. And that, of course, means executives both high and low who possess initiative. This crucial fact is lost sight of by those who operate upon the assumption that the well-adjusted young man will make a better executive in business or industry than the one who is, by test results, less perfectly adjusted socially. Political bureaucracies have always favored the man of no-enterprise, the man so well adjusted to things as they are that he will do nothing that might conceivably disturb the *status quo*. That business and industrial organizations should adopt, even in the most tentative and fragmentary way, the same stultifying policy is a development that all business-men should view with alarm. For it puts a premium on such qualities as apathy and complacence and eliminates the man who might possibly bring a bit of enterprise to organizations that are by social definition, but not always in practice, enterprising.

7

Condonation of Crime

THE ADVOCATES of the permissive home, the progressive school, and passive adjustment are mostly members of the middle middle class; and many of them no doubt moved into this comfortable category through the individual enterprise that they seemingly detest. They are, for the most part, professional people—psychiatrists, child psychologists, and educators; and so, too, are the clinicians, the teachers, and the counselors whom they have trained and sent forth to practice what they preach. Most of the parents who knowingly follow the permissive mode of child rearing must also be of middle-class status—from low to high. Few working-class parents can have the time, the energy, or the sophistication to bring up their children permissively. Few of their children will have an opportunity to attend a very progressive school, since such schools are necessarily located in the more prosperous sections of our towns and cities; and while our state and city colleges are endeavoring to provide effortless higher education for everyone, few working-class youths take advantage of it.

On the whole, then, systematic and deliberate induction into the Freudian ethic is limited to the children of middle-class parents. The ethic has, in the jargon of the Marxians, a class bias and reflects the special privileges of the higher classes under capitalistic social organization. Induction into it might be seen as one of the many ways, a rather new one, by which the *bourgeoisie* consume that excess of social values that they exploitatively extract from the working masses; and since it results in a lowering of their social vitality, it may well be one of the excesses by which they are unintentionally furthering the evolutionary process—the process that will bring

155

into being the classless society. In this view, Freud and his disciples might turn out to be unconscious *agents provocateurs,* hastening the revolution by intensifying the corruption of the capitalist masters of contemporary society—or at least that of their bourgeois hench-men.

A less doctrinaire interpretation of the class-linked aspect of the Freudian ethic might have it that the effect is simply to accelerate the dying out of men of enterprise at the top and their replacement by individuals of enterprise rising from the lower classes. There has long been a tendency, symbolized by the old American concept of "from shirt sleeves to shirt sleeves in three generations," for the exceptionally successful man so to shower his children with the prerogatives of wealth that they acquire the personal attributes of the social parasite and are incapable of maintaining the status won by their father without the aid of enterprising functionaries—lawyers, trust-fund managers, etc. So it has often happened that within two or three generations the majority of the descendants of a self-made man have returned to the class position from which he rose, thereby opening the way for enterprising members of the working classes to earn the status that these descendants have lost.

It might, then, be held that the development of the Freudian ethic and its agencies is just a systematization and codification of the haphazard and informal procedures by which some rich men have spoiled their sons, and an extension of that process to include the children of not-so-rich families. If this were true, we might anticipate an increase in the rates of social mobility; for as a higher proportion of middle- to upper-class children are inducted into the Freudian ethic, the opportunities for those children of working-class families who have, however inadvertently, acquired the attri-butes of the Protestant ethic would increase. But the Freudians have not entirely ignored the masses. And while their efforts on behalf of the masses are both limited and segmental, they are doing what they can to discourage the emergence of effective competitors for the social positions that are held, or will in time be held, by those who have been systematically inducted into the Freudian ethic.

The Freudian intervention on behalf of the masses takes at present two directions. The first, and perhaps the less significant, is by way of the professional schools of social work. The second, and the really massive attack on behalf of the masses, is by way of our courts of law and is directed toward the establishment of the principle that the individual cannot reasonably be held responsible for his actions —even though those actions are legally defined as criminal. Since the majority of those who are accused of criminal acts are members of the lower classes, if only because those classes constitute a majority of the population, the establishment of the principle of personal irresponsibility would be a sort of lower-class version of the adjustment motif; and if the criminal courts were to operate uniformly upon this principle, they would provide wayward members of the lower classes with a legal version of the permissive home and the progressive school.

The infusion of the Freudian view of man into criminological theory and criminal court practice is comparatively new; but it has built upon pre-existing foundations, coopted many jurists and other functionaries of the criminal law, and within the last two decades become a decisive factor in the legal treatment of the juvenile offender.* The result has been a partial, but highly pervasive, reversal of the traditional assumption that the individual who violates a law should in general be held personally responsible for his actions. In place of the concept of personal responsibility, the Freudians advocate and have gained considerable acceptance for the view that those who commit criminal acts are victims of society and should be treated as such rather than as willful enemies of society.

The Protagonists

The idea that the individual is not personally responsible for his actions, criminal or otherwise, stems directly from the Freudian

---

* The psychoanalyst Franz Alexander is often credited with having introduced the Freudian view into American criminological thinking. His early article, "The Neurotic Character" (*International Journal of Psychoanalysis,* Vol. 11, p. 292 ff., 1930), in which he held that the concept of disease must be extended to include neurotics, and especially those who violate the law, is still referred to by current writers as a "basic statement." An extended restatement of this basic statement is to be found in *The Criminal, the Judge, and the Public,* by Franz Alexander and Hugo Staub (Glencoe, Illinois: The Free Press, 1957).

doctrine of man. Its application to violations of the law is only a special version of the general principle; but it is one that has obvious consequences to our traditional legal procedures, and it has for this, if no other, reason met with considerable resistance. This resistance has been far more vocal, tenacious, and effective than that which has so far been put up against the intrusion of Freudianism into other aspects of our society.

The protagonists cannot be classified into neat categories of "for" or "against" holding the criminal personally responsible for his acts. But there is no difficulty in distinguishing those of Freudian leanings from those who reject the Freudian view of man. All the psycho-analysts who write on crime and the criminal are, of course, of the Freudian persuasion; and so, too, are many of the court functionaries, especially those who deal with juveniles, many of the parole officers, most of the alienists specializing in criminal cases, and some judges and penal officials. Against these are aligned, in various ways, most of the sociologists who specialize in criminology, most of the law-enforcement officers, and all the students of jurisprudence.

The most numerous, but on the whole least vocal, of the opponents of the Freudian school of criminology are the law-enforcement officials. About their only public spokesman is J. Edgar Hoover, who occasionally speaks from his unassailable position as director of the Federal Bureau of Investigation on behalf of more rigorous law enforcement, and whose *Uniform Crime Reports* provide statistical evidence of the social consequences of too liberal resort to the suspended sentence by the criminal courts and of too easy parole by local and state officials.* But from the cop on the beat to the District Attorney responsible for the prosecution of those charged with criminal acts, there is almost uniform agreement that the courts have become so lax that it is hardly worth the trouble to arrest and secure the conviction of juvenile offenders and that even the adult, professional criminal is usually back and plying his trade

---

* Some of the statements and some of the statistical data will be referred to later; but an example of Hoover's position as the spokesman for the "hard-boiled" school of law enforcement is to be found in his address, "Challenges of Crime Control" (*Vital Speeches*, Vol. 22, pp. 572-576, 1956).

within a short time after he has been convicted of a felony.* But since they are, after all, public functionaries and since there is strong public support for the practice of treating the criminal—and especially the young offender—as a victim of society, law-enforcement officials keep their opinions of current court practices largely to themselves.

Students of jurisprudence, on the other hand, are often outspoken in their condemnation of the Freudian school of criminal treatment. They see the growing popularity of the Freudian view of man, specifically the growing power in and over the courts of analytically oriented psychiatrists, as a threat to traditional legal institutions and practices. Their general position is that the law, criminal and civil, and its institutional agencies represent the accumulated experience of man over many centuries; that it is a system developed to protect our society from erosion from within; and that the current tendency to weaken the application of legal sanctions is in fact, as distinct from psychoanalytic theory, an attack upon the very foundations of our society.

The opponents of the Freudian school of criminology undoubtedly have most of the objective facts in their favor. It is not difficult to demonstrate that lax enforcement of the criminal laws is one of the important factors making for crime. Many a cop on the beat can point to the carefree hoodlum whom he has arrested time after time only to find back on the streets in a few days. The statistics on court disposition of those convicted of felonies demonstrate that even for those who are caught crime most often pays. And it is easy to prove on a factual basis that the psychiatrist's method of determining personal responsibility for criminal acts is entirely subjective and therefore inconsistent and unworthy of the name "scientific." As a matter of fact, the typical life history of the pro-

---

* All of the court and police officials interviewed for the article, "Why Law Fails to Stop Teen-age Crime" (*United States News and World Report,* January 14, 1955), agreed that softness toward juvenile delinquents is ineffective and must be replaced by firmness and punitive methods.

In 1958, New York Police Commissioner Kennedy actually undertook to reverse the long-term trend toward treating juvenile delinquents as a psychiatric or social-work problem and issued firm orders to his force to treat them as the criminals that, in law, they undoubtedly are. This extraordinary action is reported in *Time,* July 7, 1958.

fessional criminal is itself prima-facie evidence that soft treatment of the offender is one of the important determinants of crime.* But the controversy between the Freudian and the traditional schools of criminology is not likely to be resolved in terms of factual data; it is fundamentally a conflict over values.

Those who believe that society is prior to the individual—in the sense that the welfare of all the individual members depends upon the existence of an adequate society—and who hold to the view that our society is a reasonably good one would defend it against the occasional individual who is socially irresponsible by holding him legally responsible for his conduct. Those who believe, on the other hand, that only a bad society will produce antisocial members (or who accept the extreme Freudian view that society per se is bad) take the position that the welfare of the individual must in all instances take precedence over the welfare of the society; for them, our society is hardly worth preserving.

Constraint, Not Vengeance

The roots of the present controversy over individual responsibility versus individual irresponsibility go far back in Western cultural history. In a sense, the intervention of Freudian-oriented men on behalf of the rights of the individual to be himself, however illegally, without serious consequences to himself is but a final spurt in a centuries-long process of liberating Western man from the authoritarianism, religious and political, of the Middle Ages. And in the same sense, it is but an extreme expression of the humanitarianism that has been made possible over the past two hundred years and more by the growing ability of society to support its members at a level of physical and mental comfort never before known to man. In all but modern Western societies—and possibly a few small primitive groups—the pressure of numbers has been so great and so constant that many have had to die in order that any could survive. In such societies human life is inevitably held—by all except, perhaps, the possessor thereof—in small esteem.

* Many such life histories are reported by S. Glueck and E. Glueck in *Criminal Careers in Retrospect* (New York: The Commonwealth Fund, 1943).

In all the early civilizations (and even today in Russia and China) the contempt in which life was held is most clearly, although not necessarily most significantly, reflected in the treatment of those individuals guilty of violating the law. Death was commonly the penalty for crimes that we today would consider quite minor; imprisonment for any extended period was, in view of the character of prisons, simply punishment by slow death; and the practice of punishing for what were then considered relatively minor crimes by either flogging or, more often, chopping off one of the criminal's ears or hands or other body parts was almost universal. It is said that in Elizabethan England there were few lower-class members of urban society who had not been disfigured in this way and that the habitual criminal tended to disappear, piece by piece, into the grave.

The brutish nature—in modern terms—of premodern punishments for crime has led to the idea that in premodern societies punishment was administered in a spirit of vengeance; justice, it is said, operated upon the principle of retribution. And from this assumption, the Freudian school of criminology jump to the charge that their opponents are, in advocating the continuance of punishment, upholding a premodern, essentially uncivilized, doctrine of vengeance. Neither the assumption nor the charge based upon it has the slightest validity.

Retributive justice has been followed as a principle by very few peoples and then only in limited ways; and the harshness of the punishments administered in premodern societies is easily explained. Given the low value placed upon life, the destruction of one who commits a crime is the simplest and most effective way of assuring that he will not commit another crime. Simply because it is death does not make it vengeance. The widespread use of dismembering —it was common to all Asiatic societies, to those of India and the Near East, to some of the primitive societies of Africa, and to Western society prior to the nineteenth century—was likewise a deterring kind of punishment. Where it was resorted to, personal liberty was not highly valued; moreover, the social costs of imprisonment, even in the deadly prisons of the times, were excessive. The rich might be punished through the imposition of fines, and indeed often were. But the majority of criminals were without anything of which they might be deprived, except their bodies and lightly valued freedom of action. So the removal of some valued body part had the great advantage of resulting in a durable disutility and at the same time providing a constant reminder to the one so punished and to all who saw him that crime does not—or does not always—pay.

Over the past two centuries Western societies have gradually reduced the severity of physical punishments for crime. The death penalty has long since been restricted to the crimes of murder, rape, and kidnaping; and it has been totally abandoned in some countries and in some states of the United States. The lash long ago went out of fashion; and mutilating punishments had all but disappeared in Western societies by the beginning of the nineteenth century. In place of these older forms of punishment, imprisonment was gradually substituted until it became the major method of punishing the convicted criminal. But since prisons were inadequate and invariably ill maintained, particularly early in this development, a variety of procedures evolved to circumvent the letter of criminal law, such as the suspended sentence, or to lessen the severity of punishment by imprisonment, such as the granting of parole. All these developments were at basis reflections of the fact that the social value placed upon the individual—upon his life and his physical welfare—was rising as technological and other social changes brought marked and continuous improvement in the general level of life. Since the sixteenth century Western societies have become increasingly able to enjoy the luxury, theretofore unknown to many men for very long, of considering the welfare of the individual as second only to that of the state.

It was not, therefore, a change in the concept of crime and punishment that led to changing punishment practices. Now, as in times past, punishment is intended as a deterrent. Constraint, not vengeance, has always been the purpose of the law.

Born to Crime

Modern criminologists of the Freudian school have been endeavoring to bring about an abandonment of the age-old practice of punishing those who have been convicted of breaking the law. The justification for this endeavor is a theory of human behavior that is not only unproved but unprovable; nevertheless, they hold that the implications of this theory for the treatment of criminals are scientific and that all the experience of all the many and culturally varied peoples who have in the past utilized punishment as the means of discouraging crime has been in error. In this, as in other respects, the Freudians demonstrate the intensity of their faith in Freud and his works and the closed and self-validating character of the Freudian doctrine of man.

During the Middle Ages, Christian theology, rather than philosophy, provided the prevailing explanation for the fact that some men violate the law and many do not. The theory turned, of course, upon the concept of free will, which God in his benevolence had granted man, thus enabling man to choose between the ways of the devil and the ways of God himself. As it developed, secular law simply changed some of the symbols—*i.e.*, the laws of the prince or king became identified with the ways of God—without changing the underlying theory. With the rise of Protestantism and the idea that man is a rational animal, theorists tended to assume that criminal actions are the consequence of either a breakdown of the reasoning process—madness—or of ignorance—*i.e.*, of failure to understand that the act is contrary to law.

The idea that some crimes stem from ignorance may have provided the basis for the practice, which seems to have grown up first in English common law, of absolving the very young offender from the full penalty of the law on the grounds that he has not reached the age of responsibility. If so, this is one instance in which theory may have led to practice in a limited sphere. It was not, however, reversed, as in logic it should have been, when belief in man's rationality gave way in criminological theory to a strictly biological interpretation. This interpretation followed the acceptance by scientists of the Darwinian theory of evolution and was a gross distortion of it. It was, more particularly, a special application of the phrenological and physiognomical interpretations of human character that so entranced both scientists and laymen through most of the latter half of the nineteenth century. In both these latter concepts, the character (and, thus, the future) of the individual is genetically determined and revealed through physical correlates, *e.g.*, the bumps on his head or the spacing of his eyes indicate that he possesses such-and-such characteristics.

The instinctive, if not the physiognomical, interpretation of criminal behavior dominated criminological theory during the first quarter of the present century. An attempt by the sociologist Bernard to work out a complete catalogue of criminal instincts led him to realize the ultimate absurdity of instinctivism, with the result that he made one of the initial attacks upon the doctrine. As the vogue for the instinctive explanation of criminal conduct faded, sociologists entered upon the study of the social correlates of crime. Now, three decades and much effort later, sociological criminology is an established scientific discipline with a large body of factual data on the criminal and his social antecedents, and a general agreement that crime—like more normative forms of conduct—is a social rather than biological phenomenon.

Over the years a large number of particularistic theories have been posited and subjected to test, only to be abandoned—*e.g.*, the idea that it is poverty that causes crime, that criminal conduct is a social inheritance passed down from father to son, that it is the urban slum environment that impels the youth toward antisocial action, that play gangs in slum communities are the training agencies for crime, etc. Each of these and many other specific ideas about *the* environmental cause of crime have in time been proved false: so in time sociologists have come to recognize that there are many environmental factors that may, and that some constellation of some of these factors always does, enter into the making of any criminal act.* This concept of causation does not translate easily

---

* The initial, rather crude, statement of this understanding was made by Gabriel Tarde, a French jurist, in his *The Laws of Imitation* (New York: Henry Holt & Company, Inc., 1903). It has perhaps been most clearly and fully stated as the "theory of differential association" by Edwin H. Sutherland (*Principles of Criminology*. Philadelphia: J. B. Lippincott Company, 4th edition, 1947. Chapter I). It is the operating assumption of all sociological criminologists today except the few who adhere to the Freudian doctrine. Recent works that reflect or contribute to the validation of this understanding include: *Principles of Criminology*, 5th edition, by Edwin H. Sutherland, revised by Donald R. Cressey (Chicago: J. B. Lippincott Company, 1955); *Juvenile Delinquency*, by

into either preventive or repressive policy; it is too complex to serve as the basis for doctrinaire solutions to the crime problem. As a consequence, reformistically inclined criminologists and functionaries dealing with criminals have tended to ignore the findings of the sociologists in favor of the simple and dogmatic counsel of those who see crime through Freudian eyes.

The Freudian doctrine of man is neither clear nor simple; but those Freudians who have turned their attention to the criminal have derived from it a theory of the criminal act and a prescription for social treatment that anyone can understand. It is, they hold, perfectly natural for human beings to violate the law—every law, from the law that governs the speed of motor vehicles to that which prohibits taking the life of another human being. For, according to Freud, man is born a criminal—an antisocial being. Society, with which the individual is in all respects at odds, teaches the individual to repress his criminal drives and to conform to nonnatural standards of conduct. The criminal is simply one who was not fully trained to this repression or who, so trained, has been provoked by society into breaking the bonds of repression.* In either event, the criminal act is compulsive; it is neither willed nor calculated. The professional thief does not steal in order to make a comfortable living in the easiest way that he knows how; he is driven to rob homes, roll drunks, break into bank vaults, or do whatever his specialty is as a thief, by an unconscious drive. In sum, the thief has no moral or intellectual awareness of the fact that he is stealing for a livelihood.

And so with all criminal actions. The lad who, along with his

---

Paul W. Tappan (New York: McGraw-Hill Book Company, 1949); and *Delinquent Boys: The Culture of the Gang*, by Albert K. Cohen (Glencoe, Illinois: The Free Press, 1955).

* The following is the authoritative statement of this Freudian thesis: "However, within the innermost nucleus of the personality . . . it is impossible to differentiate normal from criminal impulses. The human being enters the world as a criminal, *i.e.*, socially not adjusted. During the first years of his life the human individual preserves his criminality to the fullest degree. . . . The criminal carries out in his actions his natural, unbridled, instinctual drives; he acts as the child would act if it only could. . . . The only difference between the criminal and the normal individual is that the normal man partially controls his criminal drives and finds outlets for them in socially harmless activities." (Franz Alexander and Hugo Staub, *op. cit.*, pp. 34-35.)

fellows, batters his way up the crowded highway in a stolen car or who pulls out a switch knife and slashes at their victim for the night is simply expressing his innate, and of course unconscious, antagonism to society. So, too, is the thug who murders for a price; his is not a brutal and illegal occupation, his actions are but a compulsive expression of his natural resentment of a society that refuses to let him be his natural self. The case of the man who murders his wife may be a bit more complicated; for here we get into subtleties of the Oedipus, castration, mother-fixation, and other complexes, and a full and specific analysis may be necessary to ascertain whether the wife was a mother, father, sister, or brother symbol. Basically, however, the common principle holds good; and the act of wife-murder is to be interpreted as simply a rather special form of self-expression or, to describe it another way, an act of retaliation against repressive society.

The Freudian explanation of crime absolves the individual from all personal responsibility for the criminal act and places the blame squarely upon the shoulders of an abstraction—society. Modern society is especially hard upon the individual, since it imposes upon him so many and often contradictory restraints and at the same time demands of him so much that does not come naturally to him. His criminal acts are therefore but a symptom of the underlying pathology of society, and it is as futile to punish him for the sins of society as to attempt to cure acne by medicating the symptomatic pustules. A sick society cannot be cured of its disease by removing from it individual symptoms of that sickness.

Logically, the Freudians should at this point become advocates of a revolutionary remodeling of our "sick" society. Few do, however, and for the very good reason that they apparently have only the most primitive concept of the nature and processes of social life.* To

---

* An exception is Ralph S. Banay, who would begin the reform of the sick society by remodeling its prisons. At present they are, he thinks, critical manifestations of social "sickness." They should be turned into psychotherapeutic agencies, operated, of course, by psychoanalysts (*We Call Them Criminals.* New York: Appleton-Century-Crofts, Inc., 1957).

A sociological criticism of some of the current efforts to treat criminals as mentally disturbed patients is provided by Donald R. Cressey in "Contradictory Theories in Correctional Group Therapy Programs" (*Federal Probation,* June,

them society appears as an entity apart from and independent of the individuals whose conduct is social. They entirely ignore the fact that the individual and society are but two aspects of the same thing, and that to isolate the one from the other results in conceptual abstractions that may be useful for intellectual purposes but that are not literal representations of reality. No one has ever really seen a human being who is not a part, highly dependent, of some society; and no one has ever seen a society except as the conduct of numbers of individuals.

To the Freudians, however, society is evidently more than the behavior of the members of that society. For they would absolve every individual member of all responsibility for his conduct—criminal or otherwise. The "cause" of each individual's conduct becomes, therefore, a metaphysical entity that is external to and independent of all persons. And since it is obviously impossible to cure the sickness of this metaphysical entity—even as it is impossible to change the theological will of God—the Freudians come to the position that the punishment of criminals is, like the criminal act itself, simply a manifestation of society's pathological condition. It may not be possible to prevent the sick society from producing criminals, but it is within the power of man to recognize that the criminal is not personally responsible for his crime and thus to abandon the ancient and socially pathological practice of wreaking vengeance upon him. All that this means, in fact, is that he be absolved from punishment of any sort. The sickness of the sick society will not thereby be cured, but the individual adversity produced by that sickness will at least be ameliorated.

Means of Evasion

Converts to the Freudian idea that criminals should not be punished since they are but victims of society have not yet been able to establish either in law or in practice the principle of no-punishment. But they have to a considerable extent succeeded in

---

1954, pp. 20-26). Giles Playfair and Derrick Sington have recently restated the Freudian thesis in *The Offenders: The Case Against Legal Vengeance* (New York: Simon and Schuster, Inc., 1957).

liberating the criminal from the "harsh and unreasonable" punishments decreed by law. In justice, according to their view, the criminal should not be subjected to any penalties; but the law being what it is, the best that can currently be done for him is to apply in full measure such tempering legal devices as presently exist—parole, the suspended sentence, special treatment for the juvenile offender, and the legal concept of not guilty by reason of insanity.

All these currently available devices for tempering the law with justice have evolved out of empirical experience, and each makes sociological sense when it is applied with reason. They are all operational expressions of the rising value of life, liberty, and the pursuit of happiness that has been made possible by technological and other changes in Western societies. And no one of them was evolved, as the Freudians would have us believe, as an effort to establish the principle that the individual is not responsible for his crime and must not therefore be subjected to punishment.

The now-common practice of probation, in which the offender, convicted of having committed a crime, is tentatively relieved from the designated penalty for that crime, originated in England about the beginning of the last century as a means of adjusting the traditional penalties to new concepts of what constitutes just and reasonable punishment. If, in the judgment of a magistrate, the law that had been violated was unreasonable or the penalty prescribed was excessively severe, he might release the person convicted of the crime on his good behavior, with the understanding that the convicted person would remain unpunished as long as he also remained law-abiding. The English practice of probation in time appeared here and there in this country, where it was originally called "suspended sentence," and was eventually incorporated in formal court practices, first in 1878 in the state of Massachusetts.

Closely associated with the evolution of probation theory and practice was the development of parole. The prisons of an early day were usually semi-private commercial establishments over which there was no public supervision; the operators of the prisons were paid from public funds so much per head per day. Under these conditions, an inmate who had money could buy all sorts of favors, including holidays outside, while an impoverished convict was usually destined to starve and rot away while chained—to reduce the need for guards—to the walls of his cell. During one period, English magistrates were able to circumvent the horrors of imprisonment by sentencing the more worthy criminal to exile in one of the colonies. America was for a time such a dumping place for England's undesirables; later, Australia became England's major penal colony. But as the empty places on the earth filled up and became respectable, exile became less feasible, and a new practice slowly emerged. An English prison warden, more enlightened or perhaps just more overstocked than most, established about 1830 the practice of rewarding his prisoners for good behavior by giving them credits—"marks," they were termed—toward the reduction of their sentences. Before long the marks system was being widely advocated as a way to serve two desirable purposes: the reward for good behavior encouraged the prisoners to behave and so reduced the costs and problems of imprisonment; further, the system led to the early release of those prisoners who had demonstrated their inherent goodness, thereby working in the interests of justice and at the same time providing space for new prisoners.

Over the past century the physical hazards of life in prison have been gradually reduced, and today conditions in some prisons are conducive to a long, if dull, life. But as the original reasons for parole have disappeared, new and more idealistic ones have been devised; and the parole procedures have become so much liberalized that it is now almost impossible for even the most determined convict to stay in prison for the full term to which he has been sentenced.*

The current tendency, for which the Freudian school is in considerable measure responsible, is to use probation and parole as means of evading in whole or in major part the punishments prescribed by law. Such use is in accord with the Freudian idea that

---

* As a consequence, according to J. Edgar Hoover, 63.8 per cent of those sentenced to federal prison terms in 1954 were repeaters. "If," he says, "I can judge from the reports which come to my desk daily from every section of the country, there is a growing concern among law-enforcement officials over increase in crimes by repeaters and those who have been improperly selected as beneficiaries of parole, probation, and other forms of clemency." ("The Challenges of Crime Control," *Federal Probation*, June, 1956, p. 11.)

no criminal is personally responsible for his crime and that any punishment is an act of social vengeance. It should be clearly distinguished from the use of these devices in the occasional instance when one or the other procedure seems indicated as a means of protecting society—that is, when either parole or probation may implement the rehabilitation of the criminal. Obviously, neither can reasonably be so used with the habitual criminal or the one who is well on his way toward becoming one. But all those, including not a few jurists, who subscribe to the Freudian interpretation of crime advocate the extension of these devices to all criminals. As a result, the constraining influence of punishment in our society has been gravely weakened; the criminal law has lost much of its bite; and those of us who do not, for whatever reasons, violate the criminal law have been placed in a disadvantageous position vis-à-vis those who do. For, Freudian theory to the contrary, if the criminal does not pay for his crime, the rest of us certainly will.

Delinquents Let Loose

The progressive liberalization of such traditional devices as probation and parole has weakened the effectiveness of criminal law, but it has been only an indirect attack upon the principle of criminal responsibility. The direct attack has been made by way of a determined undermining of the traditional legal distinction between one who can reasonably be held responsible for his criminal act and one who cannot. The idea of personal or self-responsibility is, it will be recalled, a major element in the Protestant ethic. But even those who, in times past, subscribed most stanchly to the Protestant ethic were apparently aware that the individual must be trained into this ethical system before he can in reason be held responsible for failure to conform to it. At any event, there grew up in English common law the practice of holding parents responsible for the criminal actions of children under seven years of age and the practice of giving children between the ages of seven and fourteen years the "benefit of the doubt" of personal responsibility.

The common-law distinction between the responsible and the not-responsible offender was for long a latent one. It enabled the courts to apply a bit of common sense to the administration of justice. During the last century, however, the distinction between those who are and those who are not by reason of immaturity personally responsible gradually became categorical and, in the process, considerably extended. By the end of the century special courts were being established, both in England and America, for the treatment of young offenders; and an entirely new idea of why the young offender should not be punished in accordance with the penalties of the law began to emerge.

In this new idea, the young offender was to be absolved from the punishment normally accorded an adult, not because he was necessarily free from responsibility, but, rather, because to treat him as an adult criminal would almost certainly make him one. Long before sociologists had begun intensive studies of the social factors that train some members of society into criminal occupations, reformers had come to the conclusion—subsequently more or less validated by sociological study—that the wayward lad who is through court procedure stigmatized as a criminal is thereby encouraged to look upon himself in that light. Such encouragement may be subtle, as when his peers accept him back into their company as something of a hero or when adults persistently treat him with suspicion simply because he was once convicted of a crime. Encouragement to the young offender to cast himself into the role of criminal can also be crude and direct, as when the convicted youth is sentenced to prison, where he will associate with hardened, professional criminals.

It was on the grounds, then, that normal penal punishment of young offenders predisposes them to become adult offenders that the reformers worked for the establishment of special courts and special reformatories for young offenders. The question in their minds was not "Is the young offender personally responsible for his crime?" but, rather, "Will punishment as a criminal discourage or encourage him to commit subsequent crimes?" Their goal was the protection of society from criminals, not the protection of the individual who has violated the law from the penalties of the law. But in recent years the special devices that were evolved in the effort to salvage the youth who had entered upon a criminal career have been taken over in considerable measure by people of Freudian leanings and put to the latter end.* The consequence has been that by and large the youthful offender, now called a juvenile delinquent to make certain that no one should mistake him for a criminal, is absolved from all responsibility for his criminal actions. It may be reasonable to assume that a child under seven does not really comprehend the difference between right and wrong, and that those between the ages of seven and fourteen may or may not do so. But it is hardly reasonable to claim that no one under the age of eighteen, or in some cases twenty-one, years of age can be expected to comprehend that stealing automobiles, tearing up school buildings, or slashing the boys from the other side of the street is contrary to law.

Few of the traditionalists in criminology or criminological practice wish to see a return to the days when youths were commonly, even upon a first conviction, sent to serve penal sentences in the company of their criminal elders. Few are in principle opposed to the modern devices and procedures for dealing with the young offender. But they know, either from scientific study of the matter or from their personal day-to-day experience, that the current tendency to use these devices to absolve the young offender from responsibility has the general effect of encouraging irresponsibility. When, as so often happens today, the youth is released, crime after crime, with nothing more painful than a judicial scolding and, perhaps, a short session with the court psychiatrist, he is being officially trained into the understanding that it is his right to violate the law—or, at any event, that he can violate the law with impunity. And when, time after time, the officials who are charged with upholding the law observe the young lawbreaker returned crime after crime to the free company of his peers, they, too, can hardly fail to wonder if justice may not in fact be blind.

* An application of the Freudian doctrine to the young offender, which leads inevitably to the thesis that he is a victim of society and should be pitied rather than blamed, is provided by Kate Friedlander in *The Psycho-Analytic Approach to Juvenile Delinquency* (New York: International Universities Press, 1947). In this view, the young offender is automatically relieved of responsibility for breaking the law and must not therefore be subjected to punishment.

Similar views are expressed by Albert Deutsch in *Our Rejected Children* (Boston: Little, Brown & Company, 1950) and David Abrahamsen in *Who Are the Guilty?* (New York: Rinehart & Company, Inc., 1952).

Sociologists have doubted that crime in America is, as the headlines frequently claim, constantly on the increase. But it is clear, at least, that over the past fifteen years the number of juvenile delinquents convicted of serious violation of the law by the courts of the United States has risen far more rapidly than has the number of juveniles in our population.* That this rise should occur during the period when the courts have been growing progressively more lenient toward young offenders can only mean that the actual number of crimes committed by youths has increased manyfold; for those—generally a large majority of the cases—who are absolved from responsibility for their crimes do not get into the records. It may perhaps be debated whether the great increase in juvenile offenses has been caused solely by the growing practice of absolving the young offender from responsibility; it can hardly be doubted, however, that this practice, based upon the Freudian theory of crime, has been a very important factor in the rapid increase of juvenile crime. It could hardly be otherwise, for every young hoodlum soon learns from his associates if not from direct experience that the cop on the beat is reluctant to make arrests, that the people in the juvenile court are a lot of do-gooders with crazy ideas about why one gets into trouble, and that the judge on the bench is a sentimental slob who treats one like a kid in diapers.

The Courts or the "Experts"?

The Freudians have not been content with the wide acceptance of their doctrine of personal irresponsibility in the treatment of the

* At least since 1945, the Federal Bureau of Investigation *Uniform Crime Reports* (Washington, D.C.: United States Government Printing Office) have recorded increases in the arrests of juveniles greater than can be accounted for by the increasing number of young people in our population. In 1952, for example, 7.8 per cent of the arrests for major crimes—murder, manslaughter, rape, and assault—reported by 232 cities over 25,000 in population were of persons under eighteen years of age; by 1957, the percentage had risen to 10.3. The 1957 report shows that over the preceding five years all juvenile crimes had increased at an annual rate two and one half times greater than the increase in the proportion in our population of persons under eighteen years of age. In recent years, persons under eighteen years of age accounted for more than one half of the arrests for auto thefts, nearly one half of the arrests for burglary, more than one third of the arrests for larceny.

young offender. They have struggled to get the principle accepted for all offenders; and this struggle has brought them into direct and open conflict with the legal fraternity. And here, as with the traditional legal distinction between the juvenile and the adult offender, the Freudians have been endeavoring to undermine a legal practice that has grown up over centuries of empirical experience.

English common law, and following it our own legal procedures, early developed a distinction between the illegal act that was one of "willful disobedience" and that which was consequent upon either inability to comprehend the law or circumstantial inability to conform to the law. Encompassed by the former category were those criminals who were judged by the magistrate to be mentally incompetent (idiots, imbeciles, and morons) or mad. Such a criminal was, in theory at least, absolved from responsibility for his criminal act; and the sentence imposed upon him, usually imprisonment, was intended not as punishment—since neither the mentally incompetent nor the mad could be coerced into obeying the law— but simply for the direct and immediate protection of society. Circumstantial inability to conform to the law was a somewhat more flexible category; it included, upon the discretion of the magistrate, the criminal act that was accidental and the one that was provoked by peculiarities of circumstances external to the offender. Murder in self-defense is the clearest of the latter type of crime; murder of "passion" perhaps the vaguest and most subjective.

During the course of some centuries the English courts, and following them our own, worked out various rule-of-thumb procedures for determining in specific cases whether the individual could reasonably be held responsible for his violation of the law or not. Some of these common-sense methods of drawing the distinction became in time incorporated into statute law; such is the case, for example, with our distinction between willful murder and involuntary manslaughter. Most remained, of sheer necessity, general principles that could be applied to specific cases at the discretion of the jurist or else made the center of court controversy between opposing attorneys.

As long as the critical decisions were made by jurists or juries on the basis of common-sense application of general principles of responsibility, the differentiations of those who were guilty from those not guilty by reason of insanity, temporary or permanent, were no doubt on the whole knowledgeable, whether or not they served some abstract principle of justice. Thus the court might, from rather intimate knowledge of the circumstances, conclude that the wife who had been murdered would drive any husband insane; *ergo*, the husband was not responsible for his murderous act. But during the last century the practice developed of bringing into court self-styled experts in mental abnormality to bear witness in favor of or against the accused. And with this, common sense tended to be replaced by utter nonsense; for the determination of sanity often became a matter of dialectics camouflaged as science.

Phrenologists, hypnotists, mind readers, and other pretenders to scientific understanding of the human mind gradually gave way in the courts to psychiatrists. The latter may not have had any greater knowledge of the workings of the human mind; but as members of the medical profession they were—as they still are—under some compulsion to maintain their personal integrity. Nevertheless, evidence provided by these experts regarding the sanity of an accused person can be just as contradictory and inconsistent as that which used to be advanced by phrenologists, hypnotists, and mind readers. So to the extent that the jurist or jury member who hears such evidence is sophisticated and unimpressed by the specious claim to scientific knowledge, he usually decides the question of sanity, not strictly in accordance with the rules of evidence and logical deduction from the evidence adduced, but in accordance with the traditional principles applied with common sense.

Here in the United States the generally accepted principle that is used to establish a defense on the grounds of insanity is one that was expressed in the M'Naghten Case of 1843. The M'Naghten Rules were a summary statement of court experience in the determination of insanity over two hundred years or more, and conservative students of jurisprudence hold that this statement has not and perhaps cannot be improved upon. But as psychiatry came more and more under the sway of Freudians, the M'Naghten Rules were attacked as antiquated, prescientific legal ritualism.* They reflect, it is charged, the ignorance about mental abnormality that existed prior to Freud's great discoveries; and they make it impossible for the use of scientific procedures in the determination of criminal responsibility.

Most students of jurisprudence are stanchly opposed to abandonment of the M'Naghten Rules, although some have been won over to the side of the psychiatrists, and a few have offered restatements of the principle enunciated in those Rules.† They claim—and they have little difficulty documenting their position—that, since the psychiatrists do not have a scientific basis for distinguishing between the sane and the mentally abnormal individual, they cannot have a scientific procedure by which to do so in actual court cases. They hold, in effect, that these "experts" are perhaps qualified to express opinions, but that they are no better qualified than is the average layman to render a judgment.

For ten years and more the controversy between the traditionalists and the psychiatrists has been fought in the legal and psychiatric literature, and by now every conceivable claim and counterclaim has been brought in as evidence.‡ To the layman, the controversy over the M'Naghten Rules might seem something of an academic tempest in a legalistic teapot. But it is in fact the focus of a strenuous and

---

* One such Freudian attack on the traditional procedure is Louis H. Cohen's *Murder, Madness, and the Law* (Cleveland: The World Publishing Company, 1952). Opposed are such writers as Henry A. Davidson (*Forensic Psychiatry.* New York: The Ronald Press Company, 1952) and Isabel Drummond (*The Sex Paradox.* New York: G. P. Putnam's Sons, 1953).

† As does Jerome Hall in "Psychiatry and the Criminal Law" (*The Yale Law Journal,* Vol. 65, pp. 761-785, 1956). This article provides an excellent summary of the controversy, a spirited and coherent attack upon the scientific pretensions of the psychiatrists, and a logical defense of the thesis that the courts rather than "experts" should continue to determine the responsibility of the individual.

‡ There are some indications that the case is going against the defenders of the M'Naghten Rules: The Report of the Royal [British] Commission of Capital Punishment, published in 1954, definitely reflected the psychiatric thesis that experts should weigh the decision regarding responsibility, even though in the case of a murder trial the jury is officially the deciding agency. A year later an American court established a rule—the Durham Rule—regarding the determination of criminal responsibility that, in the view of most lawyers, undermines the M'Naghten Rules. It has not replaced the latter in our courts, but it offers a dangerous precedent; and to lawyers, precedents are of great importance.

socially significant struggle for power. The underlying issue is whether the courts shall retain their traditional right to determine in accordance with time-tested—if unscientific—procedures the issue of criminal responsibility or whether that right shall, under some guise or other, be transferred to members of the medical profession specializing in psychiatry. Psychiatrists are already recognized in our courts as testifying experts, and their acceptance as the experts on the human mind has done much to foster the plea "not guilty by reason of temporary insanity." For they are mainly of the Freudian persuasion and, for that reason, predisposed to lend their expert testimony in defense of the accused. At any event, as the practice of relying in jury trials upon psychiatric testimony has developed, the frequency of criminal court verdicts of "not guilty by reason of temporary insanity" has definitely increased. What would happen should the right to pass judgment be in effect transferred to such experts is not difficult to anticipate; it is fear of this consequence, fully as much as fear of loss of power, that leads the legal fraternity to cling to the "antiquated, unscientific" M'Naghten Rules. Better this, they feel, than to abandon the very concept of criminal responsibility in accordance with a modern, equally unscientific concept of the human mind.

If the Analysts Win

Premodern societies have always accorded the accused lawbreaker a rigorous if not necessarily prompt brand of justice. Methods of determining guilt have varied greatly—at one extreme is the common primitive trial by ordeal, at the other the magistrate's court of old China; but whatever the method, it has operated upon the principle that it is better to convict the innocent than to let the guilty go free. And this principle, abhorrent as it may be to modern Western peoples, is functionally grounded in the fact that, wherever the means of sustaining life are dear, life itself is cheap. A subsistence, or near-subsistence, society cannot afford to put the welfare of the individual member above the interests of the whole. For, as we have seen, such societies have a very narrow margin of permissible error in all regards, including matters of legal justice.

One of the social luxuries that became possible as Western societies increased their productive and social efficiency was a progressive reduction in the severity of punishments meted out to those convicted of violating the criminal law. Another and equally significant use made of the growing social surpluses was the gradual abandonment of the old principle that justice must be cautious and err, if at all, on the side of law enforcement. In time the antithetical principle emerged: better, it was now said, that the guilty go free than an innocent be convicted. And a variety of safeguards evolved, particularly in English common-law procedure, to protect the individual from a miscarriage of justice. Thus it was to provide such protection that the jury system of determining guilt developed, and with it the increasingly complex and restrictive rules of evidence that today strongly favor the defense in any criminal trial. Thus, too, it was to protect the individual from errors of the law that the various courts of appeal were established, and weight came to be given to such irrelevancies as the technical perfection of court procedures.

All these and many related developments in criminal court practices have come close to guaranteeing that no one who is innocent of a crime will be convicted of it and at the same time to assuring that a great many who are guilty will go free. The latter may be socially calculated as the cost of the former; and up to some point modern society can well afford such cost. Perhaps we have already reached that point, for the individual is now so hedged about by protections from the law that any member in good standing of a prospering criminal organization is for all practical purposes beyond the law. And even the free-lance professional criminal is fairly conviction-proof, provided that he carries on his trade with reasonable prudence and employs a competent income-tax consultant. But there is no doubt that we are certain to run far past the point where we can afford to let the guilty go free in order to protect the innocent if the Freudians have their way.

The plea "not guilty by reason of temporary insanity," or the less formal but by now almost inevitable "I blacked out," is resorted to only when guilt is so self-evident that it cannot be obscured by any or all of the many devices now available for protecting the accused from the law. The plea, when made by the defending attorney, is in fact admission that the accused did commit the act with which he is charged; it is a claim that he is, or at the time of committing the crime was, irresponsible. The traditional means of determining legal responsibility proceed upon the assumption that everyone who commits a crime is responsible unless it can be proved to the contrary; but should the determination of responsibility be placed, as the Freudians desire, in the hands of psychiatrists, the reverse would become true. For all psychiatrists of the Freudian persuasion are ideologically predisposed to believe that no one is ever really responsible for his actions, criminal or otherwise. Should, therefore, the current infusion of Freudian theory into the treatment of juvenile delinquents and adult offenders progress to the stage where the Freudian principle of individual irresponsibility replaces the traditional idea of responsibility, our criminal courts will operate entirely in terms of the Freudian ethic, and we shall have validated the Freudian thesis. Those of us who are still constrained by law will be wholly at the mercy of irresponsible and hence unpunishable criminals, and our society will be sick indeed.

PART III

ADOPTION OF THE ETHIC

8

The New Bourgeoisie

THE PROTESTANT ethic evolved, gained advocates, and became in time the prevailing ethic of Western Europeans only because it reflected and in turn implemented changes that were already in process. Among these changes was the growth in number and social significance of independent business entrepreneurs, who operated outside the restrictive sphere of the medieval guilds and could therefore apply enterprise to the discovery and exploitation of new markets for goods and to the use of new techniques in processing, fabricating, and distributing goods. Allied with these independent entrepreneurs in a community of interest against the Church and other agencies of traditionalism were the early scientists, explorers, and political opportunists—all men of enterprise in their various ways. These were the men who in the sixteenth century gave their considerable support to the Reformation, and it was their values and sentiments that in time became codified in the Protestant ethic. As their efforts brought more and more changes to Western society, their numbers increased, and the new ethic came to prevail; and by the opening of the eighteenth century they constituted a clearly defined and powerful class, the *bourgeoisie*. It was this class that honored the Protestant ethic; and because they did so, they formed a class unique in human experience, a class that served as the driving force for the many innovations and developments that have brought Western peoples to their present social state.

The emergence of the Freudian ethic and its invasion of various aspects of current American society similarly reflect, and in turn implement, changes that are occurring elsewhere in our society. Among the more significant of these changes has been the incipient

183

decline of the *bourgeoisie*, with their attachment to the values and sentiments of the Protestant ethic, and their replacement—still only partial—by a new class that is operating in terms of the values and sentiments that are sanctioned by Freudianism. It is of course too much to say that Freud and his disciples have brought this new class into being, and thereby jeopardized the *bourgeoisie*; but there is certainly a historical concordance between the rise of the Freudian ethic and the rise of this new class, and currently each depends for its growth on the other.

It is one of the more interesting minor ironies of social history that the decline of the *bourgeoisie* should be associated with Freud rather than with Marx. Both men rebelled against bourgeois values, although they were members of the class and each was in his own way a man of enterprise. But whereas Freud was contemptuous of the moral constraints and social compulsions of bourgeois life and made them the villains of his psychoanalytic system of thought, Marx hated the class members themselves. To him, the *bourgeoisie* were the embodiment of all the evils of the ruthless capitalistic system.

The revolution that was undertaken in the name of Marx did not destroy a bourgeois class; for at the time of the revolution Russia had not yet developed a large and powerful body of commercial, industrial, scientific, and intellectual entrepreneurs. The revolution destroyed, instead, an aristocracy; and whether Russia has in the decades since evolved a professional and managerial class comparable, in rights, functions, and values, to the *bourgeoisie* of the West is a matter of considerable debate among Western students of the Russian system. At any event, Marx's hopeful prediction that the downtrodden masses of Western society would liquidate the bourgeois class has proved false; and if this class is now on the decline, as current indications suggest, the credit goes to Freud more than to any other single man. For the dissolution of the *bourgeoisie* is being wrought, not by revolt of the masses, but through the adoption by members of that class of the contra-bourgeois values and sentiments that are sanctioned by the Freudian doctrine of man. It is, so far at least, a process of self-liquidation, not unlike that by which in times past other social elites have destroyed

themselves through the abandonment or corruption of the qualities
that had distinguished them from the common run of men.

Class and Enterprise

The members of every society, however simple, are differentiated
into classes of one sort or another—into workers and managers,
owners and users, fighters and tillers of the soil. For contrary to
Marx and other utopians, some sort of differentiation is functionally
necessary. A given form of class divisions may through changes in
dependent aspects of the social order lose its utility, as when economic and other developments deprive a political aristocracy of its
functional roles and leave it a socially parasitic remnant of another
day. But class per se is a normal and invariable element of every
society; and the ideal of the classless society is at best a sort of
protest against the existing class order, and more often just an idle
dream.

Where, as in premodern China and India, and in medieval Europe, the class demarcations have been clear and the membership
of each class has been fairly stable, it is no great task to charac-
terize the various classes in terms of their distinctive qualities and
their functional roles. But sociological analysis of the class systems
of modern, highly dynamic Western societies has proved to be exceedingly difficult. For one thing, the lines between the classes are
vague and always shifting, and the membership itself is relatively
fluid. As a consequence, class members vary widely in many dimensions one from another, with much overlapping between the classes;
and there is often little social agreement as to who belongs to
which class and what are the distinguishing characteristics of that
class. This has been especially true of the American class system,
which has until now been even more dynamic and confused than
its European counterparts.* Nevertheless, we do have classes, each

---

* Even studies of specific American communities, such as that by W. Lloyd
Warner and Paul S. Lunt, have yielded varied, confusing, massive, and diffuse
data on class differentiation. The Warner-Lunt investigation of a comparatively
small New England city produced four volumes of material and a series of
theoretical conceptions of class that more or less nullified one another. The
Yankee City series, as the four volumes are now known, is perhaps most useful

of which may be distinguished in terms of some significant characteristics; and our current class system has historical roots that can be traced in a general way back to the Middle Ages.

Under feudalism in Western Europe, as elsewhere where a feudal-type society has appeared, the population was divided into two major classes—the serfs, who were tied to and worked the manorial lands, and the lord of the manor and his family. Class status was hereditary; and although there were some few free agents, such as itinerant priests, there was for all practical purposes no mobility between the classes. The decline of feudalism, the rise of the medieval towns, and with these changes the emergence of the Church and of government, the growth of commerce, and the beginnings of finance, gradually destroyed the feudal class system and gave rise to a variety of new classes, both rural and urban. The rural classes tended, especially on the Continent, to coalesce into one class of peasant proprietors; and in time the free urban workers took shelter under the protective regulations of the medieval guilds. Besides guildsmen, who although of various grades in their respective guilds formed something of a class of their own, there were in the towns Churchmen, soldiers (typically a class apart), merchant princes (whose status and powers were as much political as economic), men of finance (invariably Jews), small independent craft or mercantile proprietors, professionals (including scribes, lawyers, and doctors), and a substratum of people who made their living and lived as best they could (these ranged from wage workers through thieves to beggars).

Many factors contributed to the dissolution of the medieval class system. Eventually, the declining integrity of the Church, which had for long discouraged all enterprises except those undertaken

---

as an extensive demonstration of the fact that even here in America we do have classes, although it is impossible to specify the number and the characteristics of them. *The Social Life of a Modern Community* (New Haven: Yale University Press, 1941) is the first volume of the series.

Two of the more trenchant sociological discussions of the universality of classes and the functional necessity for them are: *Human Society*, by Kingsley Davis (New York: The Macmillan Company, 1949, pp. 366-370) and *The Social Order*, by Robert Bierstedt (New York: McGraw-Hill Book Company, 1957, pp. 401-432).

under religious auspices (*e.g.*, the building of cathedrals was sanctioned, whereas the construction of roads, harbors, etc., was not), weakened the organizational and ideological restraints on individual enterprise. It was this latter trend that became crystallized in the Reformation, giving in time religious sanction to a new ethic and a new class—the *bourgeoisie*.

The term *bourgeoisie* has fallen into disrepute, and here in America we have always preferred to say the "upper middle class." Originally denoting the members of a medieval borough, the term developed its specific social implications in the century or two preceding the industrial revolution. It came to be applied by French hired workingmen to their employers, and for a while bore something of that half-humorous affection that the phrase "the Old Man" sometimes implies today. The employers of preindustrial France were not, as a class, Protestant in faith, but they were anticlerical, for good economic reasons; and they conducted their business, as did their English counterparts, largely in terms of the Protestant ethic. And like their English counterparts, they were for the most part men of enterprise; indeed, it was just such men who developed the trade procedures and the early factory productive methods that were to lead into the industrial revolution. They were independent and individualistic, and they were self-reliant and responsible. Apparently this latter quality was what earned them the affection of their workers; for however bitterly competitive they might be among themselves, they were inclined to be paternalistic toward their employees.

As the industrial revolution got under way, first in England and later on the Continent and in the United States, the *bourgeoisie* grew in numbers and in power—political as well as economic. It was they, not the masses, who through both revolution and evolution brought representative government into being; and it was the advent of representative government that gave to the *bourgeoisie* a powerful voice in political affairs, that largely dispossessed the hereditary aristocracy, and that broke with the traditional governmental support of mercantilistic economic policy and the guild system. Meanwhile, a whole new system of urban class statuses was emerging.

Through most of the nineteenth and well into the twentieth century, the urban class system of Western Europe—and with minor variants that of the United States—consisted of five functional classes, bracketed both at the top and the bottom with a class of social dependents. The latter, which served a not very useful social function, consisted, on the one hand, of "gentlemen" and their families (remnants of the old aristocracy, men who lived on inherited wealth, and men who lived on the wealth inherited by others); and, on the other, of indigents (professional mendicants, petty professional criminals, social misfits, and social unfortunates, whose numbers waxed and waned as the local demand for labor fell and rose). At the apex of the hierarchy of functional classes were the capitalistic owners of the means of production, who tended to become after a generation or two gentlemen of leisure; beneath them, and individually only a generation from elevation to the class of capitalists, was the bulk of the *bourgeoisie;* a good span lower and as a group quite distinct was the lower middle class— the petty *bourgeoisie;* somewhat lower in status if not in income were the skilled laborers; and, providing a base upon which the entire structure rested, was the laboring class.

The functions and social characteristics of each of these five classes were fairly stable through most of the nineteenth century; but the membership of each class was subject to constant, if relatively slow, change. The class system was, in sociological terms, open. Individuals and their families might, and many did, move upward or downward. And, for the most part, it was the extent to which the given individual—whatever his class position—conformed to the Protestant ethic that determined whether he went up and how rapidly.

Much has been said on behalf of the laboring class. It has been idealized as solid, sturdy, industrious, and long-suffering—as constituting the "salt of the earth." Marx and the other theoretical socialists have invariably glorified it. They have regarded the laboring class as the producer of all economic values (this is the substance of the labor theory of value) and the members of all the other classes as exploiters. As a class, however, laboring men—*i.e.*, unskilled workers—have been and for the most part still are characteristically unenterprising and irresponsible.* These normative characteristics of the members of the laboring class can be explained as a function of class position; but that explanation does not negate the fact that most of those who have worked with their hands at unskilled tasks have been and are unambitious to the point of apathy, casual in the fulfillment of assumed obligations, indifferent in the management of their personal affairs, lacking in foresight, and unwilling to subordinate personal and immediate concerns either to abstract principles or some envisioned personal gain in the future. They have tended to conduct themselves in accordance with the values and sentiments of the medieval ethic, passively resigned to the world about them and their place in it, and suffering each day as sufficient unto itself. All they need is release from the spur of economic necessity, and they slip gratefully into conformity to the Freudian ethic.

As an individual, the unskilled workingman may, of course, be anything from a substantial citizen to a brawling and drunken sot. From his ranks have come many of those who, surmounting their class norms, have contributed greatly to society and in the process moved up in the class structure. From his ranks also have come most of the indigents—the professional mendicants of times past, and the equally professionalized and constantly increasing class of social parasites who today often live on the easy bounty of a society that is dedicated to the proposition that no one, however useless, shall know want. The laboring class as such does do most of the manual work of the world; but had it not been for others, its members would today be doing this work in the tedious and inefficient ways of a hundred or a thousand years ago.

The personal characteristics of the skilled worker—the one who has spent an apprenticeship of some sort or other learning his trade—differ markedly in some respects from those of the unskilled worker. For one thing, the skilled worker has made a commitment to his special craft and is inclined, even in these days, to take some

* Joseph A. Kahl has recently brought together and reduced to systematic analysis the various sociological and other studies of class in America (*The American Class Structure.* New York: Rinehart & Company, Inc., 1957). The evidence indicates, he thinks, that on the whole skilled workers are content just to get by, and unskilled workers are simply apathetic.

personal pride in his workmanship. Moreover, he belongs to a special and delimited occupational grouping, a fact that gives him, at least in the eyes of his fellow workers, social status. Finally, his employment has generally been more stable and more rewarding than has that of the unskilled worker; thus he has been able to learn prudence in economic and other matters. As a class, skilled workers have been and still are far more reliable and industrious than are the unskilled.

The petty *bourgeoisie*—the small shopkeeper, the artisan with his little enterprise—have begun to disappear in America, and in their place is emerging a new class of business, industrial, and governmental functionaries—bookkeepers, accountants, salesmen, bureaucrats, and other white-collar workers who operate under the shelter of large organizations. Their social status is considerably above that of the skilled laborer, although their income is often lower and their skills may be no more difficult to acquire. They do, however, seem to have a rather different life style, and this, together with their great concern with security, makes it likely that they will in time become petty bourgeois in all respects except that of independence.* The petty *bourgeoisie*, who are still a major factor in the economic and social life of Britain and Europe and who in America today, though diminishing in numbers, are still to be seen in the proprietors of the innumerable motels, restaurants, bars, and other service and mercantile establishments that line the highway approaches to our cities and towns, can perhaps best be described as *bourgeoisie* without venturesomeness. The members of this class tend to be in all respects strongly oriented toward the preservation of the *status quo*. They are, as a rule, frugal and diligent, cautious and prudent. The typical petty bourgeois may not be entirely content with his modest life; but "safety first" is his motto, and when faced with a decision, he errs on the side of security.

In their timidity and conservatism, the petty *bourgeoisie* are the

* The white-collar class is only now emerging as a distinctive class, and its characteristics are still unclear. C. Wright Mills (*White Collar.* New York: Oxford University Press, 1951) has made the pioneering analysis of this class and its development.

antithesis to the true (sometimes designated "grand") *bourgeoisie*. But like the latter, the petty *bourgeoisie* are righteously independent and self-reliant. Within their narrower purview, they are completely responsible. They pay their debts, take care of their dependents, save for their old age, and—except in France—pay their taxes in full. And although a member of this class may not have been born into it, once in it, he generally manages to stay there throughout his life and to pass on his little enterprise to his sons and daughters.

The essence of the petty *bourgeoisie* is, in sum, stability. By contrast, the only thing that has been constant through the years about the true *bourgeoisie* is their regard for the Protestant ethic. The family organization of the members of the class, their style of life, their political and other attachments, etc., have been in constant flux. The class as a whole has, in every country, suffered recurrent and marked economic devaluation; and everywhere and always its personnel has been subject to rapid change. For the members of the class have always been highly competitive among themselves and subject individually to competition from the more ambitious and enterprising members of the lower classes.

The special and historically unique characteristic of the urban class system of Western Europe and America, of which the *bourgeoisie* have been and still are the heart, is that it has given rewards, economic and otherwise, to those individuals who have adhered to and operated in terms of the Protestant ethic and has distributed these rewards in rough proportion to the extent to which the individual exhibited the values and sentiments incorporated in that ethic. Under it, the laboring man who deviated from his class norms by being industrious and self-reliant was usually able to move up a class or two; the petty bourgeois who could muster the courage to take a risk in the hope of greater profit had at least a gambler's chance of becoming a member of the true *bourgeoisie;* the maintenance of one's position in this envied class depended, in the long run, upon continued diligence and enterprise; and, finally, the most successful members of this entrepreneurial class might gain acceptance by the elite and be freed, for a generation or two, from the need to exert themselves further to maintain their position.

New Times, New Norms

The *bourgeoisie* as a class have survived wars and revolutions, liquidation through monetary inflation, political and religious persecution, and the eroding effects of the very changes that they themselves have wrought in society. For generations they have been ridiculed and taunted and scoffed at by poets, artists, and men of letters; their family morality has been jeered at by countless libertines; their taste in music, art, and *décor* has been decried by the literati ever since the time of Molière; their pretensions have been spread across the pages of a thousand novels. Still, the class survived and flourished for two centuries and more, centuries during which the Western world saw more scientific, technological, and organizational innovation than man had achieved during the preceding twenty thousand years.

But what wars, revolutions, financial disasters, discriminatory legislation, and vilification by disparagers could not accomplish, insidious social change now appears to be bringing about. The present prospect is that the *bourgeoisie* and all that they have represented—individual initiative, self-reliance, responsibility, and respectability—may shortly disappear. In both France and England, which gave rise to the *bourgeoisie*, the class has during this century gradually sold out its traditional role for the illusion of economic security; and in this process the members have become petty bourgeois in all regards except that they enjoy a slightly higher level of economic welfare.* In America the changes in the characteristics and status of the class have come more slowly and are taking a quite different form.

The primary goal of the early trade-unions, in America as else-

---

* One gets the impression that currently the countries of Europe in which the *bourgeoisie* are either holding their own or are for the moment on the ascendancy are Holland, Switzerland, West Germany, and Italy. There may be no causal relation; but in Holland and West Germany, and to a somewhat lesser extent in Switzerland, Freudianism has lost both its popular and professional following; and in Italy it never, of course, has secured much of a following, professional or otherwise. Freudianism is at least tolerated in France, and it is very strongly entrenched in England.

where, was to increase the workers' share of the material wealth produced by society. Collective bargaining was to be the means whereby workers forced employers to pay higher wages; and in the long run it did just that. But unionism also had a variety of unanticipated consequences. In the first place, the early trade-unions were highly monopolistic and succeeded in effectively reducing the labor force available to employers. As labor costs rose, employers tried—and in the main with success—to reduce, by mechanization and increasingly efficient organization of the productive processes, the work-hours required to perform a given task. This endeavor has, in America, continued up to the present day, with the over-all result that labor-productivity has risen phenomenally. But not, it is clear, through the efforts or by the intent of labor itself. On the contrary, organized labor has tended to reflect the traditional values and sentiments of the laboring class; it has given, to a considerable extent, organizational expression to such class qualities as irresponsibility, lack of enterprise, and lack of personal self-reliance.

In one significant respect unionism has, of recent years, brought about a considerable change in the status of industrial workers, if not in their primary values and sentiments. Success in the raising of wages has led, particularly here in America, to piecemeal efforts by the unions to stabilize employment, or at least to give the worker some assurance of financial security. Severance pay, company, state, union, and federal unemployment insurance, and many other procedures have been devised and forced upon employers in various businesses and industries. Currently the drive for economic security for labor takes the form of demands, still embryonic, for a guaranteed annual wage.

What all this means is that the member of the working class is gradually achieving something of the economic security that has been traditional with the petty bourgeois without assuming any personal or collective responsibility for it. Security is to be provided by employers, supplemented by the state; neither the individual nor organized labor need exercise the diligence, caution, or economic foresight by which the petty *bourgeoisie* have historically preserved their heritage. What labor seems now to want and to have obtained to a degree, if only for the short run, is to eat its bread and have it, too—to act in accordance with the traditional pre-Protestant values and sentiments, and yet enjoy the fruits of industry and prudence.

At the same time that labor has been working its way toward a position that might be called "quasi petty bourgeois," the *bourgeoisie* have been assuming many of the values and sentiments that have traditionally been associated with the laboring class. The result is the emergence, most notably here in America, of a distinctly new class. It is bourgeois in respect to its status vis-à-vis the other classes; it is bourgeois in terms of its level or standard of living; and it is composed, for the most part, of the sons and daughters of the *bourgeoisie*. But its way or style of life is in many salient respects markedly different from that of the traditional *bourgeoisie*, and the values and sentiments which it holds and in general honors are more closely allied to the Freudian than the Protestant ethic.

The new *bourgeoisie* is hardly a generation old, and it has not as yet replaced the old, traditional *bourgeoisie*. But since it is composed for the most part of men and women of early maturity and seems to include a very considerable proportion of the young business and professional people of America, the new *bourgeoisie* will become *the bourgeoisie* during the course of the next twenty years or so, unless current trends are abruptly and forcibly reversed—as they might be by a faltering of our economic order. It is, as we have seen, mainly to this newly emerging class that the advocates of permissive child rearing address themselves and from families in this new class that come the majority of children who are schooled in the progressive mode; and it is primarily the members of this class—both adults and children—who have been converted to or trained into the idea that passive adjustment to the group is the right and proper—the "democratic"—role for one to take.* So the new *bourgeoisie* has already found the ethic by

---

* "The type of character I shall describe," says David Riesman, "as other-directed seems to be emerging in very recent years in the upper middle class of our larger cities..." (*The Lonely Crowd*. New Haven: Yale University Press, 1950, p. 14). Riesman sees the development as involving a change in class type from "inner-directed," by which he means people guided by principles of conduct, toward "outer-directed," by which he means people who act in ac-

which it should live, and the means to induct its children into that ethic and its general style of life.

The Shadow of Malthus

The most tangible of the recent changes in the social conduct of the children of the old *bourgeoisie*, and hence evidences of the emergence of a new *bourgeoisie*, are the decline in the age at first marriage, the rise in the birth rate, and the increase in divorce. Together, these changes are indicators of a growing irresponsibility of the individual toward others and on behalf of his own future. The boy or girl who enters marriage in his teens, produces a sizable number of offspring, and then takes recourse to the divorce courts is in terms of the Protestant ethic wholly contemptible. Such conduct has been understandable—or at least commonplace— among members of the lower classes; but until very recently it has been considered by the *bourgeoisie* as intolerable for members of their own class. Today, however, such social irresponsibility on the part of the younger generation is not only tolerated but has come to be accepted as inevitable by most of the old and old-fashioned *bourgeoisie*.

Throughout most of human history the fertility of populations has approached their fecundity; that is, the birth rate of men— like that of cats, rats, and other lower animals—has been close to the physical maximum. And wherever this has been the case, their standard of living has remained close to the bare subsistence level; for when they have increased their production of the necessities of life, more of the children born to them have lived, with the result that there has been no surplus. The conditions of such a subsistence population may be described demographically as in-

---

cordance with standards set for them by those with whom they are in immediate, if momentary, association—*i.e.,* people who adjust passively.

In *The Crisis of the Middle Class* (New York: Rinehart & Company, Inc., 1955), Henry Grayson analyzes the historical circumstances that have brought about the rise of the new *bourgeoisie* and examines the social forces that currently seem to be changing the role of the *bourgeoisie* from that of providing the drive toward social change to that of simply aiding in the maintenance of the *status quo*.

volving a high birth rate, a high infant mortality rate, and a short life span. Concomitant social characteristics are, inevitably, a low general level of health, low value placed upon the individual, low productivity, technological stagnation, and organizational rigidity.

From time to time certain societies have temporarily escaped the cycle of permanent impoverishment. For a time, the people of Rome were able to expand their empire faster than their population and that of the conquered provinces grew. The gap between numbers and food supply was perpetuated in part by the Roman practice of pouring vast human resources into the making of war and in part by the technological advances, especially in agriculture and transport, that the Romans achieved. But once the process of expansion came to an end, the pressure of numbers against available food supplies brought impoverishment to the masses of Rome; and this in turn fostered internal decay and contributed to the final decline of the Roman system and empire.

For the past five hundred years the peoples of Western Europe have been expanding in all dimensions: territorially, organization-ally, and technologically. At the same time the population of the West, including now the North American continent, has been doubling each century. During the first three hundred and fifty years of this period the increase in population absorbed most of the increased production of food and other material goods. As a result, the general level of living at the beginning of the industrial revolution was but little better than it had been under feudalism. It was, in fact, so low that Malthus, father of modern population theory, came to the despairing conclusion that there is a natural law that precludes man's ever achieving much above a bare sub-sistence level. Under the very best of circumstances, he decided, productivity can increase only mathematically, while the enormous fecundity of man assures that the population can—and when new food becomes available will—increase by geometric progression.

Malthus succeeded in describing a condition that has in truth prevailed for most of mankind in the past, that still does prevail for most of mankind today, and that is universal among the lower animals. But along with the evolution of the Protestant ethic, and in accordance with its values and sentiments, some of the peoples of Western Europe had begun to exercise more or less deliberate control over their numbers and thereby to secure for themselves more and more of the gains in social productivity.

The *bourgeoisie* of preindustrial Europe did not, presumably, resort to birth controls to limit the number of their children. Chemical and mechanical techniques were not then available; and if husbands practiced continence, no evidence of it remains. But the number of children per mature family appears to have been considerably smaller among the *bourgeoisie* than among the laboring class and the peasants. And this seems to have come about as a consequence of the fact that, as an adherent to the Protestant ethic, no respectable burgher thought of marrying until such time as he could confidently expect to support in the comfortable fashion of his class a wife and as many children as God saw fit to encumber him with.

Postponement of marriage, which became the normal practice of the *bourgeoisie* of Europe, is a fairly effective means of reducing the birth rate, particularly where, as was the case, the man chooses a woman of his own age group when he at last marries.* The child-bearing years of women are comparatively short—from puberty to the onslaught of the menopause, which may occur any time after thirty-five years of age. If a woman marries at puberty, her theoretical potential is somewhere in the neighborhood of twenty-five children, whereas if her marriage is delayed until she is twenty-five, that potential is reduced almost by half. The theoretical potential is never reached, if only because the woman who bears a child each year, year after year, is probably dead long before she reaches the menopause. What probably happened in preindustrial Europe was that through the postponement of marriage the *bourgeoisie* kept their average mature family size—that is, the survivors of the very high infant mortality—down to four or five

---

* This practice seems to have been general and to have persisted long after the *bourgeoisie* adopted birth control as a further restraint upon numbers. An early, highly sophisticated analysis of the effects of delayed marriage among the *bourgeoisie* is provided by Benjamin Kidd in *Social Evolution* (London: The Macmillan Company, 1894, Appendix I). In 1884-85, according to data Kidd presents, the average age at marriage of English males of the "professional and independent class" was 31.22 years, and that of women of the same class 26.40.

children, while the peasant and laborer's family ran nearer to twice that number.

The industrial revolution led to a rapid increase in the relative size of the *bourgeoisie* and gave further incentive to the restriction of numbers. In America somewhat the same conditions obtained prior to the beginnings of the industrial revolution, primarily because the conqueror of the wilderness could not afford children in large numbers if he were going to hack out a home for himself in the wilderness. The ambitious lad of Colonial America tended, therefore, to delay marriage until the time when he could afford the luxury of a wife and the company and comfort of the children that she would, presumably, bear him.

Postponement of marriage seems to have been the major means of restricting the birth rate until about the middle of the nineteenth century, when a chemical means of discouraging conception gained popularity among both the peasants and the *bourgeoisie* of France. This technique soon spread to the *bourgeoisie* of England, and thence to America. The practice of birth control was vigorously resisted, usually in the name of God, by those who held to the medieval view of man; but it was rapidly taken over by all those, irrespective of formal religious affiliation, who subscribed to the Protestant ethic. And before the close of the century, the middle-class birth rate—*i.e.*, the birth rate of both the grand and the petty *bourgeoisie*—had declined to the point where the average number of children per mature family was less than three, a decline that is the more significant in view of the fact that the infant mortality rate had meanwhile declined very sharply.

Through the first four decades of this century, the birth rate in America continued to decline, most rapidly among the *bourgeoisie* (both grand and petty), but to some extent also among the urban working class, which was beginning to realize that higher wages do not automatically bring a higher standard of living. By the early 1930's American demographers were optimistically predicting that the American population would begin to level off at the comparatively low figure of one hundred sixty millions by 1960. They believed that modern industrial society had conquered the age-old problem of population pressure and that we could confidently look forward to both an increase in total social productivity and a progressive rise in the standard of living.

But the demographers failed to take into account the fact that among the various factors responsible for the progressive decline of the birth rate of the *bourgeoisie* was the Protestant ethic to which that class subscribed. It was in large part their strong sense of personal responsibility, the premium they placed upon self-reliance, and their stress upon the wisdom and desirability of postponing current satisfactions in order to secure greater future satisfactions that had led the members of the *bourgeoisie* to delay marriage and, when the opportunity afforded, utilize birth control to restrict the size of their families.

Industrialization does not automatically lead to a decline in the birth rate; it has done so only where and to the extent that the members of the society have subscribed to and conducted themselves in accordance with the values and sentiments of the Protestant ethic. Where these values and sentiments are lacking or where, as in the emerging new American *bourgeoisie*, they are being renounced, members of industrial societies father children with the same disregard for the long-run consequences to their standard of living that those of preindustrial societies display.

The New Style of Life

About 1940 the long-term downward trend of the American birth rate was reversed, and the rate of increase in our population has since been more than twice that of the preceding decade. In the 1930's the birth rate in the United States was in the neighborhood of seventeen per thousand of population per year; in the years since the war it has ranged, according to best estimates, between twenty-five and twenty-seven. And even as the long-term decline in our birth rate is attributable in major part to the old *bourgeoisie*, the major responsibility for the rise since 1940 must be placed upon members of the new *bourgeoisie*.*

* P. K. Whelpton and Ronald Freedman report in part: "The groups in our population whose birth rates were lowest in the depression years were exactly those whose birth rates rose most rapidly following the war. These were the

In the years immediately following the war, demographers presumed that the rise in the birth rate would prove to be a temporary, war-occasioned, phenomenon. Past experience had indicated that at the outset of modern wars the involved populations tend to abandon many of their peacetime values and sentiments and to adopt, for some purposes at least, a sort of hedonistic disregard for long-run consequences. At such a time it is, of course, easy to justify the violation of normal social constraints on the grounds that prudence and foresight have become luxuries that no one can— or need—afford. There is, moreover, a heightened emotionalism induced by the crisis of war, and this in itself tends to disorient and disorganize conduct, particularly that of the younger members of the society. As a consequence of both these factors, the approach and advent of a war precipitate a sharp rise in the marriage rates, a marked decline in the average age at first marriage, and in due course a considerable rise in the birth rate—legitimate and illegitimate.

The normal aftermath of wartime marriage and baby booms has been corrective postwar declines in marriages and births, to the end that in the long run the demographic effects of war have been canceled out. But in the years since World War II no such corrective changes have occurred. What were initially justified as wartime expedients have apparently become codified as normal peacetime practices. There are, in addition to the statistical data on marriages and births, a variety of indications that a real and quite possibly enduring change in attitudes toward marriage and parenthood has occurred. A generation ago the public image of the motion-picture actress was that of an unmarried, childless, and somewhat ethereal young woman. At that time the publicity directors responsible for the development and maintenance of such images did everything possible to keep their wards untainted—in the eyes of the public— by marriage or childbirth. But of recent years they seem, on the contrary, to make every effort to publicize the courtship, marriage, pregnancy, and childbearing of the stars of the entertainment

---

better educated, the white-collar workers, the urban population, the higher income groups." (*Family Planning, Sterility, and Population Growth*. New York: McGraw-Hill Book Company, 1959.)

world. It is presumed, quite possibly correctly, that such news adds to rather than detracts from the personal glamor of such stars. At any event, the current image of the glamorous woman of stage, screen, and television is not that of an unmarried and childless beauty but of a buxom girl who has accumulated a respectable number of ex-husbands and, along the way, a considerable number of children.

To what extent idealized public figures mirror the values and sentiments of real life is unknown; but there can be no doubt that the conduct of young Americans concords in many respects with what they admire in their motion-picture and other stars. Usually they marry early, produce a succession of children and, as they themselves often say, "live it up." One need only drive through the winding streets of a modern professional-class suburban residential tract to see massive evidence of these tendencies. And the fact that what one sees there—innumerable small children, matrons hardly out of their teens, each with child in hand and another in belly, big bright cars, and all the other paraphernalia of contemporary bourgeois young married life—is socially sanctioned indicates how ubiquitous the recent change in values and sentiments has been.

As little as a generation ago, it was the firm conviction of most members of the American *bourgeoisie* that only an irresponsible workingman would marry before he had become well established occupationally and had accumulated a competence of sorts. So thinking, the average age at first marriage of the members of the *bourgeoisie* had for decades risen steadily, until it became the common custom for a man to postpone marriage until he had completed his college education—including professional training, if he was going into law, medicine, engineering, or the academic life—become firmly established in a business or profession, and saved enough to tide himself through any emergency that might arise. As a result, the average age at first marriage of bourgeois males was some six or seven years greater than that of members of the working classes. But now, long after the wartime justification for early marriages has passed, there is no discernible difference in the age at first marriage among members of the new *bourgeoisie* and among members of the working classes. It has not reached the abysmal low of premodern times; and most of our children do complete their high-school education before marrying. But married undergraduate students are already so common as to be taken for granted in the colleges and universities, where for the first time special dormitories are being provided for students who have wives and children.

Not only are the children of the old *bourgeoisie* now marrying very much earlier than their parents did, but they are also producing children with a rapidity that would have appeared just a generation ago to be utter abandon. They have not, presumably, discontinued the use of contraceptives and thereby given up deliberate control of numbers. But they seem, on the whole, to want and to assume that they should have considerably larger families than did their parents. As a consequence, there is now no perceptible difference in the composition of the young mature bourgeois family and of the working-class family; on the average, both were inaugurated early in life and are composed of three and a fraction children.

The American people are in no immediate danger of being pressed by the growth of numbers back toward a subsistence level of life. Both industrial and agricultural productivity have thus far outpaced the rapid recent growth of our population. But the increase in productivity has been brought through technological and other innovations wrought by men of enterprise, members of the old *bourgeoisie*. And continued increases cannot be expected if we do not continue to produce, in addition to sheer numbers of people, a sufficient supply of men and women who are enterprising and who will, through their enterprise, provide us with more and still more innovations of a technological and organizational nature. And it is just this that seems to be jeopardized by the rise of the new *bourgeoisie*. For those who marry in haste and procreate without thought of the future lack at least two of the vital qualities of the man of enterprise—self-discipline and foresight.

There is a good deal being said and written—especially in the popular women's and family magazines—in justification of the new bourgeois practice of marrying early and having numerous children.*

---

* *McCall's Magazine* has perhaps become the outstanding defender of the new *bourgeoisie*. To symbolize this alliance, the journal has of late advertised itself as the "Magazine of Togetherness," and the term "togetherness" is now

These efforts are for the most part predicated upon the Freudian doctrine of man, and they lead, perhaps inevitably, to a sanctioning of elements of or all of the Freudian ethic. There is, for example, the argument that the younger generation has returned to the fundamental values of preindustrial society, that they have rediscovered the family and are again making it the core unit of social life. Thus, far from being an avoidance of personal and social responsibility, early marriage and numerous children constitute in fact an assumption of social responsibility that had been shirked by the old *bourgeoisie*. For is not the highest human value that of reproduction? Is not the fathering and mothering of children the very point and purpose of living? And, obviously, the earlier one starts a family and the larger it becomes, the greater the individual's contribution to mankind. That such contribution is quantitative and may lead to qualitative decline in the welfare of mankind seems to elude those who advance this particular defense of the new *bourgeoisie*. And they fail to see, too, that in terms of their argument the Chinese peasant contributes far more than the best of our young parents; for he marries earlier and fathers even more children, which is why, in part, he lives so very poorly and so many of his kind die from starvation.

A second line of defense of the new *bourgeoisie* begins with the Freudian idea that no one really wants to live in this world of ours and therefore has as his highest, if unconscious, goal a return to the womb from which he sprang. The recent orientation upon the home and family life is, so the argument goes, a seeking of security. The home and the family, once the traditional providers of security, were for some generations more or less lost to members of the bourgeois class, who tended to live as individuals, to be semiautonomous. And since they lacked roots in a social grouping, they suffered from *anomie*, wandering unloved and unwanted in the lonely crowd. But now, at long last, the home and family have been rediscovered; the new *bourgeoisie* are finding the necessary security in the early es-

---

often taken to describe the theme or motif of contemporary American life. Hugh R. King describes, in critical fashion, the present vogue for the term and something of its implications in "E Pluribus Togetherness" (*Harper's Magazine*, August, 1957, pp. 51-53).

tablishment of homes and by surrounding themselves with children. It serves them, as it did men in distant days, as a symbolic substitute for the womb into which they would but cannot retreat.

The claim that modern men are much concerned with security is a persuasive one, but that the conduct of the new *bourgeoisie* can be explained in terms of the need for security does not follow. In the first place, the old *bourgeoisie* were not unattached wanderers through the lonely crowd; they were strongly attached, by morality and sentiments, to family life. Indeed, it was this attachment that provided most of the ammunition for those who decried the *bourgeoisie* as stuffy, self-centered, and self-righteous. That members of the *bourgeoisie* delayed establishing a family until, in their demanding standards, they could afford to have one only reflects the high value that they placed upon family integrity.

In the second place, the homes and families being established by the new *bourgeoisie* are in no real sense secure. Never has the divorce rate been so high as during the past fifteen years; and never before has the financial foundation of the bourgeois family been so flimsy and so dependent upon the continuance of favorable economic conditions that are entirely beyond the control of the individual husband and father. If, as is so often asserted, the members of the new *bourgeoisie* do seek security in and through the families that they found, they are in fact doing everything possible to prejudice that which they seek. For they violate all the principles of prudence that were evolved through empirical experience by the old *bourgeoisie* and which served the members of this class long and well. The new *bourgeoisie* operate, not upon the basis of principles, but upon hope and faith; and they may possibly end up by operating as dependents upon social charity.

Then there is, finally, the idea that the new *bourgeoisie* have liberated themselves from the artificial, unnatural constraints of traditional bourgeois life. They have, presumably through heroic effort, thrown off the restrictive morality that has in the past prevented members of the bourgeois class from realizing their true selves—the moral constraints which Freud held in such contempt and which he thought were largely responsible for neuroses. In this view, to marry early and beget many children may not entirely resolve the conflict between the individual and society, but it does considerably ameliorate it. By marrying early the youth secures a socially permissible outlet for his sexual desires and at the same time a more or less acceptable mother substitute; then the arrival of children provides both parents with sublimative outlets for their libidos, further resolving the conflicts within them and between them and society. To those who accept as gospel the Freudian doctrine of man, this interpretation of the new *bourgeoisie* may make some kind of sense. But in the interpretative system of the Protestant ethic, the marital and parental conduct of the new *bourgeoisie* will be seen more simply as following the course that is least constraining and in the process ignoring the responsibilities that were the pride, if not the joy, of the old *bourgeoisie*.

More serious students of social life than those who write gaily of the joys and merits of early marriages and large families for the consumption of those who do marry early and father large families have ventured the idea that these current tendencies are adjustments to the unprecedently high levels of income. To marry early and have many children is the way in which moderns choose to consume the fruits of prosperity. The alternatives, such as reducing their economic endeavors or storing up surplus wealth for future use, do not appeal to them. They prefer, in effect, a wife and children to more leisure; and they prefer more children today to more material wealth tomorrow. It may therefore be said of the new *bourgeoisie* that they are less materialistic than the old, that their values are more altruistic than were those of the old, and their life style is ideational rather than sensate.

All this may, of course, be said. But whoever says it ignores the self-evident fact that the new *bourgeoisie* have not yet made any material sacrifices in order to secure the idealistic, altruistic, and nonmaterialistic values of family life. On the contrary, the members of the new *bourgeoisie* have raised the arts of crass materialism to unprecedented heights. They make the conspicuous consumption of the old *bourgeoisie*, which so annoyed Veblen, seem trifling indeed. Their appetite for economic goods and services is, in fact, unsatiable and held in check only by their powers to command such goods and services.

Certainly there has been a phenomenal rise in the productivity of American society; and we are currently absorbing the increase in a variety of ways, mostly experimental. Moreover, there is no doubt that the rise in the marriage and birth rates has been a powerful stimulant to business and industry, and is thus an important factor in our current level of national productivity. But none of this attenuates the conclusion that the members of the new *bourgeoisie* have in considerable numbers abandoned the old bourgeois virtues and adopted as their own the personal irresponsibility and the disregard for the future that were not long since the distinctive characteristics of the working class.* For they display the same lack of prudence in their economic conduct as they do in their marital and parental.

Living on Futures

The commercial revolution in Europe, predecessor to the industrial revolution, was founded upon a number of new principles and practices. The first of these was sound money as the medium of exchange; the second was usury at low interest; the third was the inviolability of commercial contracts. These principles and their related practices became in time an integral part of the culture of the emerging *bourgeoisie*. With the beginnings of industrial production, new principles and practices, such as that of the joint stock company, evolved; but none of the new devices ran counter to the three principles of early modern commerce. And today the vast corporate enterprise depends, even as did the merchant of eighteenth-century London, upon the existence of a fairly stable currency, upon availability of fluid capital at low interest, and upon corporate ability to fulfill its contractual obligations.

* In 1955-56, *Fortune* made a survey study of the economic and other characteristics of a sample of young married couples in the professional and middle-income group. In one of the reports on this study ("Budgetism: Opiate of the Middle Class," *Fortune*, May, 1956, p. 134), William H. Whyte, Jr., comments: "For most of the younger couples ... the older precepts of the Protestant Ethic remain the official American ideology; and they are most pleased, even insistent, that the schools should teach their children the ancient virtues of thrift. But it is in much the same spirit that many of them send their children to Sunday school, in expiation."

From the very beginning, however, the members of the *bourgeoisie* made a categorical distinction between business and private life. The former was necessarily venturesome, its future uncertain. One took risks in business; and, as has been mentioned, it was this willingness to take risks for future gains that most clearly distinguished the member of the *bourgeoisie* from the petty bourgeois. But in regard to his family, the member of the *bourgeoisie* tended to evidence the same concern for economic security as did the petty tradesman, the artisan, and the bureaucrat.

Because he was so much concerned with the financial security of his wife and children, it was the practice of the bourgeois citizen to apply to domestic affairs principles different from—but not in violation of—those that he adhered to in business. One marked result was that, although he ran his business on futures, he ran his domestic establishment on past income. He saved until he could, in his terms, afford a house of his own, meanwhile housing his family in whatever fashion he felt he could afford. He paid for current maintenance out of past or, at worst, current income; meanwhile, he saved as much as was possible for future domestic expenditures—to purchase a larger house, to buy more and better furniture, to pay for the education of his son, and—in many instances—to provide a good dowry for his daughter. And he saved, too, in order that he would leave his widow amply provided for, and that he would be assured a good headstone for himself.

Consumers' credit is perhaps as old as the debtors' prison. Members of the working class have long relied for their daily bread upon credit extended by local merchants or, through some device or other, by their employers. To be in debt has probably been the normal for members of the working class since the industrial revolution (and, before and since, for tenant farmers); such indebtedness has been one of the consequences of their low standard of living and a reflection of their lack of self-restraint and foresight. Not uncommonly the workingman went into debt to get married, and with each successive child went still further into debt. By this means he lived in a fashion that he could not currently afford; he lived, in so far as credulous or rapacious creditors would permit him, upon his future. And when the future ran out, he usually left behind only debt and impoverishment.

Within the past two decades there has occurred a tremendous expansion in the use of consumers' credit and, for the first time, widespread resort to it by young people in the middle and upper-middle income groups. The importance of consumers' credit to the producers and distributors of automobiles, electric appliances, furniture, and other consumers' goods is self-evident. There is now almost nothing that cannot be and is not being "purchased" on credit, and it has become one of the major tasks of advertising to provide the new *bourgeoisie* with reassurance that living on credit is not only the normal but the right way. Some otherwise sober economists are of the opinion that in it we have discovered the magic way to permanent economic prosperity.* They point out that money is, after all, just a bookkeeping device; that the distinction between real money and money created by a credit operation is entirely a matter of social definition; and that those who rely upon consumers' credit are, in terms of the society as a whole, not really living on futures, for the goods that are thereby made available to them have already been produced. Perhaps so, but the increasing reliance of the new *bourgeoisie* upon consumers' credit means at once the abandonment of the traditional bourgeois regard for family security and a labor-like disregard for the traditional values of personal solvency, financial respectability, and financial responsibility for one's family. Our society as a whole may not be living on futures, but the new bourgeois and his family are certainly doing so.

It is not difficult to demonstrate that a high proportion of young bourgeois families are now founded upon futures and are maintained by drawing upon futures.† Prudence has, for them, become an old-fashioned and unpalatable virtue. Their values and sentiments are

---

* On the other hand, the equally sober if not quite so conventional economist John Kenneth Galbraith considers consumers' credit one of the major evils of our present economic system (*The Affluent Society*. Boston: Houghton Mifflin Company, 1958, Chapter XIV, "The Bill Collector Cometh").

† Emily H. Huntington (*Spending of Middle-income Families*. Berkeley: University of California Press, 1957) has recently made a detailed analysis of the financial practices and standing of a large sample of middle-income families in the San Francisco Bay area. Her data generally substantiate that of the *Fortune* survey as reported by Whyte (*op. cit.*).

of, by, and for the new day. Thus it is no longer deemed necessary, or even sensible, for a young man to delay marriage until he can afford to set up housekeeping for his bride in something of the standard to which she has been accustomed. Rather, it is the current norm among the new *bourgeoisie,* as well as the working classes, for him to marry and borrow upon his future in order to set her up in an establishment better, or at least newer, than her parental home and then to proceed, borrowing upon that same future, to equip it with every device that strikes his or her fancy in anticipation of the children who will probably arrive with monotonous regularity. All that then distinguishes him from his working-class brother is that his income is higher and his indebtedness proportionately greater.

He does, of course, live in a larger house in a more desirable location; he drives a bigger and probably newer automobile; he wears a business suit rather than overalls; and he carries a brief case rather than a lunch pail. But his domestic finances are no different from, and from the old-fashioned point of view no better than, those of the bricklayer, the carpenter, the factory worker, or the clerk in the supermarket. Like the latter, he is living on futures; and that fact is obscured but not changed by saying of him that he is "renting" his house, his furniture, and his automobile. For does he also "rent" his children, his food, the vacation trips, and all the other goods and services that he promises to pay for in the future?

The members of the new *bourgeoisie* apparently consider that they are responsible and self-respecting citizens; and in their own terms they no doubt are. But their terms are those of a new, still amorphous class that has evolved during a period of economic affluence of which they themselves are in no sense the creators. Their terms, or standards, have not yet been subjected to the test of time or of adversity; and they are terms so like those that have for long ill served the working classes that only the steadfast optimist will see in them survival value. The new *bourgeoisie* currently live at a level of life far above that of the working classes; but they lead a style of life that does not otherwise distinguish them significantly from these classes. Since in the long run it is the function served by any class that determines its position vis-à-vis the other classes, one may wonder just what special function the new *bourgeoisie* fulfill that justifies their present distinctively high level of living. They may work with their heads rather than their hands, but they no longer provide the enterprise by which the old *bourgeoisie* wrought socially fruitful changes in our technology, our business activities, our sciences, and our social organization.

9

Modern Guildism

THE STYLE OF LIFE of the new *bourgeoisie* has evolved during a period of chronic international insecurity, a period in some ways comparable to that which gave rise in ancient Greece to the sensate philosophy of Epicurus. Where the future—everyone's future—may at any moment be terminated by the outbreak of an atomic war, it may seem irrational to postpone marriage simply because one has not yet achieved solid occupational status and a financial competence, irrational to delay having children simply because one cannot yet afford to rear and educate them, irrational to wait until one has money in the bank to purchase a new car, a house, or a new television set for the family room. In an age of atom bombs and constant cold war it is, according to this view, reasonable to maximize current satisfactions and to be guided only by immediate, or at most short-run, goals. Possibly there was a time when one could reasonably anticipate a long life and fairly stable social circumstances; then, no doubt, the prudent man had some chance of ultimately winning over his imprudent brother. Now anything can happen any day, and one of the more serious possibilities is that there will be no future for anyone. If and when the next war comes, all men will be equal in the sight of the atom bombs—the rich and the poor, the prudent and the imprudent, the creditors and the debtors.

But it is definitely not in the spirit of living extravagantly today on the gloomy assumption that there may be no tomorrow that the new *bourgeoisie* conduct their affairs. On the contrary, they proceed to live today with sanguine faith that there will be a bright tomorrow; and if the condition of world affairs enters at all into their calculations, they must believe that either the United Nations or the United States will prevent the coming of another war. For their style of life is predicated upon the confident assumption that the future will be not only fruitful but far more fruitful than is the present.

Men everywhere and always live their daily lives on the basis of faith; they are guided today by some sort of expectations for tomorrow. Without faith the farmer would never plant a crop; without faith the industrialist would not produce goods for future sale; without faith no man would marry. The old *bourgeoisie* were not without faith in the future; but they proceeded upon the assumption that the future was of their own making. Thus their faith in the future was simply a measure of their faith in themselves. They knowingly took occupational risks; but they were domestically conservative. They placed great value upon the economic security of the family and the status of the family within the local community; for though they had considerable faith in themselves and confidence that God was on their side, they seem to have been clearly aware that the best-laid plans of men can go astray and that occupationally their future was unpredictable and somewhat uncertain.

The new *bourgeoisie* proceed on the antithetical assumption; they assume a secure and constantly enlarging occupational future. By and large, they are family-centered men; they make much of home and of the life that revolves around it. But they change homes and community attachments with practiced ease, and many of them seem able to change wives and children almost as readily. The domestic life of the member of the new *bourgeoisie* is, thus, one of continuing instability. In it, perhaps, he finds adventure, stimulation, and excitement and through it, if anywhere, expresses his individuality. For it is in his occupation that he finds security; it is upon his occupational organization rather than himself that his faith in the future is founded.

Occupationally, the member of the new *bourgeoisie* adheres to a body of sentiments, values, beliefs, and expectations that differ little from those of the medieval guildsman. He is not, and evidently does not want to be, an individualist; he wants to be and is a member of an established organization—business, industrial, professional,

academic, military, or political. Once he has gained such membership, he assumes that his economic future is assured—that the future
of the organization is certain and the organization itself will not
let him down.

Moreover, he is confident that in the normal course of events
he will progress up the organizational hierarchy, and that with each
promotion his income will be increased and his organizational status
that much more secure. He recognizes, of course, that to gain and
hold membership in the organization he must be diligent in the
performance of his designated tasks, that he must in all respects
subordinate himself as an individual to the organizational system,
and that he cannot therefore exercise personal initiative. One of
the striking characteristics of the members of the new *bourgeoisie*
is that they are, by and large, energetic and responsible in the fulfillment of organizationally defined roles and not in the least dis-
mayed by having to play the organizational game. It remains to be
seen whether their sons, more or less effectively indoctrinated into
the Freudian ethic, will in turn consider the organizations of which
they become a part as the benevolent father who rewards filiality
with parental devotion or as the hated object of the Oedipus complex.

For the present, at any event, the majority of the mature members
of the new *bourgeoisie* are loyal and industrious members of large
and prospering occupational organizations. And they seem to have
an almost religious faith in the powers, not only of the particular
organization to which they belong, but in the powers of organization
per se. It is on the basis of this faith, rather than fear that the future
may vanish in atomic dust, that they plan their current personal
affairs.

Constraint on Enterprise

No doubt the guildsman of the Middle Ages felt something of
that confidence in the power of organization to assure his future,
and in the process relieve him of personal responsibility for it,
that seems to be the major faith of modern workers in business,
industry, and the professions. And at times and for some periods

the guild system did succeed in holding the conditions and the rewards of an occupation constant. But the guilds could not protect their members from the disturbances and disasters induced by wars, plagues, political misadventure, or the medieval counterpart to the modern business cycle. And, in the end, the guild system aided in its own destruction.

The medieval guilds began as voluntary associations of workers in a given craft or trade, and initially their function was more religious and recreational than economic. Shared occupational interests plus a special patron saint led them to foregather for worship and congenial activities. In time, each craft and trade came to maintain its own guildhall; soon these halls were being used to house single members of the guild; and thence it was but a step to the regulation by the guild organization of the work activities of the individual members. As such regulation evolved, the guild ceased to be a voluntary organization; for it was no longer possible for an individual craftsman to join or not as he saw fit. If he was to work at his craft or trade, he had to belong to the local guild; and if he gained guild membership, he thereby lost the right to do his work in his own way. He became subject to a plethora of regulations. His position vis-à-vis all the other members of the guild was specified in detail; the conditions under which he could work, how he did his work, and his reward for work accomplished were all determined for him by guild rule; and his opportunities for advancement—if any—depended upon the guild rather than his own efforts.

The guild system reduced the individual member to an organizational functionary, depriving him of the right to be enterprising and favoring the one who was by temperament or training passive and lacking in initiative. Where and when the guild system functioned effectively, it was reasonably efficient in providing the individual with economic security and comparative freedom from personal responsibility for his own economic welfare. But from the point of view of the community as a whole the guild system was exceedingly inefficient. It kept guild membership small; it restricted the hours of labor or units of goods produced; and it held prices so high that the general standard of living could not rise. Moreover, and in the long run even more disadvantageous socially, it prevented any improvements in the techniques of production. During the apex of its development and power, the guild system brought all economic life to a standstill; and in accomplishing this guild objective, it placed a high premium upon member conformity and made the exercise of individual initiative well-nigh impossible.

By the fifteenth century the many changes that were to culminate in the Reformation were giving rise, here and there, to independent and enterprising traders and men who established their own factories. Unhampered by the traditionalism of the guilds, interested in the expansion of economic activities rather than their sheer maintenance, quick to utilize the most efficient techniques and organizational procedures, these men of enterprise could easily outproduce and undersell the guilds. They had a large body of willing labor, in the persons of those who were excluded from craft and trade work by the guilds, and a ready market for goods, which were in short supply as a result of the restrictive policy of the guilds.

The medieval guild survived as a type of occupational organization until mechanization of the productive processes rendered it utterly obsolete. But its role in the economic and social life of Western peoples declined steadily through the seventeenth and eighteenth centuries, and toward the end the guild could be maintained against the competition of new and more virile forms of organization only by the force of governments that were, in terms both of forms and functions, quite as antiquated as the guilds. The political revolutions of the late eighteenth century were actually a revolt not only against a restrictive government and its hereditary elite, but against the whole system, the guilds included, that operated to limit the individual to traditional modes of life and to discourage the exercise of individual initiative.

Rule, Routine, and Regulation

Individual initiative has never been given free rein. Individualism is only a relative matter, and individual enterprise has always been and must always be subject to constraints; for a completely free enterprise system would be no system at all. It would be anarchy. Men must be organized, or they are nonsocial. But the organization of social life can be less or more fixed, thus providing either in general or in special areas of life more or less scope for individual initiative. Through the seventeenth and eighteenth centuries there was in Western Europe a tendency for more and more areas of life to become more susceptible than they had been to change through individual enterprise. Through the nineteenth century this tendency became generalized; and free enterprise in business, industry, science, technology, and the professions became the ideal if not the invariable rule. The first half of this century, on the other hand, has seen the emergence of a great many political and other constraints on enterprise. Technological developments, the unionization of labor, and the growth of political maternalism have favored the very large and tightly organized business over the smaller one. And these changes, along with the decline of the Protestant ethic and the emergence of a new bourgeois class, seem to be ushering in a new form of occupational guildism.

The modern trend toward guildlike stability in work organization is most marked in those countries that were the first to throw off the shackles of the old guildism—France and Britain. There, business, industry, education, and the medical and legal professions are for the most part so thoroughly organized that there is small scope left in them for the enterprising individual, and each organizational unit is operationally sluggish and highly resistant to change in any form. Postwar West Germany and Italy, by contrast, after a considerable period of organizational inertia, have witnessed a revival of enterprise, much of it individual in nature. For the moment, the productive organizations of the United States are ranged between these two extremes. There is, however, a distinct tendency for all of our work units to grow progressively more rather than less highly integrated and, in the process, to circumscribe opportunities for and reduce encouragement to enterprise—whether organizational or individual.

The new guildism, like the old, involves the reduction of work activities—craft or trade, scientific or professional—to rule and rote. In many instances this is being accomplished simply by the failure to abandon old procedures as new and more effective ones are evolved, with the result that occupational operations become cluttered with antiquated practices. For the most part, however, this aspect of the new guildism is coming about through deliberate bureaucratization of business, industrial, educational, professional, and other work organizations.

Bureaucracy is a type of organization that is found to some extent or other in at least some aspects of life in all complex societies. Our modern bureaucracies—political and otherwise—are usually very large, encompassing thousands or even tens of thousands of members. But bureaucratic organization is not limited to large groups. The medieval guild was always local and generally included no more than a hundred or so workers. Many a modern physicians' clinic, with even a smaller number of participants, has acquired— with apparently good reason—many of the structural and operational characteristics of a bureaucracy. Such a group may, in fact, present in microcosmic form all the characteristics of a great corporate bureaucracy, such, for example, as General Motors Corporation.

Bureaucratic structure is distinguished by the fact that it specifies, through explicit rules, the activities of each of the members and in the same fashion relates the activities of each to all the others.[*] Each member is, as it were—and often is in literal fact—provided with a book of rules to follow; these rules indicate what he shall do, when, and how. They define his role in the organization. Each such defined role in the organization is in theory, and often in fact, articulated operationally with the various roles of all or most of the other members. The result is a more or less calculated system of individual activities, each of which makes its specific contribution to the total activity of the organization.

To enable this social machine to operate under the variable conditions that invariably obtain, some of the members are by rule empowered to make decisions affecting their own work and that of designated subordinates. In a very large bureaucracy this assign-

[*] Recent sociological studies of bureaucratic structure include: *Bureaucracy in Modern Society*, by Peter M. Blau (New York: Random House, 1956); *Patterns of Industrial Bureaucracy*, by Alvin Gouldner (Glencoe, Illinois: The Free Press, 1954); and *Reader in Bureaucracy*, Robert K. Merton, *et al.*, editors (Glencoe, Illinois: The Free Press, 1952). The tendency for all human organizations to evolve bureaucratic characteristics is analyzed by Theodore Caplow in *Social Organization* (New York: Harcourt, Brace & Company, 1959).

ment of decision-making powers results in departmentalization on the one hand and hierarchical stratification of the members on the other. The bureaucratic structure consists, in effect, of a variety of organizational roles or offices, each subject to its special and specific rules and regulations, and all interdependent and interrelated in specified and delimited ways. Who occupies a given bureaucratic role or office is, in theory at least, of small importance; for a full-blown bureaucracy is not a body of organized men, but a number of men in an organization.

Those who look upon the growth of bureaucracy in industry, business, education, and elsewhere as socially undesirable usually stress its internal inefficiencies. There is certainly a strong tendency inherent in bureaucratic organizations for administrative and clerical offices to proliferate far beyond any functional need for them.* There is also a tendency for bureaucratic organizations to accumulate offices through time; for once an office is incorporated into the organization, it is seldom eliminated, even when the function that it originally fulfilled is either abandoned or satisfied by some alternative means. These tendencies, when they are unchecked by external forces, manifest themselves in a progressive growth of administrative and other personnel—clerks, stenographers, bookkeepers, secretaries, administrative assistants, and assistants to the assistants—irrespective of the need for them. To justify, or at least to occupy, additions to the bureaucratic staff, the organizational procedures may become ever more complex and devious; and this development may itself eventually require the establishment of new offices and the employment of authorities on bureaucratic protocol, specialists who can upon occasion circumvent normal procedures, etc. It is quite possible for a highly bureaucratic organization, especially an unchecked governmental agency, to become so ingrown that the personnel is exceedingly busy accomplishing nothing at all.

---

* This tendency has been reduced, in somewhat wry fashion, by C. Northcote Parkinson to what he terms "Parkinson's Law" (*Parkinson's Law*. Boston: Houghton Mifflin Company, 1957). It is, he points out, by increasing the number of his subordinates that an officeholder in a bureaucracy assures his eventual promotion. Since there may be no real need for such subordinates, they keep busy writing reports for one another to read, engaging in conferences, and preparing minutes thereof, and so on.

The fact that a bureaucratic organization can achieve an efficiency quotient, as measured by external criteria of work accomplished, of close to zero does not, however, mean that bureaucracy is per se inefficient. On the contrary, a bureaucratic organization can be exceedingly efficient in the accomplishment of routine tasks, such as the delivery of the mail; and it can provide an efficient agency for the carrying out of large-scale nonroutine operations when it is directed by enterprising leaders. Efficiency of the former type will generally obtain, even in governmental agencies, where the service rendered by the bureaucracy is visible and hence measurable. Enterprising bureaucratic leadership is in a sense a contradiction; for to the extent that a bureaucratic organization produces its own leaders—through promotion up the ranks—its leaders will tend to be men of routine rather than of enterprise. Nevertheless, under competitive conditions a bureaucracy can often violate its own normal procedures and accept the imposed leadership of enterprising men. It is the ability to do this that has so far made it possible for many American corporations to be at once highly bureaucratic and competitive.

Actually, the inherent tendency for bureaucratic organizations to evolve and accumulate nonfunctional offices and to develop cumbersome and costly procedures is often more than offset by the mechanical kind of efficiency that such organizations can achieve. Moreover, efficiency is in most areas of American life not a particularly important matter. Indeed, some of the current problems of American society (what to do with agricultural surpluses, how to occupy the leisure that results from the reduction in working hours, even how to eliminate the chronic congestion of our highways) stem directly from the fact that we are exceptionally efficient in the production of goods and services. And in some instances, no doubt, bureaucratic inefficiency may work to the advantage of society; this would be especially true of governmental agencies that have been established to fulfill some socially impracticable function. No doubt the economic—to say nothing of the political—difficulties of postwar Britain and France are in considerable measure a consequence of bureaucratic inefficiency; but for the United States, at least, the critical disadvantage of the trend toward bureaucratization of business, industry, education, and the professions is that bureaucracy fosters a noncompetitive system and gives preference to men who are unenterprising.

The work role of the unskilled and semiskilled—even of the white-collar—worker is much the same, whatever the nature of the work organization. He is assigned a task and required to accomplish it in accordance either with traditional techniques or the rules specified for the job. This is not true of the professional and semiprofessional worker—the technician, the scientist, the teacher, the accountant, the salesman, the administrator, etc. For such people, who make up the bulk of the *bourgeoisie* today, the nature of the work organization makes a great deal of difference. The more bureaucratic the organization, the less they can operate as enterprising individuals.

The rules and regulations that define the functions of each office in a bureaucracy have, of course, been designed by men; but in a going bureaucratic system these rules and regulations operationally represent a higher, and quite impersonal, authority over which the individual who occupies that office can have little if any effect. Thus if in his personal judgment any or many of the rules under which he operates are antiquated, cumbersome, overly restrictive, or whatnot, it behooves him to keep his conviction to himself and to adhere to the rules with apparent good grace. For it is an ideological presumption of every bureaucratic organization that the organization (often characterized as "the home office") knows best and that it is, in some inexplicit way, both omniscient and omnipresent. An officeholder may, in collusion with one or more of his fellows, momentarily circumvent a hampering procedure; but a successful bureaucrat does not resent or fight against the established procedures. He is far more likely, in fact, to develop a vested interest in them.

To anyone who has been inducted into the individualistic values and sentiments of the Protestant ethic, subservience to the rules and regulations of an office may appear to be a humiliating violation of the dignity of man. It certainly reduces severely the scope of action and forces the bureaucratic officeholder to rely as a worker upon the wisdom and judgment of the bureaucratic system rather than upon his own personal abilities. He cannot, therefore, secure the kind of personal gratification that comes from doing something on one's own—from assuming responsibility, exercising initiative, or excelling one's associates. His long-run welfare depends in the first instance upon his earning a reputation both among his occupational peers and superiors of being sound, and in bureaucracy the soundness of a man is measured by the meticulousness with which he adheres to the rules of his office. If he performs his designated functions effectively—that is, if he does what is required of him promptly, does no more, and does nothing else—he will be well liked by his associates, and can be expected to be promoted up the hierarchy in accordance with the rules affecting promotion. If he deviates in any significant degree from the procedures officially designated for him, he can expect to acquire the reputation of being a troublemaker.

The bureaucratic officeholder is, moreover, discouraged by the nature of the bureaucratic system from assuming any personal responsibility for the operation of the organization as a whole. He is normally responsible for some clearly defined department, section, or subsection of the bureaucracy; and he is given some specific discretionary powers over it. How well, in terms of bureaucratic standards, he operates that unit will ultimately, no doubt, affect his personal standing with his organizational peers and superiors; but since the functions of that unit are largely prescribed and since his decisions directly affect only his own subordinates, he need only adhere scrupulously to the rules and regulations to earn the reputation for being a sound administrator. And whenever he is faced with an extraordinary problem, the solution to which may conceivably affect the operation of other departments or sections, he can evade personal responsibility in one or another of the approved bureaucratic ways. The simplest method is the referring of the matter to superior authority—a process commonly described as "passing the buck." More devious, but greatly favored in the higher echelons of all modern bureaucratic organizations, is the diffusion of responsibility through the mechanism of group-made decisions.

The idea that a number of people are somehow better qualified than is any one of them to solve problems of organizational policy is by now deeply embedded in the folklore of contemporary American business, industry, education, science, and even of the military forces and the medical and legal professions. It provides the ideological justification for the now common practice of referring all major organizational problems to a committee, and of delegating responsibility for the making of decisions to such a group rather than to a single individual. In theory, the group-made decision will be a superior one, for in theory there occurs within the properly democratic atmosphere of such a group operation a synthesis of the best qualities of the various individual members. The idea that a group can produce a superior solution to an organizational problem is simply the converse of the concept, discussed earlier in connection with the cult of adjustment, that the democratic process enables the individual to fuse with others to form a group without in any way losing his identity as an individual. In the bureaucratic use of the democratic process, the purpose is not that of preserving the integrity of the individual members but of relieving each member of any personal responsibility for whatever it is that the group decides to do.

Thus in a variety of ways the bureaucratic organization encourages and enables the individual officeholder to avoid the strains, so inimical to the psychic welfare of the Freudian man, of competition with his fellows; he can proceed about his tasks with confidence and assurance that what he is doing is right and proper, for it is so defined by the organization; he need have no qualms about his future, for the organization provides him with the security that, the Freudians hold, is necessary to his mental stability. That in return for all this he surrenders his right to have opinions and prejudices of his own, to take risks and make mistakes, and to exercise initiative in the hope—however faint—that he may discover something new or a new way to accomplish something old, he will probably never know or, if he does, care not at all.

Business and Bureaucracy

The decline of competition between the members of the new *bourgeoisie* has been paralleled by an equal or even more effective elimination of competition between members of the laboring class.

For they, too, have found security in the protective embrace of organization. The bureaucratic organization of business and industrial enterprises has of itself tended to regularize their employment and standardize the conditions under which they work. But more than this, they have evolved their own guildlike union organizations to protect each from the many, and the many from the danger that the one might through misguided and selfish enterprise attempt to improve his personal station in life. In so doing, they have inadvertently encouraged the bureaucratization of business and industry, deliberately destroyed the free market for labor, and—intentionally or not—more or less closed the door of opportunity to the individual who is by the misadventure of birth a member of the laboring class.

One of the conditions that gave rise to the industrial revolution was the existence of a considerable body of free—that is, organizationally unattached—labor. The conventional interpretation is that the industrial revolution, by disturbing prior forms of organization, produced this body of free labor. As industrialization progressed, it did indeed undermine the guilds and accelerate the release of workers from agriculture; but the mechanization of the productive process was more a response to than a cause of the availability of free labor. Changes already in process, including the rapid increase in the population, had produced a considerable surplus of workers; and by the middle of the eighteenth century the towns and cities of England, France, and the Low Countries were supporting—at subsubsistence levels—large numbers of unemployed people.

The coming of mechanized factory production, first in textiles and in England, provided new employment opportunities and in time greatly reduced unemployment both in England and on the Continent. The condition of the wageworker during the early phases of the industrial revolution was not, in modern terms, an enviable one; but the coming of industrial production did provide the worker with employment, which was at least a gain over the unemployment that had previously been his lot.*

---

* Social historians have produced a large literature devoted to critical portrayal of the condition of the laboring class in early industrial England and elsewhere. In contemporary terms, that condition was intolerable; but when compared with the economic and social circumstances of the free, and generally

As a consequence of the industrial revolution the productivity, agricultural and industrial, of all Western nations steadily and at times very rapidly increased. Some, but far from all, of this increase in material wealth was absorbed by the increasing population; some was, perhaps inevitably, dissipated through wars and revolutions; and, of course, the productive potential was seldom if ever achieved. By and large, the net gain in production was distributed among the various individuals and classes of individuals in society in accordance with market-place supply and demand. The laissez-faire economists maintained that the laws governing supply and demand assured that each component involved in the production of goods—capital, management, labor—secured a return commensurate with its contribution to that product. But here and there workers discovered that, theory aside, they could increase their share by monopoly of the local labor supply.

The early trade-unions were but modern versions of the medieval guilds; they were local, they brought together skilled or at least semiskilled workers, and they monopolized and regulated the supply of such workers for the local employer. By the middle of the nineteenth century, however, there began, here in the United States, the integration of local trade-unions into national organizations of those working in a given craft; and some of these national unions were eventually combined into the American Federation of Labor. By the end of the century the idea of skilled workers combining for purposes of joint bargaining with employers was thoroughly established in American life, and the trade-unions had become reasonably responsible agencies for the representation of skilled workers in the market place.

Two factors, both peculiar to the United States, retarded the growth of trade-unions and mitigated against the organizing of unskilled workers. The rapid development of industry in America, together with the availability of new lands, resulted in a chronic shortage of skilled labor; there was, at least by comparison with the

---

unemployed, worker of the preceding period, it appears very advantageous. Only recently has anyone thought to make such a comparison (in *Capitalism and the Historians,* Friedrich A. Hayek, editor. Chicago: University of Chicago Press, 1957).

countries of Europe, little need to create an artificial shortage of skilled labor through monopoly by trade-unions of the supply. At the same time, the supply of unskilled labor was being constantly replenished by immigration from Europe (and, for the West Coast, from Asia). Since the demand for skilled labor was high, the ambitious unskilled worker could more easily, or at least more surely, increase his income by acquiring some craft skill than by combining with his fellows in a militant union organization. And since circumstances favored the independent business entrepreneur, the ambitious skilled worker was more inclined to set up shop for himself than to devote much time and effort to trade-union activities. Thus the drive toward unionism was tempered here in America by the relatively high rate of upward mobility; as long as the American economy was both prospering and expanding, the trade-union slogan, "In union there is strength," had very limited appeal.

A number of factors converged during the early years of the great depression to make workers, unskilled as well as skilled, eager to gain the shelter of union organization. Immigration of unskilled workers from Europe had been shut off by legislation shortly after World War I, and the worker low on the economic ladder had no new shoulders upon which to climb; the demand for all kinds of labor had, for the moment, sharply declined; and the prospects for personal advancement by learning some craft skills or setting oneself up in some independent enterprise were, again for the moment, exceedingly slim. The old, established trade-unions were, in true guild tradition, unwilling to take in new candidates for unionism; so the union movement began to take on a new direction and, at the same time, a new objective. The new direction was away from trade- or craft-unions to industrial unions—that is, unions including all the workers in a given industry in one organization, irrespective of the differences in their trades or other characteristics. The major new objective was economic security, an objective that, though produced by the massive unemployment of the depression, has persisted into the war and postwar years.

The effect of the old trade-unionism had been to increase, at least in some places and times, the skilled worker's share of the national product; but this form of unionism placed only limited constraints upon the business entrepreneur, since normally only a small proportion of his employees would be both skilled and unionized; and for the same reason it did little to check upward individual mobility. The advent of the new, industrial type of labor organization has, however, contributed to the historical trend toward large-scale and bureaucratic business and industrial organizations and has at the same time bureaucratized the position of the individual worker. Though this development is far from complete, organized American labor is already for the most part committed to a policy of stability in all respects and at all costs. The wage escalator clause, through which wages are tied firmly to the cost of living, has become standard in the labor contracts of steel, automobile, and other large industrial organizations. The guaranteed annual wage that is the current goal will, no doubt, also be tied to the cost of living. Through such methods the industrial unions propose to establish a floor under labor, providing every class of worker with an assured minimum wage. At the same time, the industrial unions have been endeavoring, with considerable success, to establish seniority as the principle upon which hiring, firing, and promotions are to be based. Forgotten, or ignored, is the fact that wage floors usually turn out to be also wage ceilings, and that where seniority rules, merit is seldom rewarded.

The new unions are highly bureaucratic of necessity; and the goals to which they aspire are certain to make the individual worker increasingly a function of his designated role—both within the union and within the organization by which he is employed. As this is happening, the opportunities for the individual worker to distinguish himself from his fellows by his own efforts and thus, perhaps, improve his personal position are steadily contracting. Union rules, unemployment and pension rights, seniority rights—all these and many other factors tie him to the job he has, and discourage if they do not actually preclude his moving in search of a better place. Thus in many ways the new unionism tends to freeze the position of labor in the economy and the position of the individual worker in the labor force.

If present trends toward stabilizing the position of labor continue, upward mobility—so long the ideal of the American people—will become a thing of the past; and the laboring class will tend to become a hereditary caste, or system of castes, each with its own fixed function and status. But long before then the debilitating consequences of this rigidity will have reduced the American economy, and indirectly the entire social system, to a monolithic structure incapable of any enterprise. For as the labor force is brought increasingly into large, bureaucratic, and quasi-monopolistic organizations, the opportunities for the independent business entrepreneur are diminished, and the advantages to large organization, established labor relations, and quasi-monopolistic control of sources of supply and of the market for goods are intensified.

It should now be evident that the modern American businessman must operate in a climate of bureaucracy rather than, as in times past, one of comparative freedom. He is, as will be shown shortly, controlled from above by a wide variety of political agencies, each a bureaucratic organization with some specialized function and with inherent tendencies toward stabilizing all that it affects. He is controlled from below by bureaucratic union organization; and the pressure upon him will be to stabilize his operations in order that labor can be assured constancy of wages and employment. Moreover, organized labor in considerable measure designates for him how he shall use his various types of workers; it requires that he honor seniority rather than merit in the employment and advancement of the members of his labor force; and it does everything in its power—which is considerable—to discourage him from displacing workers by introducing new productive processes.

Under these circumstances it is no wonder that business organizations are becoming increasingly bureaucratic themselves; for only by becoming bureaucratic can they adjust to the bureaucratic demands upon them. The wonder is that American business organizations have been able to maintain any semblance of dynamism; and it speaks for the enterprise of the leaders of American industry and commerce that they are still able to maneuver in new directions the unwieldy organizations over which they have command. The present leaders are, of course, products of the older and freer enterprise system; and it remains to be seen what their successors, products of bureaucracy and skilled mainly in the arts of bureaucratic routine, will do when they come to assume command.

Science Falters

Traditionally business entrepreneurs have been the promoters, the practical exploiters, of technological and other innovations produced by others. Occasionally, as was the case with James Watt, the two functions have been combined in the person of one man; but the personal qualities that are essential to innovative achievement are different from those that make for a man of practical affairs. Until well toward the close of the last century, most of the innovations that were put into practical use by enterprising businessmen were the work of inventors who proceeded toward their goals empirically—by raw trial and error. They were experimentally minded mechanics, tinkerers, amateur chemists, etc. Neither Henry Ford nor Thomas Edison, for example, was a sophisticated engineer, mechanical or otherwise. Although Goodyear discovered the processes of vulcanizing rubber—upon which the rubber industry of today is based—he was not a chemist, and he made his discovery more or less by accident. But in every field of human endeavor there has come a time when the possibilities of successful innovation through empirical methods have been exhausted and further innovation has depended upon the application of scientific knowledge to the solution of problems. At this point the empiricist has been displaced, and the innovator trained in science has taken over.

Achievement in applied science differs only in degree from innovation and discovery in pure—or, as it is now termed, "basic"—science; like the pure scientist, the applied scientist must have individual initiative. But the goals of applied-science endeavor are by comparison short-run, the chances of success are by comparison high, and the consequences of success are by comparison immediate and tangible. As a consequence, the applied scientist need not be so strongly self-motivated as the pure scientist; his labors can be bought, and his labors and those of others can be organized without too great danger of dampening the individual initiative that is essential to innovation. Both industry and government have taken advantage of this possibility; and the products of chemical, pharmaceutical, metallurgical, petroleum, and other commercial and governmental research laboratories have provided us with a steady stream of new products.

Applied science is, however, more a consumer of than a contributor to scientific knowledge; and for the most part additions to scientific knowledge have come from those traditional citadels of freedom from practical concerns and social constraints—the universities.* During the Middle Ages the universities were very loosely organized islands of free inquiry in a sea of theological authoritarianism. They may at times have produced nothing but random discourse on unimportant matters; but they developed and maintained the concept of free inquiry, and they transmitted this as an ideal to successive generations of students, some few of whom abandoned philosophical speculation in favor of scientific discovery. Such discovery requires not only individual initiative but adequate social support—a favorable climate in which to work. And that means a reasonable degree of freedom for the scientist to pursue his own interests, however futile they may seem to others, and financial support while doing so. Some of the early scientists were men of wealth; some secured wealthy and tolerant patrons; but most lived and worked in universities, if only because there was no other way by which they could continue their impractical endeavors.

General acceptance of the scientist as a potential social asset was long delayed. Indeed, he was often scoffed at and sometimes even stoned. The scholar who translated a bit of Sanskrit might be honored as a man of esoteric wisdom, but the scientist who experimented with electrolysis was more likely to be defined as a puttering old fool. As the findings of such fools were gradually translated into practical applications (Pasteur's application of biology to the salvation of the French wine industry was one of the earliest and

---

* This is clearly pointed out in William Cecil Dampier's A *History of Science* (New York: The Macmillan Company, 3rd edition, 1944).

That almost all of the new ideas—including technical innovation—of the past half century have come from men who were not attached to corporate or other integrated organizations has been demonstrated by John Jewkes, David Sawers, and Richard Stillerman in *The Sources of Invention* (New York: The Macmillan Company, 1958).

more dramatic of such developments), the work of scientists was re-evaluated; and for the past century or so "science" has become synonymous with "progress." It seems odd, therefore, that no very important new provisions have been made for the perpetuation of scientific endeavor.* The technician's need for new scientific knowledge is rapidly increasing, and the problems of the scientist are becoming ever more complex. But even the university, though still, as it was a hundred years ago, the primary center of scientific work, has of recent years lost some of its traditional freedom to subsidize and otherwise encourage scientific endeavor. For the university, like the business enterprise, is being constrained from above and from below and is, in self-defense, developing guildlike attributes.

Our major privately supported universities were evolved on the European pattern and were dedicated to the enlargement as well as transmission of knowledge. They provided considerable support, therefore, to pure research, scientific and otherwise. Our state universities, on the other hand, have always been politically obligated to provide masses of undergraduate students with something called a "general education" and large numbers of advanced students with training in such practical matters as engineering, business, law, and medicine. Nevertheless, the better of the state-supported universities have endeavored with considerable success to emulate the private institutions in their stress upon the enlargement of knowledge.

At about the turn of the century, many of the private universities began, for economic reasons, to take on more and more of the educational functions of the state university—i.e., they established professional schools and began to cater to the interests of undergraduate students. As they did so, they became economically—if not politically—obligated to provide what the student (and parental)

---

* The spate of self-criticism generated in the United States in 1957 when the Russians successfully launched earth satellites led to a verbal overhauling of the science training in our public schools and universities, of which the *Life* series "Crisis in Education" (*Life*, March 24, March 31, and April 1, 1958) is representative. Educational administrators rushed into the public print with promises that high-school courses in science would be increased and their quality improved, and government officials made reassuring noises about future encouragements to pure-science research.

market demanded, and were to that extent distracted from the pursuit of knowledge. There thus came about a leveling of the distinction between the private and the best of the public universities; and from the point of view of science, what was lost to one was gained through the other. But in the years since World War II, both private and public universities have been under great and increasing pressure to abandon the quest for pure knowledge and to devote their resources to the transmission of knowledge, mainly practical, and to research of an applied nature.

During the depression and war years the recruitment of scientists fell off markedly; moreover, during this same period a considerable proportion of our scientific personnel was drawn away from the universities into governmental and other nonacademic fields. By the end of the war, the scientific manpower in the universities was seriously depleted; and it was then that the universities were called upon to double their prewar enrollments. This demand stemmed, in considerable part, from the federal subsidy of veterans; and it coincided with the development of a new and unprecedented source of research funds—the military contract-research program that was instituted shortly after the war.

The military authorities made, and continue to make, a great show of interest in pure science. Their research projects are, in fact, often designed with pure-science objectives. But experience has shown that, although such a project may get under way as one in pure research, it usually suffers redirection before very long.* This perhaps is inevitable. The contracting agency, a military bureaucracy, must provide justification to higher authority for the moneys spent on research, or at least make a good case for results achieved in order to secure further funds for research; and pure research can seldom be justified in this manner. It must be supported (and undertaken) on faith that ultimately—years or decades hence—new knowledge will be forthcoming and that sometime or other this

---

* William H. Whyte, Jr. ("The Strange State of American Research," *Fortune*, April, 1955) has estimated that of the $38,000,000 that the United States government spent on social-science research during 1954 only $2,000,000 went for basic (pure) science projects. The proportion is no higher for the physical and biological sciences.

new knowledge will combine with other knowledge to provide the basis for some practical innovation. Moreover, once a pure-science endeavor is under way, it must be left entirely free to proceed in whatever direction the investigator happens to desire, a luxury that no bureaucratic organization, least of all a military agency engaged in preparing for war, can possibly afford. On the whole, therefore, those university scientists who have become involved in contract research have been lost to pure science. Many of them, in fact, have found themselves—pleasantly and profitably, perhaps—removed from research entirely. The military contracts are invariably big operations, and under them research is programmed. This means, in the first instance, that the research process is largely planned in advance and that the actual work is done by a large number of men, each assigned some special and limited task. It also means that the scientist who accepts responsibility for such a project inevitably becomes the administrator of a complex bureaucratic organization, whereupon he ceases to be a research scientist and is reduced to the role of a research entrepreneur.

The recent development of governmentally sponsored contract research has accelerated the trend toward large-scale, highly organized research projects in the universities that was earlier begun by the private foundations. The early scientists had needed little more than free time and freedom from interference in order to do their work. Even for physicists and chemists, equipment had been simple and mostly homemade. But as each of the several sciences advanced, research became ever more costly. There is still scope for the conceptualist, who needs only access to an adequate library and pen and paper. But the experimentalists, those who grub out the evidence from which the conceptualists make their projections, now need some and often much expensive equipment and numbers of field or laboratory assistants. As this need began to arise, it was, for the most part, the private foundations that provided financial subsidy to university scientists.

The foundations have of late years been subjected to a good deal of criticism, much of it justified. Whatever its initial objective may have been, the large foundation has always in time come to favor large, highly organized research projects in one or another of the currently fashionable scientific problems. And the reason is not difficult to ascertain. The foundation may have started out under the enthusiastic—and possibly misguided—leadership of one man; but in time it has invariably developed bureaucratic organization and all the bureaucratic protective devices. Of the latter, the system of boards and committees through which the disposition of funds is determined is perhaps the most common. Each of the larger and older foundations has evolved complex procedures whereby would-be researchers must apply for funds and even more complex procedures of screening and evaluating such applications. The whole operation is designed, of course, to assure effective and efficient distribution of moneys; but it tends to operate to just the opposite ends. For one thing, only those academicians who have made a career of wrangling funds out of foundations will have the necessary skill, the requisite personal contacts, and the patience with bureaucratic procedure to do so. Such specialists in negotiating with the foundations are not necessarily competent to formulate and carry to completion a piece of truly scientific research. Thus the foundation system tends to favor the man with promotional interests and abilities against the individual who, however competent as a scientist, lacks both the skill and the patience to sell himself and his project.

Moreover, the elaborate procedures by which foundations evaluate applications for funds are costly; and unless the project is a big one, the foundation overhead may well be greater than the grant. So strong is the tendency for foundations to favor large projects that it is a standing academic joke that, if a man needs ten thousand dollars, he had better ask for a hundred thousand. The marked tendency to favor conventional over ingenious and exploratory projects stems, on the one hand, from the fact that foundation decisions are made, ostensibly at least, by committees and boards and, on the other, from the inherent timidity of all bureaucratic organizations. Only a very bland proposal is likely to be acceptable to all of ten or twenty men; and only an exceedingly safe project is likely to secure bureaucratic sanction. To the scientist, the findings of a true scientific quest are unpredictable; after all, if they could be predicted, it would be unnecessary to undertake the quest. But to the foundations, such a quest is fraught with danger. It might uncover nothing at all; worse, it might reveal some socially unpalatable truth (this is a particular hazard in psychological, sociological, and economic research).

The progressive degradation of pure-science research in our universities is not entirely a matter of economics. It reflects in considerable measure a change in the academic climate itself. The old idea of the university as a loose association of individualists—if not outright eccentrics—each going his independent way has all but disappeared.* Administrative office, once held in mild contempt by the scholar, has gained in stature and power; and organization—of courses, of schools, of interdepartmental programs, and of research —has become the order of the day. As administrators are taking over and organization is coming to be valued above men, the dedicated teacher-scholar is inevitably going out of fashion and being replaced in favor by the academic bureaucrat. The latter is, in general outline, hardly distinguishable from his brother in business or industry—less prosperous by far, but almost equally subservient to the rules and regulations of his professorial office. This means, in varying degrees, teaching his designated courses in a safely routine manner, doling out grades in a protectively lenient way, and playing a good game on a variety of academic teams—on the curriculum committee, perhaps, or on the committee responsible for conducting some interdepartmental course, or on the committee for research in something or other. If he is an exceptionally ambitious man, he will of necessity curry administrative favor in the manner of the ambitious man in business or industry; and he will, most particularly, seek to gain acceptance as a sound research man—and

---

* "From the general ethos of our society comes the notion that cooperation is always superior to isolation and teamwork to solitary work, a notion easily extended from persons to entire disciplines. Teamwork carries connotations of democratic *camaraderie*. Individual work bears the odium of snobbish, aristocratic exclusiveness. The present tendency toward the exaltation of the co-operative research team over individual research almost causes one to wonder if ultimately the practice of individual investigation by the single scholar working alone may not come to be looked upon with suspicion as a kind of solitary vice if not evidence of subversion." (Adolph S. Tomars in *Modern Sociological Theory*, Howard Becker and Alvin Boskoff, editors. New York: The Dryden Press, Inc., 1957, p. 503.)

hence grants of funds—by one or more of the foundations. Then before long he will be in his own right an administrator of a research project, from which position it is only a step to becoming an assistant dean, and so to administering those who were less ambitious than himself.

Organization Takes Over

A generation ago the American businessman and the university professor were the polar types of the man of enterprise, and each in his own way acted mainly in accordance with the Protestant ethic. The professor struggled, usually against social indifference, to extend the frontiers of human knowledge and to transmit knowledge to the students from whom would come his successors, the technicians, and the professionals. The businessman struggled, usually with social acclaim to speed his labors, to apply human knowledge to the satisfaction of human needs—often, certainly, only to the satisfaction of his own need for wealth, but in the long run at least inadvertently to the needs of mankind. Today the independent businessman has in the main been replaced by the organizational officeholder. The university professor is beginning to suffer a similar fate. The university is undoubtedly the last stronghold of individualism; but its walls are crumbling, and its faculty are being mobilized not to repel the invaders but to meet them on common organizational grounds. Should the current trends persist, within another generation the tradition of free inquiry freely engaged in will have disappeared from university life; and knowledge will have returned to the organizational—and authoritarian—bondage from which the medieval university helped rescue it.

The bureaucratization of business enterprise and university life is an exceptionally clear reflection of the general decline of the Protestant ethic and an organizational expression of the emergence of a new ethic. The organizational developments are in the direction of large-scale guildism, and the new ethic is that complex of values and sentiments that has here been termed the "Freudian ethic."

The new guildism, like that of the Middle Ages, relieves the individual of personal responsibility for his own welfare; it frees him from the strains of interpersonal competition; and it provides him —in Freudian terminology—with an organizational substitute for the womb, which is his natural habitat. The Freudian ethic sanctions individual dependence upon organizational support; it justifies the subordination of the individual to organizational roles and procedures; and it assures the individual that adjusting passively to the group—the organization—is natural, whereas striving for individual achievement is false and artificial.

The new *bourgeoisie* have taken to the new guildism with complete confidence in the power of organization to assume and fulfill the responsibilities that they individually ignore. They apparently believe that man has at long last and for the first time discovered— presumably through the magic of science—that the organizational whole is more than the sum of its individual members and that, therefore, an organization of individually passive and unenterprising men can operate so effectively and be so adaptive to changing external conditions that it will assure each member lifelong health, wealth, and happiness. They apparently also believe that, should some misadventure afflict the particular organization to which they are occupationally attached, the protective powers of government will take over where those of business, industrial, professional, or academic organization have failed.

10

Political Maternalism

THE EMERGENCE of the new guildism would not have been possible without the support and encouragement of that special kind of organization that we call government. The guild as a form of organization is a sociological anomaly. Its bureaucratic structure gives to it great internal resistance to change, and in this sense high survival value. It can absorb and nullify the efforts of deviant members to reorganize the structure or modify its established procedures; it can digest such organizationally foreign objects as new techniques; and it can often survive an almost total loss of functional significance. On the other hand it is not a self-sufficient organization, for it invariably supplies some specialized service. Since it tends to provide this service at maximum rather than minimum cost, it is vulnerable in competition with any less bureaucratic agency.

The early medieval guilds often resorted to force, exercised by their own members or for them by hirelings, to discourage upstart competitors and thus to preserve their monopoly over their special craft or professional activity. In time, as the medieval towns grew both in size and complexity and political organization evolved, the guilds came to have a more or less symbiotic relationship with the agencies of political authority. In some instances the towns were ruled by a council of guild masters, who used law and the law-enforcement agencies to enforce guild regulations upon the entire community. In others, where the separation of economic and political powers was at least nominally clear, the law-enforcement agencies enacted and enforced laws that gave monopoly rights to each of the various guilds in the town. Frequently such laws were

237

justified as necessary to protect consumers from exploitation by unscrupulous craftsmen and traders; for example, the authorities would establish minimal standards for bread, and then grant to the local bakers' guild sole right to supply townsmen with bread of this quality. In return, the guilds provided political authorities with a reliable source of revenue and with equally reliable, since highly organized, popular support.

By the fourteenth century, the guilds and political authority had in most parts of Western Europe become integrated on a local basis into a monolithic system of control. The political organization provided the coercive basis for preserving guild monopoly, with the guilds supplying the economic means for maintaining the political agencies. The centralization of political authority that came with the rise of nationalism somewhat weakened these local structures, and kings and princes occasionally attempted to destroy by legal fiat the concordance between political and guild organization. It persisted, nonetheless, and retarded the development of individual economic enterprise, until the industrial revolution and the political revolutions that it fostered brought the entire system to an end.

Enforced Monopolies

The history of the medieval guilds does not provide us with a standard against which to evaluate the organizational trends of contemporary American society, but it does provide suggestive parallels. As with the early medieval guilds, early efforts on the part of both business enterprises and labor unions to gain monopoly positions almost invariably led to extralegal use of force. The business that could neither buy out its competitors nor ruin them by uneconomic competition might then employ gangs of hoodlums to sabotage the properties and intimidate the customers of its competitors. It was in part by these latter means that the original Standard Oil Company almost, but not quite, secured a monopoly over the production and distribution in the United States of petroleum products. Labor unions, too, frequently used force in the effort to prevent nonunion members from working in the craft over which they claimed jurisdiction; and both employers and unions resorted to force, each against the other, in the effort of each to achieve monopoly powers over the other.

More rapidly than in the case of the medieval guilds, but in quite similar ways, political authorities came to sanction and protect through law the "rights" of organized business and equally organized labor. Those rights are far from being today as monopolistic as were the rights of the medieval guilds; the concordance between economic and political organization is far less complete than it was during the Middle Ages; and both forms of organization are now national rather than local. It is, however, already certain that the ability of highly bureaucratic business, professional, and labor organizations to survive depends now, as did the guilds in the Middle Ages, upon their achieving and maintaining a monopoly position.* And it is equally certain that this position is now, and for the first time since the industrial revolution, being fostered by local, state, and federal political agencies.

To some extent, political intervention in the affairs of business and labor was made inevitable by the resort to force on the part of both business and labor that stemmed from their monopolistic endeavors. Thus the growing concordance between modern economic and political organizations can be interpreted as simply a means whereby political authority maintains peace between economic organizations. There is no doubt that most of the early laws governing business and, later, most of those intended to prevent labor violence and encourage peaceful settlement of disputes between labor unions and employers were directed to this simple end. Long since, however, the police powers of government, American as well as European, have been extended far beyond this simple objective. They have come to include, first, the protection of individual mem-

---

* A few of the studies of this tendency are: *Challenge to a Free World*, by W. Berge (Washington, D.C.: Public Affairs Press, 1946); *Retail Trade Associations*, by H. Levy (New York: Oxford University Press, 1944); *The Concentration of Economic Power*, by D. Lynch (New York: Columbia University Press, 1946); *Giant Business: Threat to Democracy*, by T. K. Quinn (New York: Exposition Press, Inc., 1953); *Monopoly and Social Control*, by H. A. Wells (Washington, D.C.: Public Affairs Press, 1952); and *Monopoly in America: The Government as Promoter*, by Walter Adams and Horace M. Gray (New York: The Macmillan Company, 1955).

bers of society from too grievous economic exploitation and, second and quite recently, the protection of economic organizations—business enterprises, professional groups, and labor unions—from unfair competition either with individuals or with other organizations.

What may well, then, have originated simply as an effort to preserve the peace has now evolved into a system of politically supported quasi monopolies that differ mainly in size and scope from the guilds of the Middle Ages. In the process, the political principles that obtained for more than a century and a half have been abandoned, and new and more inclusive principles have been developed. In that process also, governmental agencies have proliferated at a constantly accelerating rate and have expanded even more rapidly. With each advance and extension of political control, organizations, especially large organizations, have been granted further rights, the rights of the individual being to that extent reduced. All this has come about in piecemeal fashion, without any consistent ideological guidance, in response to the demands of various self-interest groups and with the tacit consent of the general public. Yet its cumulative effects are those of a major revolution in our way of life.*

The fact that this revolution has been accomplished by peaceful means seems to have obscured the fact that the changes accomplished constitute a reversal of prior principles and practices. Everyone is presumably aware of the fact that government was called

---

* Every taxpayer over the age of forty must be painfully aware of the recent tremendous growth in the size and scope of our various governmental agencies. Those who came in late and are consequently inclined to accept as normal the high level of current governmental activities may find the following comments illuminating: During the nineteenth century the governments of the United States seem to have cost in taxes between 6 and 8 per cent of the national income as measured in dollars and to have employed less than 4 per cent of the labor force. Currently governmental employees constitute 14 per cent of the labor force and the costs of government close to one third of the net national product. Should the upward trends of the past twenty years continue, the United States would be completely socialized by 1975.

A detailed and carefully documented study of the changes in the scope, character, and social costs of government in America between 1900 and 1949 is provided by Solomon Fabricant in *The Trend in Government Activity in the United States Since 1900* (Washington, D.C.: National Bureau of Economic Research, Publication No. 56, 1950).

upon to rescue the American people from the crisis of the great depression, and apparently almost everyone assumes that government did do so. But few Americans seem to be clearly conscious of the fact that what began as emergency actions by the government during the depression years have been continued and even extended during the postdepression, postwar period. The changes in the scope and role of government in recent years have been characterized by some who are critical of them as "creeping socialism"; but this term hardly begins to suggest the magnitude, the rapidity, or the significance of what has been occurring.

For one thing, recent changes in America as elsewhere have made the classical controversy over capitalism versus socialism entirely meaningless. We have already exceeded the hopeful expectations of the socialist theorists, Marxians excluded, in socializing the means of production and in determining the distribution of what is produced; and we have accomplished this in ways quite different from those that were proposed by the socialists. In so doing, we have violated a major tenet of both capitalistic and socialistic, Marxian included, ideology. Both ideologies had great, although differing, faith in man, the one in the powers of individual initiative to produce social values, the other in the perfectibility of man; whereas our recent extensions of governmental control have been based upon the implicit assumption that man is neither individually competent nor collectively self-reliant. Much of the recent extension of governmental functions has been based upon the implicit assumption that man is fully as weak and inherently incompetent as the Freudians profess him to be. On this morbid assumption, governments are assuming a responsibility for the welfare of each individual citizen and each class, category, and organizational unit of citizens that is essentially maternalistic; for governmental agencies are currently expected to bestow benefits without demanding anything of equivalent value in return.

Many a government has been looked upon and to some extent has operated as an impersonal, large-scale father of fathers. As a sort of institutional patriarch of its citizens, such a government has been more or less paternalistic in function. As with the traditional paternalistic role, it has assumed protective functions; but also in accordance with that traditional role, it has demanded obedience and sacrifices from the citizen in return for its protection—in fact, to make such protection possible. In contrast, the current trend in most Western governments, the United States included, is toward a functional role within society somewhat comparable to that of the properly permissive mother in the family. Each governmental agency (excepting the police and those collecting taxes) is supposed to grant rights, political and otherwise, to all who fall within its jurisdiction in order that none shall suffer adversity through their improvidence, incompetence, or misadventure; and it is supposed somehow to make such helpful grants without imposing obligations upon the citizens. For such would, in the current view, be both undemocratic and counter to the nature of man.

Politics and the Prevailing Ethic

The political revolutions of the latter eighteenth and early nineteenth centuries, both here and abroad, did not follow the current textbook pattern. They were not the product of discontent among the masses; they were not spontaneous uprisings of exploited peasantry or town laborers who had endured much but come at last to the breaking point; nor were they irresponsible and wantonly destructive. The 1789 French revolution did, it is true, get badly out of hand; and before it had run its course the rabble of Paris was using the guillotine for its own sadistic pleasure. But even in France revolution was brought about by leaders of the *bourgeoisie* as a calculated, and ultimately effective, means of releasing men from their bondage to the past. That past was represented by the landed aristocracy, a heritage of feudalism, and by the restrictive regulations of the guilds and the political controls that had grown up through the Middle Ages to secure the monopoly position of the guilds, all of which were delaying the full flowering of the age of enterprise.

The political philosophy underlying these revolutions was both simple and forthright: Government is an evil, but a necessary one. The only valid function of government is the use of force to prevent individual members of society from using force in the pursuit of their personal ends. The least evil government is, therefore, one that is constantly accountable to the socially responsible members of society. Neither the hereditary elite nor the working class can be entrusted to use the instrument of government with that parsimony which is essential if it is to maintain a balance between the evil of anarchy, on the one hand, and the twin evils of autocracy and demagoguery, on the other. Only government of and by the *bourgeoisie* can, that is to say, truly serve the interests of the people; for it is they who are the socially responsible members of society.

The governments of postrevolutionary Europe and North America were, with the partial exception of always ambiguous France, largely under the control of the *bourgeoisie;* and they quite naturally gave political expression and sanctioning to the values and sentiments of the Protestant ethic. In a negative way they did this by repeal or nonenforcement of the maze of laws that had for long hampered entrepreneurs. Many of these laws had grown up during the commercial revolution to prevent the free exchange of goods with other nations—a political effort that was predicated upon the assumption that the wealth of a nation is to be measured by the gold in the king's treasury; *ergo,* sell goods abroad, but buy at home. The remainder of these laws were a heritage from the Middle Ages, old laws affecting the ownership and use of real property, especially land, and equally old laws supporting the restrictive and monopolistic practices of the guilds. The revocation of such laws did much to lift the dead hand of the past and thus enable men of initiative and enterprise to expend themselves in the application and further development of the new techniques of production. The results were not always or immediately conducive to the common good; but the opportunity to experiment, unhampered by restrictive legislation, was essential to the development of industrial society.

Equally vital, and some would say even more important, was the positive encouragement that the postrevolutionary governments gave to men of enterprise. That encouragement consisted, in principle, of forcing all members of society to be responsible, both individually and collectively, for fulfilling their contractual obligations.

One of the distinguishing characteristics of the *bourgeoisie* was that they were as individuals morally bound to enter into no agreements that they could not reasonably expect to fulfill and to honor to the full those into which they did enter. Foresight, prudence, and integrity were essential to respectability, in economic as well as marital and other realms of life. The aristocrats and landed gentry were subject to no such scruples; and the rising class of urban workers often had neither the will nor the means to fulfill the contractual obligations that they undertook in the grim struggle for sheer survival.

Law is at best a fragile substitute for moral standards; but the laws governing contract that were enacted by the postrevolutionary governments did give the honest and economically responsible man some legal assurance that others would behave toward him as he was morally bound to behave toward them. They enabled him to collect rents from his tenants, to recall an absconding business partner, to force customers to pay for the goods they bought from him, and so on. They also led to a rapid growth of debtors' prisons, to an increase of indentured labor, to the corporate form of business enterprise, and, in time, to the charge that government was of, by, and for business.

The effort to obtain conformity by all members of society to the core values of the Protestant ethic through the force of government was accompanied, with somewhat less success, by an attempt to make government itself a responsible agency. The national governments of medieval and early modern Europe were often highly personal and always irresponsible, most particularly in respect to economic matters. Taxes were levied in the most whimsical fashion, and the rights to collect were often simply sold to the highest bidder; the currency was frequently debased in order to make a royal profit; and the contracts entered into in the name of the king were no better than the king's marriage vows. In so far as the government represented anybody outside the king and the court, it reflected the values and sentiments of the landed gentry, who while they made much of honor on the field of battle and in the chase had no morals whatever in regard to economic matters.

It was in considerable measure because the early governments lacked integrity that private bankers were called upon to finance and provide the medium of exchange for the commercial revolution. The private bankers, such as the house of Rothschild, guaranteed that the gold in coins that bore their mark was fine and true to weight and that the banknotes they issued would be redeemed upon demand or at a stated time and place in gold or its equivalent. None of the then existing national governments could even give assurance that they would be in power a year hence or that, if they were, they would be both willing and able to redeem a pledge.

With the beginnings of the industrial revolution the need for economically responsible government became crucial, for the private bankers could not supply the large quantities of stable currency that were necessary if the new techniques of production were to be exploited. The contractual arrangements between traders were then, as they still are, relatively short-run affairs; and what is important to the trader is that the monetary terms specified in his contract to buy or sell will remain valid until the transaction is completed—that, for example, the gold sovereigns specified in his agreement to buy or sell will be of the same gold content then as now. The monetary needs of the early industrialists, on the other hand, were far more complex; they needed a rapidly increasing supply of money that would at the same time be relatively stable in terms of its purchasing power over the years. The cost of building a factory was very high; and whatever return the investment brought, if any, came only in the course of years. The private bankers had for long made gold their basic measure of value; and since the gold supply was fairly constant, they in this way achieved a degree of monetary stability. They could not, however, in the same way provide the greatly increased quantity of that medium that was needed. Government, on the other hand, could—and often did—offer an inexhaustible supply of monetary tokens (promises to pay in gold or silver); but unhappily their value, as measured either in gold or goods, was subject to rapid decline. What was needed by the rising class of industrialists was a monetary medium that had the stability provided by the private bankers and the quantitative flexibility provided by fickle government. The two ends are inherently incompatible; but a workable compromise was achieved by the postrevolutionary governments through the nationalization of currency based upon gold.

Political leadership by the *bourgeoisie* did not succeed in achieving governments that were wholly responsible, either in economic or other respects. It did, however, develop governmental forms and procedures that gave some semblance of stability to the governing process, that reduced the role of personal whimsy, and that made the governors subject to both the law and the people—essentially the middle classes—whom they represented. No government has ever operated for long and in all respects in terms of the Protestant ethic; but during most of the nineteenth century the governments of Western Europe and North America came closer to that ideal than any government has before or since. Moreover, it was to a considerable degree the fact that these governments represented and to some extent operated in terms of the Protestant ethic that made possible the rapid development of industrial technology and the emergence of what is now contemptuously termed the "capitalistic system."

The decline, most marked during the past quarter century, of the old *bourgeoisie* has been accompanied and no doubt accelerated by parallel changes in governmental policies and practices. In the long run, it may be assumed, people get the kind of government that they want or, at least, deserve. While the *bourgeoisie* were on the ascendancy, economically and politically, Western governments tended to force conformity to some elements of the Protestant ethic upon those classes of the population that were not by cultural training industrious and foresightful and, at the same time, to operate at least minimally in the same terms.

The recent and rapid assumption by government of responsibility for the welfare of the individual citizen and of economic and other kinds of organizations is closely related to the rise of the new *bourgeoisie* and the growth of guildlike characteristics in business, industrial, professional, labor, and other work organizations. Without the former, the latter developments would have for the most part been impossible; and only to the extent that governmental effort is successful can the latter maintain their present estates. Should the currently responsible governmental agencies fail to maintain full employment, easy credit, steadily but slowly rising price levels, including those of agricultural products, and all the other maternal benefits to which the new *bourgeoisie* as a class, unionized labor as a class, and the various occupational organizations through which the members of both classes secure employment have become accustomed, every individual, every class of individuals, and every organization would then be thrown back upon its own resources. The result would, no doubt, be catastrophic.

There is no real reason to think that man is inherently weak and incompetent, that he is individually incapable of assuming responsibility for his own welfare, that his organizations are thus by nature fragile and in constant need of protection, or that only through constant and indulgent political ministrations can a society be kept operating effectively. This idea of man, so ardently propagated by the Freudians, has, however, during the past few decades been given political validation; and as governments have assumed maternal responsibility for maintaining society, the individual citizen and his organizations have tended to acquire a dependence upon a political maternalism that differs only in form and degree from the maternal love, affection, and permissive care which the Freudians believe are essential to the psychic welfare of every child.

Of, by, and for Organized Groups

The nature of political maternalism may be summarized by saying that, in assuming responsiblity for the welfare of its various citizens, government relieves them of responsibility for themselves, thus discouraging initiative and self-reliance, and that in the attempt to fulfill this assumed responsibility, government necessarily becomes itself irresponsible. How long an irresponsible government can actually fulfill its assumed responsibilities remains to be seen. Limited attempts of this sort have been made throughout the history of civilization, both in the West and the East; and all have sooner or later come to a bad end. There would appear to be certain inherent disadvantages to reliance upon government as the means of securing the production and distribution of social values. There is certainly an inherent danger in placing too great reliance for the maintenance of a society upon any one agency or any one system of agencies, political or otherwise. And there is no good reason to believe that modern governments are any better qualified to design and bring into being the good society than were the governments of five hundred or five thousand years ago.

All these doubts apply, of course, to *any* attempt to determine by political means the basic structure and processes of society. Military conquerors have sometimes succeeded in establishing themselves as the political elite of the society that they conquered; more often they have either exterminated the native population or been in time absorbed into the indigenous society. Seldom, if ever, have they been able to produce through forceful means the kind of social system that they have desired. Political conquest, such as that by a revolutionary junta dedicated to the creation of a better—or at least different—society has always been short-lived; and the enduring results have been trivial in comparison with the effort expended and the chaos produced.

What most clearly distinguishes our own current heavy reliance upon government from past experiments—including such varied ones as those of ancient Rome and modern Russia—is that it has evolved from within rather than been forced from without. It is an oversimplification to say that the political maternalism of modern America is a response to the public will; the American people are not one but many things, and politically as well as otherwise they differentiate into a wide variety of unstable publics. There is, however, a world of difference between the coercive and propagandistic procedures by which the Russian people have been made to accept—however superficially—the bureaucratic rule that is ideologically supposed to bring into being communal society, and the legislative procedures by which we have established new political agencies and expanded the functions of old ones. Under our political system, designed and put into operation, as it was, by the old *bourgeoisie*, new legislation invariably reflects the will of some block of voters rather than simply that of our legislators or political administrators.

Many of the recent extensions of political authority have in a sense been forced upon us, but by scientific, technological, and organizational changes rather than by political bodies or political self-interest groups. Perhaps there is no need for us to have public-health agencies; but if we did not, the death rate would be very much higher than it is now; for our current high spatial mobility, the fact that we derive our foodstuffs from widely scattered sources, and the fact that we live for the most part in dense urban aggregates combine to make us extraordinarily susceptible to epidemic diseases. The biological sciences have, fortunately, enabled us to devise protective measures; but such measures cannot be put into effect by individuals or, even, by voluntary associations of any sort. They must be enforced, and usually over large numbers of people.

What applies to public-health agencies applies also to many of the other political agencies, local, state, and federal, that we have brought into being. If we are to use the products of Detroit, we must have public roads and regulate conduct upon those roads. If we build our houses of wood, we must have a governmental agency to put out the fires that will occasionally occur. If we are to perpetuate the forests in order that future generations may have wood, we must have public forest preserves. If we require that our children be educated at public expense, then we must have the political machinery to collect school taxes and maintain the schools.

It is impossible to determine how much of our present political apparatus has evolved to provide these and comparable public services. Public education absorbs nearly one fifth of the total governmental manpower (or woman power); and of course a very considerable proportion of the money and manpower expended by local and state governments goes into the provision of streets and roads, drainage and water supply, the protection of persons and physical properties, etc. Nor can there be any doubt that some of the recent increase in governmental agencies and expansion of governmental functions is to be accounted for by increasing demands for such public services; our cities are growing bigger, the propor-tion of children higher, our road and highway systems more exten-sive and elaborate, etc.

But the major part of the expansion, at least of our federal govern-ment if not that of local and state governments, is to be accounted for by the depression, wartime, and postwar enlargement of our military establishments on the one hand and development of social welfare and other maternalistic endeavors on the other. The former is by far the most significant quantitatively. Defense, including atomic-energy development and foreign military aid, has taken one half and more of the total annual national budgets since the end of World War II. For the first time in our history we are a military power—one of the two great military powers in the world. The effects upon our economy are, of course, profound. The ability of military agencies to direct the disposition of more than 10 per cent of the national income gives them great power over those industries that produce military equipments, enables them to influence the direction of technological research and development, and makes the military career attractive to considerable numbers of ambitious young men who might otherwise go into socially productive activities.

The money costs of our new political maternalism, with the exception of the social-welfare and the agricultural programs, do not loom large in the budgets of either the federal or state and local governments. They may account for the direct disposition of no more than 5 per cent of the national income. This figure is, however, misleading for two reasons. First, many of our current maternalistic measures are simply matters of law and law enforcement, and do not show up in budgetary terms. Such is, for example, the case with federal fiscal policy, whereby the supply of money and credit is manipulated. Second, the fact that governments now draw off nearly one third of the national income in taxes means that methods of levying taxes have become a profound influence upon the conduct of business and industry and, what may be even more important, upon many of the decisions made by the individual members of society—occupational choices, level of endeavor, time and occasion for retirement, disposition of income, etc. Moreover, political maternalism combined with the new guildism seems to encourage, as we have seen, those forms of conduct characteristic of the new *bourgeoisie.*

Through the nineteenth century and well into this century our governments tended to reflect the values and sentiments of the old *bourgeoisie,* and thus to operate in considerable measure upon principle—responsibility, integrity, and regard for the consequences to society at large. The transition to political maternalism, which became marked during the New Deal period of the 1930's, was accompanied by an equally radical—although only implicit—shift from government by principle to government of, by, and for specific organized vested-interest groups. Established interest groups have always exerted pressure upon governments, ancient and modern, autocratic or democratic; and no government or governmental agency has ever been entirely able to ignore such pressures. Within the last twenty-five years, however, the political will to resist the demands of large blocks of voters—in particular, business, labor, veterans, and agriculture—seems to have all but disappeared. It has become a part of our political mores for legislators and political administrative agencies to see themselves as caterers to the public will, so much so that political scientists have come of late to define the function of government as that of brokerage.*

To the extent, evidently considerable, that our governments are now operating as brokers, bringing together the conflicting demands of various self-interest groups and resolving through legislation or administrative decree an exchange of values, they are functioning on an organizational level very much in accordance with the current rules for good parental care. Everyone (every strong pressure group) is right and should have his wants promptly satisfied, and nothing of course should be demanded of anyone in return. Such political acquiescence cannot possibly lead to the granting of everyone's demands, but it does tend to result in a devious political robbery of Peter to pay Paul and of Paul to pay Peter. It also makes for contradictory, improvident, unstable, and irresponsible political action.†

---

* The broker-role concept of American government is defined and accepted as desirable—or at least inevitable—by James McG. Burns and Jack W. Peltason in *Government by the People* (New York: Prentice-Hall, Inc., 1952. Chapter 18). There is an interesting parallel between David Riesman's thesis that the American personality type has shifted from what he terms "inner-directed" to that of "outer-directed" and the political change from government by principle to government by popular demand.

† As just one example, and a minor one at that, of the kind of contradiction that arises when government attempts to give every interest group what it desires, consider the fact that the United States Department of Agriculture is currently endeavoring to reduce the production of price-supported agricultural products by paying farmers to remove land from cultivation (the so-called

Political Irresponsibility

Applied to professional politicians, the phrase "political integrity" is hardly more than a juxtaposition of contradictory terms. Whatever the society, whatever the nature of the political system, the professional politician corrupts means to ends; and his one constant end is to gain and maintain political position. It is for this reason that the rules for success in politics promulgated by Machiavelli are as applicable to contemporary America as they were to fifteenth-century Italy. But a political system, as distinct from the men who occupy its policy-making offices, may operate with a high degree of organizational integrity. Wherever the law becomes traditionalized or, as is more often the case, it is reinforcement of tradition and those who administer that law are either steeped in this tradition (as lawyers and jurists tend to be) or else bureaucratic functionaries (as are most political administrators), government operates with remarkable consistency through time and with extraordinary freedom from corruption.

The politicians of an earlier day were probably no better or worse than those whom we elect to office today; but the demands made upon them were quite different. The modern politician is expected to serve his constituents in much the same manner as the properly permissive mother is required to serve her children. He is expected to give but never to receive; that is to say, every special-interest group in the society expects special political aid and support of some sort or other from one or more of our governmental agencies without giving anything—except, perhaps, re-election of the politician —in return. Such expectations are based upon the assumption, which currently prevails, that government can and therefore should assume responsibility for the welfare of everyone and everything. The hard fact is, however, that government is rarely a creator of social

"soil bank program") while the United States Department of Interior is annually spending hundreds of millions of dollars to bring new (mainly arid) land into cultivation. For details of this and other contradictions in the political pampering of American agriculture, see Charles M. Hardin, *The Politics of Agriculture* (Glencoe, Illinois: The Free Press, 1952).

values. It may arrange for the production of social values, as it does when it applies tax funds to the construction—by private contractors—of roads; it may remove discouragements to the production of social values, as it does through criminal law; and it may direct the distribution of social values, as it does when public funds are applied to the support of indigents. But government is by its very nature an agency of control rather than creation; so what it gives to Paul it must take from Peter, and what it confers on Peter it must derive from Paul.

One of the tangible consequences of the recent efforts of government to contribute to the welfare of contradictory self-interest groups has been the abandonment of financial integrity. Wars in particular and economic crises in general invariably brought about some suspension of sound bourgeois practices and permitted such expedients as debit financing of government and more or less deliberate debasement of the currency. In some instances, such as post-Napoleonic France and post-World War I Germany, governments abrogated all prior financial commitments, with devastating results to whole classes of citizens, usually and most destructively the middle classes. Nevertheless, for well over a century Western governments struggled, sometimes against great counterpressures, to maintain some semblance of financial integrity. All professed adherence to the principle of the balanced national budget, except during the exigencies of war. And all made heroic efforts to maintain a stable currency, either through reliance on the gold or on the bimetallic standard.

Germany lost her political integrity during and immediately after World War I; and with the rise of the Nazis to power, fiscal policy became an instrument of power politics and, subsequently, of war. France never did recover from the emergency measures, financial and otherwise, that were taken during that war; but the other Allied nations returned, as quickly as circumstances permitted, to or toward the balanced budget and a stable currency. On the whole, then, the principle of governmental responsibility persisted until 1931, when England and the Scandinavian countries abandoned the gold standard and, with it, the idea that a government should finance current expenditures out of current income. The United States held on for another year; but immediately upon assuming office, the government of President Roosevelt withdrew minted gold from circulation, took the United States off the gold standard, and set industriously about priming the economic pump with printing-press public moneys. The direct effects upon the economy of these and related moves are impossible to evaluate. These measures did, however, mark the end of a very remarkable period in political history, a period during which most governments had adhered with reasonable fidelity to the principle of financial responsibility.

The abandonment by the United States and other nations of the gold standard and the principle of the balanced budget was presumed to be temporary. It was generally believed that, with the passing of the economic crisis, we would return to the old political morality. But the crisis of the great depression led imperceptibly into the greater crisis of World War II, and that in turn has led to the anticipated crisis of World War III. Each succeeding crisis has been made a justification for perpetuating and intensifying the original crisis measures, until by now the concept of a financially responsible government is hardly more than a memory in the minds of nostalgic elders. Even the economists have for the most part capitulated, discarding the views of their old prophet Adam Smith in favor of the new-day doctrine of John Maynard Keynes.

In the dark years of the depression, the English economist Keynes found a satisfactory rationale for the economic antics of his and other governments. In times of national economic crisis, he decided, even as in times of war, political principles must give way to economic expediency. Specifically, the principles of a balanced national budget and a stable currency should be abandoned; and the government should undertake to stimulate business activity by every available means, including financial subsidies to business and industry, legalization of price fixing, publicly financed building and other projects, and an increase through doles and in other ways of consumers' buying power.

Keynes's goal, increase in the national production, was the same as that of the laissez-faire economists and fully in accord with the Protestant ethic; but his means were in direct violation of the principle of responsible government; and whatever he may have intended, the events of the past twenty-five years have demonstrated that irresponsible government tends to be self-perpetuating. The monetary measure of the irresponsibility of modern governments is the rapid rise in public debt and the progressive decline in the purchasing power of the monetary medium. In so far as the countries of Western Europe are concerned, much of this, though by no means all, can be accounted for by the economic stress of World War II; for since the war only Holland and West Germany have made any real effort either to get government onto a pay-as-you-go program or to stabilize their currency. Except for Switzerland, other governments of Europe have become habituated to debit financing and recurrent devaluation of the monetary medium. In these countries inflation has become chronic. That chronic inflation is now a consequence of political maternalism rather than of economic crisis is suggested by the fact that the national debt of the United States has continued to rise during the years since World War II and the real value of the dollar to diminish, although the total national production of goods has been increasing rapidly.

Some economists have concluded that the constant rise in our national production has been caused by inflation; and on this assumption they advocate "controlled" inflation as a desirable political policy. The assumption is dubious, and the idea that it is politically possible to foster inflation and at the same time keep it under control is hardly tenable. Monetary devaluation, once begun, is a self-perpetuating process that can be checked only by economic catastrophe. It is a complex parallel to check-hiking and to the less spectacular but in the end possibly quite as disastrous practice of progressive borrowing on futures to pay for current maintenance. Unquestionably it has been political efforts to give financial support or favor to various and contradictory self-interest groups that have resulted in progressive postwar inflation in the United States as elsewhere. Many of these efforts, such as that of the Federal Housing Authority, which was established during the depression years to stimulate the building of homes, were no doubt perfectly sound emergency measures. Some of them, such as the parity price support program for agriculture, may not have been sound even as emergency measures; but their inception can at least be justified on the grounds that under the economic crisis that existed almost any action was better than none. The trouble is that, having been established to meet a momentary and special economic problem, such measures are seldom abandoned with the passing of the crisis. Rather, they accumulate, each new measure generating dependence upon it by some or many interest groups (including the governmental bureaucracy established to administer it).

As maternalistic governmental measures accumulate, they tend to produce crises necessitating new maternalistic measures. Thus as debit financing, agricultural subsidies, politically encouraged mortgage debts, and other measures pushed up the cost of living, the time came when organized labor refused to enter into long-range contracts with employers. Labor did not want to be committed to dollar wage levels while the value of the dollar was declining; on the other hand, employers could not program their operations on the basis of short-run labor contracts that might end in prolonged and contentious negotiations with labor unions. The conflict was resolved, with the encouragement of interested governmental agencies, by the now widely used "escalator clause" in labor contracts, by which wages are periodically adjusted to changes in the value of the dollar. Since that value has continued to decline, the result is periodic increase in wage levels; and each such increase in wages contributes in turn to further decline in the value of the dollar.

The economic improvidence of the new *bourgeoisie* is undoubtedly related to the fact that the members of this class have come to maturity during a period of inflation. During a period of rapidly rising prices, individuals are encouraged to purchase goods rather than accumulate savings, and to borrow heavily on their future in order to invest in such relatively durable goods as houses, furniture, and automobiles. They anticipate that their monetary incomes will rise as prices rise and that, therefore, they can expediently borrow in order to make purchases at present prices. Inevitably, their borrowing for advance purchasing makes its contribution to the inflationary process. When this process will come to an end, and what social and economic dislocations will in the end terminate it, it is impossible to predict. But when that time comes, government will, no doubt, be expected to protect everyone and every major organiza-

tion from adversity—to protect debtors from the demands of
creditors; to protect creditors from defaulting debtors; to prevent
wages from falling (for the unions will undoubtedly abrogate the
escalator clause should the cost of living start to decline); to maintain full employment; to hold up agricultural prices on the one hand
and corporate profits on the other; and to do all this while tax income
is sharply declining. For just as a child who is pampered and guided
grows in dependence with the passing years, groups that are
indulged by maternalistic government become ever more reliant
upon political support and protection.

II

The Security Goal

POLITICAL MATERNALISM is by no means new. Governments have often given special rights and privileges to some favored class or group within the social population. But until very recently political maternalism has always been narrowly restricted to one or two special-interest groups; and under these conditions Paul was definitely and visibly robbed to pay Peter. Today the granting of special benefits by government has become generalized; the goal is for government to give everyone everything he needs and to relieve him of personal responsibility for his welfare.

It is perhaps possible for a patient and sturdy mother to give to her progeny all the protective attentions that they demand of her; she gives, as it were, of herself. But government cannot give of itself; what government gives to one it must take from others. The special privileges, subsidies, or protection from competition that it grants one individual or class of individuals can be procured only by imposing new obligations, taxes, or constraints on some other individual or class. The net effect of systematic political giving-and-taking-away may conceivably be greater momentary security for all; the long-run consequences are a matter of speculation. But it is obvious enough that security provided through governmental action can be had only by increasing reliance on coercion as a means of control.

The effectiveness of any political action rests ultimately upon the threat of force. A governmental agency that is dealing with private contractors may rely upon economic incentives, and the one that is distributing gratuities can depend upon the avarice of its dependents; but the money or other value used in these ways has to be extracted from citizens in the form of taxes or a reduction of rights, and few citizens pay taxes willingly or voluntarily renounce established rights. A properly maternalistic government may endeavor so to balance political gratuities and political deprivations that each interest group within the population will think that it is securing more than it gives; * but while the effort to do so may foster a considerable degree of abstract loyalty to and approval of the government, it does nothing to reduce the need for coercive threats to make laws and administrative rulings effective. It is one thing to approve of a law or regulation on principle and quite another to give up wealth or valued rights as demanded by that law or regulation. So, as every government since that of Rameses I has known, a law without teeth is but empty words on the statute books.

Coercion versus Social Controls

Coercion, both the sanctioned kind exercised by established government and that relied upon by thugs and bandits, is universal; and apparently, there are some things that can be accomplished in no other way. Properly exercised force can induce individuals to pay taxes and renounce some valued rights, although there are always some limits to what any government can secure from its citizens in this way. The threat of force can deter individuals from doing some things that they might otherwise undertake to do, although, again, there are always some limits, as the history of crime so clearly demonstrates. The threat of force, though more commonly its application, can under certain conditions induce actions that would not otherwise occur—such is the mechanism of slavery, of indentured labor, and of military conquest.

Except during times of war and revolution, however, coercion is quantitatively the least important of the forces that control the conduct of the members of society. Even in modern society, where

* David M. Potter (*People of Plenty.* Chicago: University of Chicago Press, 1954) has observed that it is only during a period of rapidly rising national production that government can maintain the illusion that it gives to all more than it takes from any. In his view, then, current political maternalism is a consequence of rather than a condition making for the present high levels of income.

the scope of governments is Brobdingnagian, most of the behavior of any individual is a consequence of habit, of calculated self-interest, or of conformity to social—as distinct from political—controls. He pays his taxes minimally and reluctantly; he drives his car more or less in accordance with the legal regulations; but most of what he does he does because he wants to, because he thinks it economically expedient or socially desirable to do so. That most of what he does is at least within the law simply reflects the fact that even in our society most law is legal reinforcement of cultural and local standards of behavior, of what is considered right and proper, and actively affects only those few individuals who are inclined to violate the standards.*

The inherently limited role of coercion in determining social behavior is most clearly seen when attempts are made to prevent or to induce change by political action. The early modern governments attempted to preserve the traditional rights of the landed gentry and of the guildsmen; but while these efforts to prevent change may have delayed the industrial revolution, they did not prevent it. Today our own government is attempting, with little success, to prevent the industrialization of agriculture—a matter that will be discussed in some detail shortly. Many current political efforts are directed toward bringing about social changes that are deemed socially—or perhaps just politically—desirable. When the area involved is both limited and tangible, as it is, say, with urban slum clearance and mosquito abatement, such efforts may be quite effective. When the change sought through legislation is one that is already well under way, legal reinforcement may perhaps somewhat accelerate it; such is, possibly, the case with federal effort to bring about educational desegregation in our Southern states. When, however, the change desired is extensive, complex, and contrary to existing trends, political reforms almost certainly fail. Whenever any considerable proportion of a people are opposed by

---

* A detailed analysis of social controls as one of the major determinants of individual conformity to social norms and of the relatively slight role of law in producing socially acceptable individual conduct is provided by Richard T. LaPiere in *A Theory of Social Control* (New York: McGraw-Hill Book Company, 1954).

habit, by self-interest, or the powers of social controls to what is politically demanded of them, they rebel; and the change does not occur.

The Freudian concept of man may lend a sort of ideological support to the prevalent idea that only through legislation—*i.e.*, governmental coercion—can anything be achieved. For if man were, as the Freudians hold, born with innate and enduring antisocial drives (or, as some of them describe it, born a criminal), then nothing short of force would keep him acting in a reasonably civilized manner. Moreover, if, as they also believe, man were by nature such a weak and inherently incapable creature that he could do nothing that is socially constructive without external compulsion, then nothing short of inclusive political coercion would induce the members of society to produce and distribute the social values that maintain a society. That such a society would, in their own terms, be self-defeating, in that the conflict between each individual and his society would be unendurable, can be ignored; for there are other and far more definite reasons for believing that the scope of coercive control, and hence the ultimate powers of political action, are far less than the advocates of political maternalism realize.

All the current efforts to give protective political rights and privileges to every individual citizen, every class of citizens, and every organization through which citizens operate to secure their livelihood are attempts to produce calculated changes in the society; and all are predicated upon the assumption that social changes can be planned in advance. This assumption is at best wishful thinking; but it is made by all legislators and political administrators, today as in times past, and is upheld by all advocates of some specific social reform. Legislators and political administrators, in accordance with the customary obligations of the offices that they hold, must proceed as though they had some foreknowledge of the social consequences of their actions; social reformers can be, for the most part, dismissed as people with very admirable intentions. But no one, not even the social scientist, can predict the social effects of even minor reformistic endeavors—political or otherwise; and unless it is possible to predict in advance the social consequences of any new form of action, it is patently impossible to plan or program any change in the society. The most that can be said is that calculated attempts to bring about social changes will undoubtedly produce many and mainly unanticipated social consequences.

Decline of Individualism

We cannot as yet predict what a given change in a given aspect of society will lead to. We can, however, evaluate the consequences of past changes; and it is already evident that political maternalism has thrown the social balance against the man of enterprise, erected many discouragements to the generation and expression of individual initiative, and rendered more or less obsolete the values and sentiments of the Protestant ethic. Like the occupational guildism to which it lends support, political maternalism has already given considerable advantage to the man of no-enterprise, to the social conformist, to the willing dependent; and in so doing it has provided a rather favorable climate for the individual who exhibits the passive characteristics honored by the Freudian ethic.

With each extension of political maternalism the individual is devaluated, and organization—in this case political—is exalted; for with each such extension some class of individuals is deprived of the pre-existing right to determine, for good or ill, their own conduct in some respect or other. As this right is taken from individuals and nonpolitical organizations of individuals, it is transferred to some centralized political authority. It may be held that under our system of representative government—local, state, and federal—political authority expresses the public will and, hence, cannot deprive citizens of the right of self-determination. But since even under our most felicitous political system a political authority can through any single action express the will—that is, cater to the special interests— of only a small proportion of those who come under political jurisdiction of that authority, every such action is more or less contrary to the will of the majority. That all in the end secure some such representation does not change the fact that most of what any political authority does is contrary to the will of most of those whom the authority represents.

One of the distinguishing characteristics of early American society was the prevalence of the idea of local self-determination—of the inherent right of a number of people to determine for themselves to what principles and practices they would collectively subscribe. The principle of local autonomy was manifest in the New England Town Meeting; in the federation—rather than actual unification—of the colonies; in the persistence of the idea of states' rights—*i.e.*, of the sovereignty of the state as a political unit; in the strong and until now largely successful resistance to national integration of public-school education; in the separation of church and state, and the local autonomy of all the Protestant churches; and in the reliance upon the principle of federation rather than integration in the activities of a wide variety of organizations from college fraternities to labor unions.

There is still a tendency for Americans to cling to the principle of local autonomy in nonpolitical matters; but for a century and more, changing circumstances have forced a gradual and reluctant retreat from the practice of local autonomy in political matters. The coming of the railroad, for example, ultimately necessitated federal in addition to state regulation of this device; the coming of the automobile required the integration of local road systems into first state and then national webs; and the advent of large-scale wars rendered the old state militia system ridiculous. During the past quarter century, the principle of local autonomy has been all but abandoned. The growing willingness of the American people to submit to centralized political authority is, of course, but an aspect of their growing reliance upon maternalistic political protection, but it is an aspect of this general development that specifically jeopardizes the traditional role of the individual in American life.*

* In *Individual Freedom and Governmental Restraints* (Baton Rouge: Louisiana State University Press, 1956), Walter Gellhorn analyzes three of the many ways in which the trend toward political centralization encroaches upon the freedom of the individual: in the growth of administrative powers to deal more or less finally with personal interests; in the varied controls over reading; and in the increasing restrictions on occupational choice and the right to aspire to another status in society.

The assumption that under our political system control from centralized political authority is nonauthoritarian since it is "democratic" is critically examined by Richard Paston in *Democracy Is You* (New York: Harper & Brothers, 1953); and the dangers to individual freedom of any sort of social planning

Any transfer of authority—religious, economic, or political—from small, local groups to a centralized representative of many such groups reduces by that much the possibility of deviation between such groups and the individuals composing them, increases by that much reliance upon fixed rule and regulation, and shifts by that much determination of group behavior from interpersonal give-and-take to impersonal bureaucratic operations. In such matters as highway construction, traffic control, and public sanitation, the advantages may all lie with centralization of authority and what stems from it. As more and more aspects of social life come under the jurisdiction of centralized authority, political or otherwise, there is, however, a progressive reduction in the scope of individual enterprise and in the social value placed upon initiative.

In interpersonal relationships, such as those that obtain among the citizens of a small town or among a community of persons in a large city, each individual tends to be judged in terms of his total personality—or, at any event, in terms of the many facets of that personality known to his associates. Thus any act of his will be evaluated more or less in terms of his local status and particular reputation. If, for example, he is known as a hard-working, responsible, and henpecked husband, he may be excused for occasionally disturbing the peace when in his cups, whereas the same action might be condemned in some other member of the community. If he is considered an excellent driver, his fast driving may be sanctioned, whereas that of a known poor driver might be deemed dangerous to the community. If he is known as honest, loyal, and of good intentions, he may be permitted to make atheistic pronouncements and speak ill of the government.

As authority becomes centralized and impersonal, judgment of individual conduct and control over it become atomized. Rules, regulations, and laws necessarily apply to specifics of behavior and can take little if any account of the context in which behavior occurs. The neighborhood grocer may be tolerant of a man who fails to pay his bill on the first of the month, taking into account such personal considerations as that the man's wife has been ill,

---

are examined by Friedrich A. Hayek in *The Road to Serfdom* (Chicago: University of Chicago Press, 1947).

that his car broke down and had to be repaired, or that he habitually pays his bills two weeks late. The tax collector, however, makes no such exceptions to the rule that taxes are to be paid by the day specified in the law. The tax collector and those who framed the tax laws assume that any individual who fails to pay his taxes on time is willfully evading the law. They, like every centralized authority of every kind, must operate upon the principle that all the individuals who are subject to the law are comparable in terms of their personalities and their circumstances; for laws and administrative regulations and rulings are of necessity categorical and cannot take into account such variables as intent, integrity, and extenuating circumstances.

We today like to congratulate ourselves that in the eyes of the law all men are equal; but it is the very fact that they are that makes law and administrative regulation a dehumanizing form of social control, one that tends to bring out not the best in man but the bare minimum, just that amount that is demanded by the law or regulation. In both formulation and enforcement, any law, administrative regulation, or other act of centralized authority is predicated upon some idea of what is normal to all those who will be affected by it; and since the greater the number of people who are included within it, the wider the variations among them, what is normal is exceedingly low. Thus in the formulating of highway regulations, good and very bad drivers, drivers of excellent motorcars and weary jalopies, and drivers who are stone sober and those who have had a drink or two must be taken account of; and the result, inevitably, is a mass of restrictions unnecessary for a considerable proportion of those who drive the highways. The same sort of thing obtains with more complex forms of centralized authority; the law operates in terms of and for the average man under average circumstances, and all others must conform to his limitations.

As a result, centralized authority, especially that of a political nature, makes for the forcible homogenization of the members of society. In so doing, it reduces the range of permissible individual variation; it penalizes all those with exceptional ability; and it gives the advantage to the indifferent fellow who by inclination and circumstance more or less fits the average. Under such authority individual excellence has no worth; and, being valueless, it is discouraged. Under such authority such otherwise valued human characteristics as industry, honesty, generosity, and most especially initiative count for nothing. In the eyes of the tax collector, the dollar earned by hard work is no different from the one won at the race track; if both are of record, they are equally subject to tax. In the mind of a politician, one vote is as good as another; the fact that one voter beats his wife and has never done an honest day's work in his life while another is as kind and honest as the day is long makes no difference at the polls.

The progressive centralization of authority tends to bring about, if not an actual reduction to the average of those who fall under its authority, at least outward conformity to the behavioral standards that are set by such authority. The man who exceeds the average in some respect discovers in time that it is easier, safer, and quite as rewarding to do no more than the law expects of him. He may not become dishonest simply because the tax laws operate on the assumption that all men strive to evade paying taxes; but since the many laws that affect him presume him to be a mediocre and irresponsible fellow, he may eventually conclude that there is no point in going out of his way to assume responsibilities. Moreover, to the extent that the law provides maternalistic protection for him, he may find that he really has no very clear alternative to becoming personally irresponsible.

There is still another way in which the progressive centralization of political authority discourages individual initiative and self-reliance. With each extension in the scope of political action, the proportion of the social population that lives in and through political bureaucracy is increased. Socially valuable as the services of a given agency of government may be, it is still true that every such agency more or less effectively reduces those employed by it to working robots and effectively deprives them of any opportunity to display initiative, or any other distinctive quality, during working hours. As members of the labor force are drawn into political bureaucracy, society is deprived of individuals some few of whom might otherwise contribute to its development. And as more and more members of our society are incorporated into political bureaucracy—civil and military—they tend to obtain an occupational standard of economic security that must be met if not exceeded by business, industry, and other kinds of work organizations.

The Man Behind the Plow

There is no clearer demonstration of the way in which political maternalism discourages or perverts individual enterprise, of the distinctly limited powers of control through coercion, and of the inability of political authority to predict the actual social consequences of its actions than what has happened to American agriculture under the benevolent rule of government during the past twenty-five years.

The man behind the plow has often been a symbol of industry, thrift, and social integrity; but in point of fact his status in all the great civilizations of the past has been low, and his outstanding characteristic has been stubborn resistance to change in any form. Fellah, slave, serf, peasant proprietor, tenant farmer, or share cropper, he has always produced the foods and fibers needed by society in a laborious, traditional manner; and in many times and places he has slowly destroyed the land upon which he and his urban brothers were dependent. It may be that only those devoid of imagination, lacking in curiosity, and incapable of thought have been able to endure the brutish and unending struggle to extract a harvest from the reluctant earth; or it may be that physical exhaustion from that struggle has precluded thought, deprived the agricultural worker of his zest for life, and reduced him to plodding in the footsteps of his father and of his father's father. Whatever the reason, the man on the land has rarely been a man of enterprise. Proof of this is the painful slowness with which agricultural technology has evolved and the even greater slowness with which new techniques have been adopted by the farmers of the world.

An agricultural revolution of sorts accompanied and abetted the industrial revolution in Western Europe; but it consisted mainly of changes in land holding, land usage, and kinds of crops, and involved very little in the way of new technology. Today, as in times past, most of the land of Western Europe is cultivated by peasant proprietors; and although they obtain good yields from their little lands, they do so in ways not greatly different from those of two centuries and more ago—by brute strength, age-old skills, and bestial endurance.

With the settlement and conquest of North America there emerged, possibly for the first time in human history, a truly enterprising man behind the plow. His prototype was, no doubt, the industrious and independent New England farmer, who had brought with him the Protestant ethic and who cleared and cultivated his rocky soil with contempt for European traditions. He grew to maturity when he discovered and settled the vast and fertile lands west of the Appalachians—the Ohio country. No doubt it was the existence of this untouched body of potentially productive land that enabled the pioneers to evolve a unique system of land utilization and an unprecedented agricultural way of life. But had they not been for the most part men of enterprise, the opportunity thus afforded them would not have been utilized.

The agricultural development of the South was enduringly prejudiced by the early establishment of the plantation system by which first rice and later cotton, tobacco, and in the Gulf regions sugar cane were produced by slave labor. The share cropping and subsistence farming systems that first supplemented and, after the Civil War, replaced the plantation system were hardly better. On the whole, indeed, the farmer of the South has been and still remains a man of no-enterprise and, too often, of little industry. North and westward, however, the pattern of agricultural development was that set by the farmers of the Ohio country. Whether he was a prospering Indiana farmer with a quarter section of good land, a sodbuster, a cattleman, or an Oregon pioneer, the man on the land tended to be enterprising, proud of his independence, jealous of his right to gamble with the weather and the crops as he saw fit, willing to risk all that he might win large stakes, and willing to try out new and more effective tools and seeds and cultivation techniques. Such, at least, was the ideal man on the land; and the ideal did in fact exist, although it is possible to exaggerate his numbers and ignore his limitations.

From enterprising men on the land came, directly or indirectly, over the course of a century most of the important developments in agricultural technology—the mechanical reaper, barbed wire, the disk cultivator, the gang plow, rust-resistant wheat, the silo, the Missouri mule, and the tractor that eventually displaced it. Through the initiative of such men and through their willingness to apply the products of the initiative of others have come at length a mechanization and systematization of agricultural production that are now the hope of the underfed peoples of the world—and they have been, in major part, an American development.

The role of government in all this was by no means slight. First the pioneering settler, afterward the established farmer, was encouraged in his endeavors by our federal government. He was provided with some military protection, inefficient and erratic though it was, from marauding Indians; he was escorted through the plains; and he was given ownership of new lands on most favorable terms. The advance of the railroads for his convenience was fostered by the granting of blocks of public lands; and, later, land-grant colleges, county agents, and a variety of devices were resorted to in the effort to make the latest technical knowledge available to the farmer who wanted it. All this was done in accordance with the nineteenth-century view of government as a socially responsible agency dedicated to the support of responsible individuals.

The results were far from the utopian ideal. The very success of the farmer as a producer combined with the uncertainties of world marketing to bring occasional financial crises; and there were always the hazards of weather, of drought, flood, hail, or frost. But what he could not sell at a profit, the farmer and his family ate; and even when the harvest failed, there was some food for man and beast. Though his work was always hard and his profit often small, he had his cherished freedom from political restraints, his economic and personal independence, and a goodly chance of leaving this world better off financially than he had been upon his arrival in it.

Within the brief span of a quarter century, however, the farmer who approached the American bourgeois ideal has passed largely into history to be replaced to some extent by the agricultural industrialist but in the main by the farmer who is, in all but his material standards of living, a new-day version of the age-old peasant. He does not live, it is true, in terms of ancient superstitions, cultivating his land in the manner of antiquity. He drives a new tractor over his fields, he plants the newest strains of wheat or corn or soybean or cotton, he sprays his crops with the latest deadly chemicals, and he listens to the nightly weather reports on his radio or television set. He also has running water in his house, flush toilets, a good car in the barn, a deep freezer filled with processed and packaged foods, quick access to modern medical care, and many other fine products of industrial society.

The American farmer prospers, for the moment, and his way of life is in many salient respects fast approaching that of his urban middle-class brother; but, like that brother, he has lost the values and sentiments of the old *bourgeoisie*—lost to a great degree his enterprise, his independence, and his freedom. For he has now become, in an odd and still vague manner, a bureaucratic functionary; as the pampered darling of a benevolent Congress, he is the recipient of the maternal ministrations of one of the largest and most complex political bureaucracies ever designed by man— the United States Department of Agriculture.

Political subsidy of agriculture is nothing new. All the premodern governments of Europe favored agriculture over trade and commerce, and to some extent or other robbed the town to buy the peasants' favor. It was only when governments came to represent the growing *bourgeoisie* and thus to operate more in terms of the Protestant ethic that they withdrew their positive support of agriculture; and this withdrawal was, except in England, no more than a temporary change of policy. First in France and soon elsewhere on the Continent, government shortly returned to the aid of agriculture, mainly on the grounds that military necessity demanded self-sufficiency in foodstuffs. Governmental subsidy did not, however, change the role or character of the peasant; it merely enabled him to survive as and in the mode of a peasant and to direct his efforts increasingly into the production of agricultural commodities favored by subsidy but often of small value on the open market.

Here in America, on the other hand, the transition from a government that encouraged but did not sustain the man on the soil to one that assumes responsibility for his welfare has brought—or more probably only encouraged—an abandonment by the farmer of the Protestant ethic and his adoption of a system of values and sentiments which are somewhere between those of the European peasant and the very modern Freudian. The modern American farmer expects to do his daily chores and plow, seed, and cultivate his fields; and even his government expects him to. It is now assumed, however, both by the individual farmer and his government, that he can do these things only if he is free from fear—that is, only if he is assured that his labors will yield a profit. Since, in the long run, security has its price, he must cultivate his fields in the prescribed mode, plant the crops that are price supported, plant no more than his allotted share—unless he is shrewd enough to circumvent the rules—and when at last the harvest is in, fill out all the proper forms.

The degradation of the American farmer began, as have most maternalistic programs, with a series of crisis measures during the dark years of the depression. It culminated in the emergence of a new concept of the American farmer, of his role in American society, and of the need to save him from extinction by lavish political patronage. During the decade following World War I, American agriculture had suffered through the decline of world markets for wheat, cotton, dried fruits, and other export products. With the advent of the depression, the domestic market contracted; at the same time there was a considerable movement back to the land. Then came the successive dry years of the Western plains, when the plight of the dust-bowl farmers served to dramatize the sad condition of all American agriculture. Congress, under the New Deal, rushed somewhat belatedly to the rescue, and the Department of Agriculture was given what amounted to a mandate to save the farmer.

Under the then Secretary of Agriculture, Wallace, there soon evolved what may best be described as the nostalgic theory of the American farmer; and on the basis of this theory there in time developed a vague program for his total and permanent salvation. The American farmer, according to the theory, is not only the salt of the earth; he is the foundation upon which rests the greatness of American society. From the pleasant, friendly, industrious but rewarding life down on the farm have come the men who have made America what it is; for the city draws not only its sustenance but its virtuous people from the rural village and the rural home. The American farmer was not, in this view of him, really a man of sturdy character—and certainly not one of enterprise; rather, he was a humble, kindly, decent man who with his equally humble, kindly, and decent wife produced the good but also enterprising men who built cities and ran industries and, quite incidentally, staffed the Department of Agriculture. Unfortunately, however, industry was destroying the way of life that gave industry, and all of industrial society, its necessary manpower. The rural way of life was being corrupted. Farmers were losing in the struggle to make a living on the soil; and as their returns from honest agricultural endeavor diminished, they were being enticed by the gaudy offerings of urban society. The rural church was in a sad state of decline; the rural village—together with the rural banker, the rural merchant, and the country doctor—was withering away; and the farmer himself was more inclined to listen to the radio than plow his fields and raise good sons.

To save for America the agricultural way of life became the dedicated goal of the Department of Agriculture; and with the sanction of Congress a plan of sorts eventually emerged. The key to the new program was, of course, financial security; and the key to this, in turn, parity prices (or 90 per cent thereof) for the basic agricultural products. Further, the Department of Agriculture, with all its many hands, was to divert its efforts from its traditional activity of aiding the farmer to aid himself and turn its attention to the provision of rural social welfare. The farmer must be taught to enjoy the old-time rural way of life, to revive the communal practices of yesteryear—folk dancing, church sociables, etc. He must be aided to recapture the integrity and co-operativeness of the old farm family. To these ends and for related reasons he must be encouraged to abandon the forms of agricultural specialization that had grown up under economic adversity and return to the diversification and relative self-sufficiency of the premodern farmstead.

To the rural ideologists of the 1930's, the goal of the various political measures taken to aid agriculture was in fact if not in statement to return the American farmer to his preindustrial, premechanized condition. They would, in effect, increase the relative numbers of Americans on the land by depriving them of those technological and other advances that had led to a flight from the land. Somehow, it never occurred to them that they could not accomplish this through political means or that the means they used might bring forth consequences quite different from those they anticipated.

The first major disaster to the program came with the advent of war. Overnight, emphasis shifted from reducing production in order that the price-support program could be maintained to fostering increases in production. In the new crisis, everything possible was done to undo whatever had been accomplished; the man on the land was encouraged to bring all his land back into cultivation, to concentrate on the production of grain, cotton, meat, or some other basic product, and to mechanize as fully as wartime circumstances would permit. By the end of the war the more enterprising of farmers had prospered so greatly and become so much imbued with the spirit of production that they were well on their way toward becoming agricultural industrialists. Contributing to this trend were the scarcity of agricultural workers, new developments in fertilizers and in insecticides, and before long a series of new agricultural machines; and providing the stimulus for this new revolution in agriculture was the assurance that the price of the basic agricultural products would not fall, no matter how vast the supply.

With the end of the war, the Department of Agriculture returned, albeit wearily, to the goal of reviving the old agricultural way of life. Apparently there was little if any awareness that between the war and their earlier efforts there had been set under way a revolution that could not now be checked; for reliance was still placed upon price supports and, to check the rising tide of price-supported products, acreage limitation and other constraints upon the farmer. Of recent years, many of the large-scale industrial farmers have concluded that the farm program is running toward disaster and that they at least might be better off freely competing in a free market. Meanwhile, however, the very programs that were intended to keep the marginal farm family down on the farm have helped to drive them away; like the small businessman, the little and unsophisticated farmer has often found it impossible to keep up with the increasingly elaborate bureaucratic regulations through which he was, presumably, being enabled to survive.

The present structure of political incentives to produce or not to produce, to put land into cultivation or to withdraw land from cultivation, has had the obvious and short-run consequence of burdening the American people with ever-increasing surpluses of high-cost agricultural products, which they must hold in storage and try to dump at cut-rate prices on foreign markets.* It has held the domestic market price of the staple foods and fibers so high that substitutes have tended to replace them—margarine for butter, synthetic fibers for cotton, etc. It has led to uneconomic use of land and of the seed, fertilizer, and labor that make the land produce. But it has not done what all these political antics were intended to bring about; it has not brought back the good old days of the self-sufficient, integrated, respectable, and responsible farm family. On the contrary, it has quite inadvertently fostered the industrialization of agriculture. At the same time it has relieved the smaller, the only quasi-industrialized, farmer of the need to be enterprising. It has made him a dependent, a prosperous ward of the Department of Agriculture, a man so much habituated to protection from adversity and so much accustomed to operating within the framework of an elaborate system of bureaucratic controls that he takes them all for granted.

* An attempt to rationalize this contradictory and unsystematic system is provided by Ronald Mighell of the United States Department of Agriculture in *American Agriculture: Its Structure and Place in the Economy* (New York: John Wiley & Sons, Inc., 1955). A critical evaluation has been made by Lauren Soth in *Farm Trouble* (Princeton: Princeton University Press, 1957). Recent developments in the struggle to keep the unworkable system of agricultural controls working are reported by *Time* in the following articles: "A Place to Prune" (April 8, 1957, p. 78); "The Soil Bank Fiasco" (July 22, 1957, pp. 68-69); "The $5 Billion Farm Scandal" (August 19, 1957, p. 12); and "A Blow at Parity" (August 4, 1958, p. 15).

According to His Need

Political subsidy and protection of productive individuals, classes of individuals, and organizations have as their correlate political aid to the nonproductive, all of whom are adversely affected by the special rights and benefits that are granted to the productive. Those who have passed their productive period may find their savings, their pensions, and all their other careful preparations for old age sharply reduced in value by rising prices and higher taxes. Those who live, and perhaps have always lived, on a small fixed income will be similarly impoverished. And the higher price levels, if not the rise in taxes, will hurt all those who have learned to live without labor, worry, or visible means of support.

Inevitably, maternalistic government grants the major favors to blocks of voters; and, again inevitably, the modest unorganized members of society must contribute some of the values that are thus dispensed. They may have very little to lose, some almost nothing; but what they do have is vital to them. Reduce the widow's mite by ever so little, and she may be deprived of her independence; deny the beggar the right to beg, and he might even have to work to allay his hunger; tax the petty businessman just a little more, and he may well go under.

It is one of the more interesting, and in some respects most reassuring, aspects of recent American social history that as government has taken over increasing responsibility for the welfare of business and industry, of organized labor, and of agriculture and has given various forms of aid to the professions, it has also extended protection of a sort to various categories of nonproductive citizens. The development under federal auspices during the 1930's of what came to be called the "social security program" can be variously explained —as a logical culmination of the long-time trend from private to public charity; as a manifestation under severe crisis of the humanistic tradition; or as a practical political method of heading off the various mass movements (of which the Townsend Old Age Pension Plan was the most vigorous) that were generated by the depression. Probably all three factors were to some extent or other involved.

At any event, it is clear that the Social Security Act of 1935, which is the base upon which all else now rests, was the culmination of a series of early depression crisis measures, each one of which had been designed to give aid to some class of impoverished persons.

The various crisis measures (administered by such agencies as the Federal Emergency Relief Administration, the Public Works Administration, and the Civil Works Administration) were presumed to be temporary; and the National Industrial Recovery Act under which they had been established was at any event declared unconstitutional in 1935. The Social Security Act had the general effect of consolidating the various emergency programs and of putting the whole on a permanent and, in theory at least, self-maintaining basis. The administrative bureaucracies that have grown up to administer the Social Security Act are marvels of complexity, especially at the federal level; and the integrity with which unemployment compensation, old-age pensions, and other welfare funds are distributed by local and state agencies would seem to be, the difficulties considered, remarkably high. Practices vary, of course, between states; and in general the more prosperous the state, the more effective the welfare program—as a result of which, beneficiaries, particularly old-age recipients, tend to congregate in those counties and states that will do the most for them.

The idea that government—local, state, and federal—should assume responsibility for supporting those who are incapable of earning their livelihood is by now thoroughly established in the mores of American society. There may still be some doubt in the minds of many Americans that the program should be indefinitely extended until it covers, in the British fashion, everyone from the cradle to the grave. (The medical profession has mobilized to check agitation for national health insurance; and if the various current private hospital and medical insurance plans can keep pace with the constantly rising cost of medical care, there is little likelihood of serious public pressure for the socialization of medicine.) But that politically provided social security is desirable almost no one now doubts. Such criticism as has appeared applies mainly to the economics and equities of the current program. Neither the unemployment compensation nor the old-age and survivors insurance annuities are really self-maintaining insurance programs. The income available for un-employment compensation will decline whenever severe unemploy-ment makes heavy demands on the fund; and the frequent extension of social security coverage, combined with the constant aging of our population, makes certain that general tax funds will eventually be needed to keep up old-age payments. Although the social security program was established during a period of relatively low national income, it is the belief of many economists that it is a fair-weather operation and that it will precipitate almost as many problems as it solves should we encounter a prolonged period of declining national productivity.

This possibility and the questions of equity in the administration of the program are, however, procedural matters that can certainly be resolved in time. Quite different is the fundamental and generally ignored—if not outright taboo—question of the long-range effects of social security upon the character of the American people. There can be no clear and certainly no final answer to that question; but it is the vital one, and to neglect it will not dispose of it.

The avowed premise upon which all social legislation since the time of the Elizabethan Poor Laws is based is that no one should suffer need in a society that is physically capable of feeding and providing some sort of physical shelter for all its members. This premise is by no means a universal one. Although tribal societies have tended to operate on the principle of share and share more or less alike, the great civilizations of the past have, on the contrary, tolerated starvation in the midst of comparative plenty. There was a functional basis for such social ruthlessness toward indigent mem-bers; for it was true of those civilizations, as Malthus was later to claim was true of early industrial England, that if the poor were fed, then there would simply be more poor to feed, until in the end no one would have enough to eat and the "natural" checks to population increase would come back into play—that is, until starvation, which normally affects first and mainly the society's indigents, would in-crease the death rate.

In modern America our productivity—to say nothing of our theo-retical potential productivity—is for the moment so very high relative to our population numbers that only the most farsighted of pessimists could fear that the vast complex of social security measures by which we today practically guarantee that no one shall know want will produce an overwhelming tide of indigents. These measures do, however, add up to a political reversal of the principle of "to each according to his worth" and a partial application of the socialistic principle of "to each according to his need." This latter principle, which has never actually been tested in full and in practice, either presupposes that the production of the necessities of life is somehow already assured or else, in the Freudian manner, assumes that society from which all services must flow is different from its membership— that all the members could individually be socially irresponsible and there would still be a productive society.

The inescapable fact is, however, that any going society is from one point of view a system of reciprocal exchanges in which most, if not all, of the members pay in some coin or other for what they receive. The exchange procedures are always complex and usually devious, and spurious values enter into the making of many of the exchanges. Nonetheless, to survive through time, the system must so operate that most of those who receive goods or services from the society also return to the society equivalent values. Otherwise social productivity declines, if only because more and more individuals endeavor to leave those social roles that demand much and pay little and to gain entrance to those that pay much and require little—to become mistresses rather than wives, thieves rather than working-men, dependents rather than supporters of dependents.

In all relatively stable social systems, primitive as well as civilized, the rates of exchange between individuals and between groups have been standardized. This no doubt has made for equity, but it has also discouraged the individual from making exceptional effort. Upon the death of his father, the eldest son might, for example, step into his father's shoes, whether he had been an especially good son or not; and however diligent and enterprising a younger son might have been, his rights as brother of the new head of the family would be limited to those fixed by custom. And so, in one way or another, have been most if not all of the reciprocal relations in premodern societies.

One of the special and unique characteristics of the capitalistic system has been its distribution of social rewards in accordance with the individual's actual or anticipated contribution to society of social values as measured by market-place exchanges rather than by fixed, traditional standards. The system has never worked perfectly. Market-place values are often false, and a good salesman may inflate the value of the service he renders. Moreover, there are many socially valuable services—kindness toward others, for example—that do not ordinarily enter into market-place exchanges. Nevertheless, the capitalistic system has tended far more than any other one to distribute social values "to each according to his worth." It is this, as much as any other factor, that has made it an enterprise system—one that rewards enterprise and penalizes individual sloth, irresponsibility, and stolidity.

All societies have tolerated some irresponsible individuals—the black sheep, the ne'er-do-well, the village drunkard, etc.—who probably have earned their keep by providing the responsible members of society with horrible examples, objects of mild contempt, and material for gossip. Some societies have maintained in addition a class of persons in a nonreciprocal status—a decadent aristocracy, a band of thieving gypsies, or a class of professional beggars. Such irresponsibles have, however, been recognized as parasitic; and although they have been tolerated, their numbers have not ordinarily been permitted to increase; they have been granted just sufficient of the society's wealth to live but not to multiply.

Now we find a society—our own—beginning to abandon the universal principle of reciprocity and to provide through political means for the maintenance of a potentially unlimited number of members who are not required either to have contributed or to be likely in the future to contribute anything—material or otherwise—to the society. It is now quite possible for a reasonably determined irresponsible to progress, from childhood through youth and maturity and into old age, from welfare agency to welfare agency and from this social provision to that, without having made more than a token effort to take and hold a remunerative job. Moreover, he can do all this while failing to support a series of equally irresponsible wives and fathering an unchecked number of children who may, with social permission, simply follow in their father's footsteps.

The fundamental question is, then, how far is it possible to go in implementing the principle of "to each according to his needs" without establishing conditions so favorable to personal irresponsibility that the proportion of chronically irresponsible members of our society will constantly rise, not alone through natural increase, but also because the growing burden upon responsible members turns for them the balance in favor of becoming irresponsible recipients of the values produced by others? There is certainly some point at which even the most respectable and responsible man will begin to look with envy at the now equally respected but irresponsible one. The former may have a newer and bigger car, a finer house, and even some money in the bank; but if the effort to get and maintain these, in the face of constantly rising demands to aid his unproductive fellows, becomes too great and if the number and status of the latter pass some undesignatable point, he may decide to join them. Eventually the problem would arise of just who is going to provide social security for everyone.

The Freudian ethic does sanction everyone's living irresponsibly upon society, and the Freudian theory of man assures us that no one can really be expected to be socially responsible. But neither Freud nor any of his disciples or lay followers has ever explained how it is possible for society to provide security—psychological and otherwise—for each of its several members if no one of them can endure the strain of contributing to the support of society.

12

The Latent Danger

SINCE MOST of the social philosophers of the nineteenth century, or at least most of those who gained a following, believed in social progress, they faced tomorrow with hope and courage. They foresaw, each in his own way, a future that would be far better than the present, even as the present was far better than the past had been. It was their firm belief that man had at long last discovered that society was of his own making and that he could, therefore, remake society to suit his own best ends. This prospect was, of course, in complete accord with the Protestant ethic. Indeed, in the view of most nineteenth-century social philosophers it was the full flowering of the Protestant ethic that was to bring about further social progress.

At least here in the United States much of what the philosophers of social progress hoped for has come into being. The first half of this present century brought us two costly world wars and a long period of economic stagnation; but it also brought us the highest material standard of living that man has ever known, a standard of material welfare that is shared if not equally at least equably by the majority of the members of our society; it brought the lowest death rates and the longest average life span in the history of mankind, a progressive reduction in the average work week and in the physical strains of work, and many other tangible gains.

Nonetheless, the most conspicuous of modern social philosophers have, with few exceptions, been pessimists—men of little hope who have viewed the future glumly. Oswald Spengler seems to have set the fashion just after World War I with his wordy contention that the West was on the decline. Later, Vilfredo Pareto was exhumed to give a pseudoscientific explanation for the coming of the great depression; and not long ago the doleful writings of the Dane Sören Kierkegaard were translated and republished as suitably expressive of the discouragement of our times. Through it all we have heard repeated pleadings by such men as Pitirim Sorokin that we abandon this appalling industrial civilization of ours and return to the calm and comfort of the good old Middle Ages. And not even Arnold Toynbee, most hopeful of the recent crop of social pessimists, has been able to do more than pray that we will somehow respond to the challenge of our disintegrating way of life and start anew to build the good society that we have somehow lost.

Though our politicians during their campaigns often sprinkle their speeches with predictions of such desirables as reduced taxes, increased prosperity, and eternal peace, our more serious prophets see only major disaster on ahead. We shall either blow ourselves into extinction in the coming war that will end all wars by ending mankind, or we shall secure the peace and assure our survival only by foregoing everything that makes life worth living. (George Orwell's *1984* explores this latter alternative.)

There is certainly some possibility that we will make a remarkable mess of our affairs, although one may seriously doubt that we can actually terminate human life on this planet. Certainly we now have unprecedented powers of physical destruction; and it is conceivable that we may, in the not too distant future, apply these new powers to mutual self-destruction. The total extermination of man is, however, so simple a solution to the problems faced by mankind that it is not at all likely to come about. Nor are the prospects of our becoming, in the interests of military security, a nation—to say nothing of a world—of human automatons obedient to the every command of a small ruling clique any more probable. We have, it is certainly true, moved somewhat in the direction of becoming automatons in some specific respects. Who does not now quite unthinkingly shift from the accelerator to the brake when the stoplight turns red? Who does not now accept, however grudgingly, the inevitability of answering the innumerable and impertinent questions asked by the Federal Bureau of Internal Revenue each year and paying tribute to it? And how many of us have really fought the growth of what have been euphemistically described as "security measures" but are in fact a kind of latter-day Inquisition?

However, man is a stubborn creature, and a society is both so complex and so much a product of the past that it cannot be completely mechanized and brought under the absolute control of political organization. We shall no doubt see a further expansion of our military establishments, and the trend toward more government and less personal freedom may very well continue. Long before 1984, however, a more insidious and portentous trend in our affairs may make itself apparent.

There may be little truth in the old saying that truth is stranger than fiction, but there is no doubt that it is far more complicated. A man may die abruptly, and even from self-inflicted causes; a man may be transformed in a relatively brief period from one who is reasonably normal to one who is definitely psychopathic. For a society, however, there are no such dramatic potentials. A society does not die, disintegrate, or become megalomaniacal overnight. Many a society has changed in directions that have led ultimately to its disappearance, but change of this sort has always been both inadvertent and gradual. It seems always, too, to have escaped the notice of those who have been affected by it.

The kinds of changes that are noted and remarked upon are seldom the changes that, in the perspective of a later age, prove to have been the society's undoing. The Romans noticed that they were losing battles, that their Legions were being forced to withdraw from the provinces, that "barbarian" hordes were encroaching on their preserves, and that a new faith—Christianity—was gaining adherents in Rome itself. But these self-evident developments were only symptoms or indirect consequences of subtle, antecedent changes that had gone largely unobserved. Rome had become the center of a great and exploitative empire because its people had been sturdy and aggressive brigands who had learned and applied the arts of military, political, and economic organization. With the passage of centuries, however, the masses of Rome developed qualities of passive parasitism; and through this slow dissolution of their Spartan qualities the peoples of Rome themselves brought erosion to the Roman system and a fading of the glories that were Rome. The peoples of other societies have, to put a vastly complex matter simply, eaten themselves out of topsoil or worn themselves out in sacrificial supplication of their gods. Whatever the route to historical oblivion, it has always been slow and it has usually been unapparent to those who have traveled it.

The Unintended Consequence

It is the thesis of this study that many of the changes that have been of late years occurring in our society are malfunctional and that they will, if they continue uncorrected, constitute our unrecognized road to disaster. The particular changes that have been analyzed here involve quite different aspects of our society—ideological, procedural, and organizational; and they take such dissimilar forms as a growing preference for the permissive mode of child rearing and the growth of political maternalism. These changes are being wrought by men of many kinds and various functions—by psychiatrists and child psychologists of the Freudian persuasion, by permissive parents and progressive teachers, by welfare workers and impressionable judges, by managers of business and industry and leaders of labor and academic life, and by politicians and political administrators of many sorts. Moreover, they are being demanded or welcomed, or at least passively accepted, by almost everyone.

All these changes, varied as they are in source, in form, and in purpose, seem to be converging in such a way as to constitute a general social drift—a movement of many parts to produce one common and unintended consequence. That consequence is a slowing down of the rates of change in our society, a progressive reduction in its dynamism, a trend toward social stability. Every one of the changes that have been here discussed has as its recognized and avowed objective the provision of more security for some kind or class of individual—the protection of the infant from stressful experience; the school child from competition and strain to achievement; the college youth from the need to excel; the young hoodlum from the pangs of punishment; the employer from competition with other employers; the workingman from competition with his fellows; and the nonworkingman from the normal consequences of the fact that he does not work.

To a considerable extent these changes are actually increasing the security of various classes of individuals in our society. But every change is also reducing the range of permissible individual variation, for it demands, no doubt as the necessary price of security, increasing conformity by the individual to socially imposed standards of conduct. Thus every change is to some extent destroying those social conditions that have been conducive to the perpetuation of the Protestant ethic, to the generation of men of enterprise, and so to the continuation of the age of enterprise.

On the positive side, these various changes may be seen as contributing in one way or another to the emergence, the social sanction, and the social maintenance of a new ethic, an ethic that translates into action as apathy and indifference. This new ethic presupposes that man is by inherent nature weak, uncertain, and incapable of self-reliance and that he must, therefore, be provided by society with the security that is his greatest need. Since the most outstanding and most popular proponent of this view of man has been Sigmund Freud, the newly emerging ethic has been designated by his name.

It is perhaps possible to conceive a society in which the Freudian ethic prevails and in which, therefore, the members tend to demand much each of the others and to give little each to the others in return. It is perhaps possible that, in view of the many nonhuman agents of production that are presently at our command, the level of life in such a society could be acceptably high. That society would, necessarily, be a stable one—a self-maintaining and unchanging system; if we were to achieve this condition, we would, in our own particular way, have reached the goal of all utopianists—a society in which every member lives the calm and complacent life and drifts from birth to death without excessive effort, without strain, and entirely free from fear in any form. If we were to achieve this blissful social state, it would be only just to acclaim Freud as our Messiah. He hated and despised society as he knew it, but he would no doubt have approved a society so admirably suited to the Freudian man.

There is, however, slight likelihood that Freud will be honored as the savior of mankind, although there is some possibility that he may be remembered as the prophet of doom. For we are currently moving, in many salient aspects of our life, toward a condition of social stability that is altogether incompatible with the nature of our society and the circumstances under which it operates. The old agrarian societies, with their relatively simple technology, could and often did achieve considerable stability; century after century the members could rely upon the same traditional tools, skills, knowledge, and forms of organization to maintain them in the impoverishment to which they were accustomed. In the very long run a society might peter out or be overwhelmed by the members of a stronger and more dynamic system, but in the short run social survival could be accomplished by social stability. All modern societies, however, most especially our own, are caught up in a perpetual race against disaster.

Freudianism and the Future

The danger is not, contrary to what our social philosophers have been telling us, that we may shortly wind up in a cloud of atomic dust or become slaves to a system of military-political security. The difficulty is, rather, that we must keep on changing our society and changing it at a constantly accelerating rate if we are to keep it going; for a modern industrial society constantly changes the conditions on which it thrives and in order to survive must be dynamic technologically, organizationally, and otherwise. We may wish for a time of social stability; we may, individually and collectively, long to relax and to do tomorrow just as we did today. But if we do, we shall most certainly lose some valued possession—freedom from irksome labor, freedom of speech, freedom from disease, or freedom from hunger. In no phase of life, excepting perhaps the arts, will the devices of today produce tomorrow exactly what they do today.

The reasons are apparent although often brushed aside. Modern American society—and to an almost equal extent the same is true of the other societies of the Western world—is so very complex and its multitudinous arrangements are so precariously balanced that they will not operate effectively without constant adjustment. An old-fashioned clock may run on for years with no more attention than a weekly winding; it will never tell the exact time, but it will keep going. A modern chronometer, on the other hand, which is capable of keeping time with great accuracy, must be kept adjusted or it will cease to function. The same sort of thing is true, in a way, with any modern society. It is not a single social system, but a vast complex of interwoven and interdependent systems; and like a complex, multiphased machine, it must be worked over constantly. A bit of wear here or there may seriously disturb its delicate balance; a failure in one of its many constituent parts—if, for example, medical science should fail to maintain its present functions—may well destroy the whole.

Moreover, no part of this extremely complex whole can continue to fulfill its present functions without successfully solving an endless series of new and imposing problems. We are, for example, destroying our natural resources at an unconscionable rate; and of recent years the factor of population numbers and composition has become, for the first time in America, a matter of considerable concern. Both trends, the rapid exhaustion of resources and the rapid growth in our population, if unchecked or uncompensated for, will depress our material standard of living.

Nor are these the only ways by which, through failing to remain socially dynamic, we might come to a bad end. We could lose out in the battle with the lower organisms; some new disease strain or some new blend of old diseases could weaken or destroy us; the struggle to keep our plant and animal crops free from diseases could lead to the use of poisons too toxic for us; our current tinkering with nature could give the rat or some equally enterprising creature an opportunity to overrun us—as one famous biologist sincerely fears, or perhaps hopes. We could through our increasing consumption of the fossil fuels and metals so pollute the air on which we are dependent that no man would be able to venture into the open without a mask and a tank of manmade stuff to breathe; or we could, in returning so much carbon to our atmosphere, so upset the complex and delicate balance of forces, thermal and otherwise, that provide us with our present climates that our climates would change radically and in directions adverse to us. A slight rise in world temperatures would, for example, be sufficient to melt the icecaps and submerge under the seas much of the land upon which we dwell.

There is, thus, nothing certain about the social future. Neither is there anything in the nature of things that precludes our preserving and extending the mode of life that we have evolved. The fact that many of our social philosophers currently view our future with strong misgivings is significant in that it reflects a rather widespread adoption of the Freudian view that man is socially incompetent, but all talk of social destiny or inescapable fate is simply a symptom of a general unwillingness to make the effort to do and keep on doing what is necessary to maintain our way of life. If man fails in the battle with the bugs, is overwhelmed in a flood of babies, runs out of topsoil, smothers in smog, or in some one of the various other ways fails to solve the problems of social adaptation, it will be only because he has given up trying.

It should now be evident that we cannot hope to maintain ourselves in anything like the fashion to which we have become accustomed if we continue to crawl in ever increasing numbers under the temporarily protective shelter of security organizations of one sort or another. It has been men of enterprise who have brought us to our present state of development, men who have operated in terms of the Protestant ethic. Over the past two centuries and more it has been men of enterprise who have evolved our crafts and technologies, developed our sciences, devised and diffused new and more effective forms of social life, and explored and exploited our physical and biological resources. If we are to preserve the advantages, material, psychological, and social, that these developments have made possible, we shall need now, and on through the future, other men of enterprise—others who will, through their industry and initiative, continue the extension of our scientific knowledge of this earth and the people on it, continue to work changes in our crafts and technologies, and continue the evolution of new and appropriate forms of social relations. And if we are, further, to enjoy what a century ago was termed "progress," we must produce and give scope to a steadily increasing proportion of such men. It is in view of this necessity, rather than of some inherent evil, that the decline of the Protestant ethic and the emergence of the Freudian is an occasion for concern. For only if these trends are checked by men of enterprise, can we for long continue as the most fruitful society that man has ever known.

INDEX

Index

A

Abrahamsen, David, 172
achievement, 17, 130
Adams, Walter, 239
adjustment, 121, 147
  courses on, 126, 150
  cult of, 151
  passive, 135, 194
  popular concept of, 130, 135
  of primitives, 98
Adorno, T. W., 90
agricultural revolution, 267, 273
agriculture, 268
  industrialization of, 260, 273
  subsidy of, 251, 269, 272
Agriculture, Department of, 251, 270
Alexander, Franz, 157, 165
Alger, Horatio, 24, 130
anal type, 36, 95
anomie, 5, 72, 203
anthropology, 47, 97
apathy, 64, 146
Aquinas, St. Thomas, 50
authoritarianism, 60, 160
  in the family, 90
  in the school, 123
authority
  centralization of, 262
  political, 244, 248
autonomy, local, 106, 263

B

Bacon, Sir Francis, 29
Banay, Ralph S., 166
Barnett, Homer, 8
Baruch, Dorothy, 97
battle fatigue, 85
Becker, Howard, 149, 234
behaviorism, 45, 52
Bennett, M. E., 150
Berge, W., 239
Bestor, Arthur, 113
Bettelheim, Bruno, 97
Bierstedt, Robert, 186
birth control, 197
birth rate, 195, 197, 199
Blau, Peter M., 217
Boskoff, Alvin, 149, 234
bourgeoisie
  decline of, 184, 192
  grand, 191
  new, 187, 194, 220, 236, 250, 256
  petty, 188, 190, 193
bureaucracy, 217
  corporate, 217
  and enterprise, 153, 219
  in foundations, 233
  in industry, 218
  political, 267, 270
  and science, 232
  in unions, 226